DESPERATE TIMES

The Summer of 1981

Desperate Times, The Complete Issues, 1-6

Maire M. Masco

Prologue by Wilum Pugmire

FLUKE PRESS

Tacoma, WA, USA
2015

Published June 17, 2015 by
FLUKE PRESS
6918 East "I" Street, Tacoma, WA 98404
www.flukepress.com
Editorial and production services: Gillian Gaar , Colleen Grey, and Wendy Katz.
Design: Linda DeSantis
Cover: Art Chantry

Library of Congress Control Number: 2015909347
Masco, Maire M., 1962-
Desperate Times: The Summer of 1981/Maire M. Masco
Includes indexes and bibliographical references.

ISBN-13: 978-1938476013
ISBN-10: 1938476018
1. Desperate Times—Newspaper—Fanzine. 2. Seattle Music—Grunge, 3. History of Rock Music

Printed in the United States of America

DEDICATION:

To all the cool people who shared the Seattle summer of 1981 with me.

Except the Boppo Boys. You guys were a pain.

CONTENTS:

ACKNOWLEDGEMENTS

Thanks Mom, for putting up the deposit for the typewriter rental. My bro, Tom; thanks for being in a garage band and letting me sleep on your couch (god-you-saved-me). And Joe, my middle sib, you are the best bro ever. Kisses to Shawn, Art's sis Cindy, and Boz for being a great survivor and drama queen.

Lastly, if you never got it before, Art, you are the MAN of my life. 'Tis true, rock on.

Thanks for encouraging me to document Desperate Times for posterity.

PROLOGUE

by Wilum Pugmire

DELICIOUS DESPERATE PAST

Great Yuggoth, how can it have been so long ago? 1981 was the year that completely changed my life — indeed, it was then that I found what is now a core component of my persona. Punk rock was still a new and mysterious beast in Seattle. I was working at Southcenter Shopping Mall, and I remember listening to some co-workers talk about punk shows: "Yeah, they beat each other up and vomit on each other while the band is playing." I was, at the time, a little disco fag, going to queer bars and moving along on beer-stained dance floors. Punk sounded like some kind of monstrous aberration. Then I saw Loud Fartz and Heidi Weispfenning[1] on the route #150 bus going home, and I was mesmerized. Loud looked so totally hardcore, and Heidi was beautifully Goth, with white face makeup and blood-red mouth. The innocent exhibiwtionist in me suffered throes of inner ecstasy. How fabulous, I thought, to be able to dress like that. I knew that to qualify for such sartorial splendor, I would need to authentically appreciate the music.

I bought three artists: the Sex Pistols, Dead Kennedys, and David Bowie. They were all too weird for me, and I was deflated. I wasn't going to dress punk if I couldn't get into the noise. I could be new wave, I thought — it's just pop and disco on speed. I came close to buying a DEVO jumpsuit at a shop in Pioneer Square (now I wish I had). I attended a "Save the Wave" concert[2] at the Showbox Theater, carefully observing the correct way to pogo dance. I heard new wave kids discuss punks, noting that "they put safety-pins in their leather!" Although their words were disapproving, their voices were laced with a kind of awe.

Punk was beguiling. I kept an eye on gigs at the Showbox, and decided to attend the International Punk Explosion. I had just gone to a barber and had all of my hair shaved off.

---

[1] Ed. Note. Loud and Heidi were known throughout the city for their outrageous fashion style based on early punk. Loud, a member of the band the Fartz, was the first person I saw with a Mohawk haircut, and Heidi was the first person I saw using crazy color in her hair.

[2] Ed. Note. See "A Few Words About Radio" for more information on radio in the 1980s.

Standing right up front near the stage, I was astounded when some rad punk women came up to me and ran their hands over my head. "Nice. Smooth," they told me. I had never in my life felt that I was "cool" in any way. I liked feeling cool very much. And then the music began, and live hardcore swept over me and pierced its anchor into my heart. My sad little boring life suddenly had aspects of becoming *fun* and *adventurous*. I was 29 going on 30 and in need of a big change in life.

Punk rock changed my life that night — it gave me my life. For the next three years, the hardcore way of life was all I cared about. I found a new family, beautiful and dysfunctional. Looking over these old issues of *Desperate Times* has reminded me of those days and of those beloved messed-up souls. When I began doing *Punk Lust* I approached it as a kind of journal in which I would record my life in the punk scene. Reading *Desperate Times* has that same effect, reminding me of gigs and geeks that I have long forgotten.

It's great, too, to read these old issues today, and see the budding of what the Seattle Scene would become. In Vol. 1 No. 2, we have a letter from Mark McLaughlin that begins: "I hate Mr. Epp & the Calculations! Pure grunge! Pure noise!"[3] I had forgotten about my own wee write-up on Husker Dü in that issue, and reading it brought that night back as if it were only yesterday, hanging out at Wrex (such a great club) and thrashing to such excellent bands. Reading about the Gorilla Room benefit concert at the Showbox reminded me of when The Enemy sang one of their old punk numbers just for me, and that reminded me of how I used to go see the band whenever they played at Baby O's, half a block away from the Gorilla Room. Gawd, the Seattle music scene gave me so much to do with my time, my life. It introduced me to many of my finest friends, and it opened my mind to forms of music about which I would otherwise have been clueless. It gave a lonely young man a sense of family such as he has never again experienced.

The music is still wonderful, and this is another great asset of having these issues of

---

[3] *Desperate Times*, No. 2, pg. 1. Ed. Note, see my comments on pg. 8-9.

Desperate Times republished now: they serve as a valuable guide to good music, the fab noise of the early eighties, a variety of original sounds and approaches to music. Much if not most of the old music is still available in new form, such as MP3, and there are videos of the old bands to be seen on YouTube. Thus these wonderful old issues serve to channel information regarding the way-cool bands of the past. The value of these old issues, thus, is priceless.

Wilum Pugmire
August 2012
Seattle, WA

INTRODUCTION

by Maire M. Masco

WHAT I DID ON MY SUMMER VACATION

Desperate Times was a fanzine published in Seattle during the summer of 1981. It was a fanzine because we wrote only about what we cared about, we basically wrote for our friends, and we did it for fun. There were just six issues, but this short-lived 'zine was kind of remarkable. First of all, *Desperate Times* was actually a bit more than a 'zine — it was a newspaper, with regular sections, advertising, articles with bylines, and photo credits. We had an Editor and an Art Director. Today, *Desperate Times* could be a really good blog. But 1981 was a long time before personal computers, the internet, and smart phones became ubiquitous. *Desperate Times* was printed with real ink, on newspaper stock — something you could hold in your hands.

When I recently came across a complete set of issues, I was stunned that such a collection was extant. My band management files, phone books, promotion notes, and press releases were lost years ago, along with my precious concert "staff" stickers[4] and posters. Paging through the 20-year-old newsprint was surreal: a combination of acid flashback, high school yearbook, and sheer astonishment at what we had done. There was also a bit of *memento mori*, as I sadly recognized the names of people who had died over the last couple of decades. Damn. When I was working on *Desperate Times*, I never thought I'd live to be 30, let alone 50.

BACK IN THE DAY...

In the '70s and '80s, word of mouth was the primary means of promotion in the music scene. Xeroxed flyers were important, and the exceptionally cool ones were called posters. There were a few music magazines around, like the *New York Rocker* and the *New Musical Express (NME for short)*, that covered punk and new wave bands; there were also 'zines like *Search & Destroy, Slash, Touch & Go, and Flipside*.[5] But we mostly picked up music news at the record store. You and your buddies would

---

[4] *Desperate Times* No. 3 pg. 2 for pictures of Neil Hubbard's backstage passes for the Gang of Four concert tour.

[5] Danny Baker, *Sniffin' Glue & Other Rock-n-Roll Habits: The Catalogue of Chaos, 1976-1977*, illustrated ed. (Sanctuary Publishing, 2000). The UK fanzine *Sniffin' Glue* was perhaps the most infamous 'zine of this period, but I never saw a copy of it in Seattle.

spend hours looking through the bins searching for new releases or rare copies of records you'd heard about but didn't have. Import records were often considered better for the simple reason that they were more expensive and harder to find. That was pretty simplistic. But you just *knew* that a record from Rough Trade would be better than a record on Casablanca.

Communication in general was also obviously slower in the days before the internet. Heck, in 1981 young people did not have their own phones.[6] Our idea of "texting" was leaving graffiti messages in the bus stops and bathrooms we frequented. Tesco Vee, the genius behind the *Touch & Go 'zine* and record label in Lansing, Michigan, wrote: "The internet in all its immediacy will see to it that neither an idea, nor a fanzine, will ever be allowed to percolate, fungate, and grow to fruition in this modern age. The Web will see to it that said idea is co-opted, bastardized and rendered passé with 24 hours."[7] Like vinyl records, the printed page was saved and savored over time. These physical objects create a psychic link between our emotional experience and our personal histories. I suppose that's what drives collectors to collect and the rest of us to get nostalgic.

THE ORIGINS OF FANDOM

The prolific science-fiction author Frederick Pohl (b. 1919) wrote about his experiences with the fledgling sci-fi community beginning in the late '30s.[8] A group of authors would meet to encourage and critique each other, and in the process they created fandom. Pohl is rather self-effacing about their writing efforts ("the craftsmanship was poor"), but also points out that these early writers laid the groundwork of the genre for future authors: "Their insights and innovations provided capital on which all of us have since drawn." He also described the development and importance of fandom, crediting it as "an auxiliary force and seedbed." Pohl's ad hoc club, The Futurian Society of New York, was made up of authors and fans.

---

[6] Mobile, personal, or cellular phones were not widely used until the late 1990s. In the 1980s, telephones were rented from the phone company and hardwired to a physical location. It was expensive to have a telephone, and it required having a bank account and a home address, two things a lot of young people simply didn't have. Beepers were the model of mobile communication. Drug dealers and pimps used beepers but still had to resort to a pay phone to speak with their clients.

[7] Tesco Vee and Dave Stimson, authors; Steve Miller, ed. *Touch and Go: The Complete Hardcore Punk Zine '79-'83.* (Bazillion Points, 2010), XII.

[8] Frederik Pohl, *In the Problem Pit* (Bantam Books, 1976). See essays "The Way the Future Was" and "Golden Ages Gone Away."

Pohl also writes: "Not all of our work was aimed at the paying markets, for all of us had our own little fan magazines — mimeographed or hectographed, published in editions of a dozen or a hundred copies, in which we wrote invariably rotten amateur stories and sometimes quite good scathing attacks on everybody else." What is so charming about Pohl's comments is that as a senior don he can look back and call the work "rotten." There is a spiritual lineage between *Desperate Times* and these early sci-fi writers.[9] Reading through its pages, I find lots of rotten material, although only one mention of Johnny Rotten. We also had an attitude that demanded dismissiveness of all contemporary culture and aesthetics. We liked a good "scathing attack" as a method of social commentary, but mostly as a way to define what we were, by telling everyone else what we were not.

We fancied ourselves as rebels rallying against the status quo. In that sense, we arrogantly claimed to take a page from the Dadaists during the First World War. They, too, self-published treatises against The War and popular culture, and promoted their form of anti-art. Marcel Duchamp[10] created sculpture based on found objects. His most famous piece was a urinal which he called "Fountain." Whether we were mocking or copying Duchamp is not clear, but we proudly included a picture of the urinal at the Gorilla Room in our paper.[11] Everybody got the message, even if the message was difficult to verbalize. It was important and deconstructive and nasty. We thought we were so clever.

Let's be clear: *Desperate Times* was a selfish and rather vain venture. We were non-conformists who lived in a communal house. We were all involved in the music scene in one way or another. If you didn't play in a band, you made posters or promoted concerts. The all-important stereo was pieced together like a Frankenstein monster from the best parts people had to contribute. (The only thing that trumped a stereo in status was a car, but no one at DT[12] House had a car.) There was a constant pull and tug between individualism and community. Youth is a wonderful thing,

---

[9] And be honest, some of those concerts looked a little like a Star Trek convention. Or maybe my memory is confused with *The Rocky Horror Picture Show.*

[10] Marcel Duchamp (1887-1968) was the most influential of the Dadaist and Surrealist artists of the 20th century. "The Fountain" is a readymade sculpture rejected by the Society of Independent Artist for inclusion in their 1917 Exhibition. The porcelain urinal was modified only by a fake signature, "R. Mutt, 1917." Curiously, the original sculpture vanished, although numerous copies are on display in museums around the world. I have one in my garden.

[11] *Desperate Times*, No. 3, pg. 7.

[12] Many communal houses had their own monikers. Often the name referred to the primary band that lived or hung out a particular house. DT House obviously refers to the *Desperate Times* newspaper that was produced there. Other communal houses in Seattle carried names like Holy War Cadets House, The Telepath House, and Dogma House. Zee Whiz Kids had a series of houses or building with unique names, e.g., The Under Arms.

after the fact, but in the moment the experience is pretty smug, filled with a chronic hunger and a determination not to be common. At the same time, we were terrified of being completely alone. We didn't trust adults who had voted Reagan into office. I am reminded of Peter Fonda's character in the 1966 movie *Wild Angels*:

> "We want to be free! We want to be free to do what we want to do! We want to be free to ride.
> And we want to be free to ride our machines without being hassled by The Man.
> And we want to get loaded. And we want to have a good time!
> And that's what we're gonna do. We're gonna have a good time. We're gonna have a party!"

Our desire to party didn't negate a genetic understanding of business and politics. Club promoters were always stiffing someone and going under. We knew they were bad businessmen. An ongoing issue was who got paid in the music scene. As a general rule, the rental hall and the soundman always got paid. After that it was a bit flexible. In one fit of populist uprising, we called for a strike against a certain promoter who didn't pay the bands.[13] It was silly.

We also knew something about the great radical history of Washington State. We'd heard about the Wobblies (Workers of the World) and the Suffragettes (women's suffrage for voting rights). We were pro-worker even if we didn't have jobs. My "womyn" friends and I considered ourselves feminists. We believed in civil rights, even if we really didn't know many people of color; they'd be welcome, if we could find some.

1981 was pre-AIDS, so we didn't have that to worry about (everybody seemed to get chlamydia instead and was on tetracycline at one time or another). A few of us knew about the Polaris nuclear warheads across Puget Sound at Naval Submarine Base Bangor.[14] That was bad. Some of us wore Greenpeace buttons on our jackets, but by 1981 those had become passé and were replaced by Dead Kennedys buttons.

We were easily bored and often confused. We were creative, inventive, sometimes even gifted, but mostly self-centered, with a political objective that even to this day I can't define. Although we fashionably hated big business, we secretly desired to be rich, to have freedom from money and the constant worry of paying the rent or purchasing food. We ignorantly co-opted images and messages;

---

[13] *Desperate Times*, No. 4 pg. 10, and No. 5 pg. 1-2, editorial and rebuttal.

[14] In 2004 the Bangor Naval Submarine Base was renamed the Kitsap Naval Base. It is still one of the largest stockpiles of nuclear weapons on the planet, and is homeport for at least twenty nuclear submarines. The base is about 15 miles due west from Seattle across Puget Sound.

as long as it fit the groove, it didn't matter. We had no intention to make *Desperate Times* like a Thomas Paine[15] -style "Common Sense" pamphlet, but like modern-day colonialists, we did want to fight for our rights and defend our freedom. Sometimes we behaved badly and smelled. But we cherished our own autonomy. We were young, and we ruled the roost, at least in Seattle's University District. There were other clowns on the Eastside and in West Seattle, but we didn't have too much contact with them. This sounds trite and melodramatic. But that was really how it was in 1981 in Seattle for me and my friends. We loved the music — most of the time — and we wanted a scene, a happening, a place to hang with our friends (preferably on a bus route). *Desperate Times* was a cute adjunct to the gestalt of color, tone, attitude, and companionship of the times, coupled with a sincerely bizarre idea that we could change things. It was even more bizarre that it actually did change things. How could we have known?

THE SEATTLE MUSIC SCENE

Many people have written about the "Seattle Scene" of the 1990s — the golden age of Nirvana, Soundgarden, Pearl Jam, Mudhoney, and heavy drugs. It was the grunge era, and by that time *Desperate Times* was long gone and forgotten. But the 'zine is nonetheless a part of the grunge heritage, and an important part at that. For example, the term "grunge" first appeared in print to describe a Seattle band in *Desperate Times*.[16]

Here is the story…Mark Arm wrote a fake letter to the editor for the first issue of our little newspaper. Using his real name, no less, he poked fun at his own band, Mr. Epp & the Calculations, by calling their music "pure grunge" and explaining in the letter that he preferred the repetitiveness of classical composer Phillip Glass. The inside joke was that Mr. Epp & the Calculations was not really a band at all. It was group of kids from Bellevue who pretended to have a band, and put up posters with great lines such as "Mr. Epp — Bigger than the Beatles!" and "Mr. Epp — Coming Soon!" and "Mr. Epp — Deader than the Grateful Dead!" Everyone knew about Mr. Epp from the posters, but no one had actually heard them play.

At *Desperate Times* we had some discussion about the letter. The reference to Phillip Glass was a little confusing, but the main question was what the word grunge meant and if it was a

---

[15] Thomas Paine (1737-1809) was a political activist and writer of the American Revolution.

[16] See the letter to the editor in *Desperate Times* No. 2 pg. 3, from Mark McLaughlin, aka Mark Arm. McLaughlin was poking fun at his own band, Mr. Epp & the Calculations. He later fronted the band Green River, considered by some to be the *original* grunge band, and continues to perform in Mudhoney.

word at all! A lot of hardcore music was completely unintelligible, so maybe grunge was referring to grunting vocals? We all thought it was a funny word and supposed it referred to some kind of garage rock — you know, a home brewed-type of sound that was grimy, dirty, and sloppy. Unknown to us, the term grunge had been used before to describe music, but for us it was a comical, made-up word, like an onomatopoeia. Later the record label Sub Pop turned the term into a marketing phrase for Seattle rock, and the rest is history.[17]

Desperate Times provides an amazing view into the variety of the music that was being played and listened to in Seattle in 1981. The 'zine had a sense of purpose that helped create an environment conducive to wildly diverse forms of expression. Authenticity and sincerity were valued over skill and aptitude, although there was some very good musicianship going on in the scene. Action mattered, but it was the intangible energy behind the action that made it something special. The pressure to create unique personal expression in Seattle cleared away irrelevant rules and guidelines. It was our own Cambrian explosion of evolution[18], where anything was possible. The sheer variety, range, and dissonant scope made the music scene in 1980s Seattle memorable.

The cognitive dissonance of the scene was delightful and entrancing. There was a certain amount of naughty pleasure to admit that you enjoyed an experimental art band as much as a thrashing hardcore band. My production company with Dennis White was called Pravda Productions, named after the Soviet newspaper meaning "truth" in Russian.[19] As a concert promoter, there was no problem about including a rockabilly or a reggae act on the bill with a

---

[17] As far as I am concerned, the term grunge, as the term is used today, originated with Mark Arm's letter to *Desperate Times* and was commercialized by the Seattle based record label, Sub Pop.

[18] The Cambrian explosion describes the massive diversification of animal life around 530 million years ago. The term was popularized by Stephen Jay Gould's 1989 book *Wonderful Life*. It does not surprise me at all that the Burgess Shale fossil bed, which is the best example of the Cambrian explosion, is located in the Pacific Northwest, ever the hotbed of innovation and radicalism. The fossils date to 505 million years ago, remarkably preserve the soft-bodied creatures of that time, and are proof of convergent evolution. Punk culture is an example of convergent evolution in that a similar cultural expression appeared in several different and unconnected places at the same time.

[19] Get it? Our tag line was "Truth in Management and Production," but the newspaper Pravda was the propaganda arm of the Soviet Communist party. But the real joke was me making business deals, "This is Maire Masco with Pravda Productions…" Remember the cold war was still quite active in 1981 and the Soviet Union was called the Evil Empire by US president Reagan.

[20] Fake bands, like Mr. Epp & the Calculations and the Thrown Ups, didn't really play songs as much as get up on stage and swagger around making noise, and they were beloved for their bravery as much as their buffoonery. A similar term was "fuck bands," which referred to bands that existed for one night, as in, a one-night-stand. Corrine Mah came up with the term when these improvised jam sessions began to name themselves.

headlining punk band. Fake bands were equally admired and given a turn on stage.[20] Stylistically, it was equal-opportunity mayhem. The Seattle music scene in the 1980s was like the best Waldorf school ever![21] You were encouraged to be yourself, take a stand, challenge authority, and share your toys. The key to success was to make the most of what you had and to be ready for opportunity. Sure, we felt disenfranchised and had all that angst stuff going on. But we also had social ideals that were brand new to us, and we considered ourselves to be people on the frontier. We wanted to fight the bad guys and create a new age. A *real* new age, not a spiritual "new age" as popularized by Ramtha channeler JZ Knight and reincarnation spokeswoman Shirley MacLaine. We fancied ourselves as pragmatic, more political and social than philosophical. We really hated Ronald Reagan.

THE SUMMER OF 1981

1981 was a little before the modern DIY (do it yourself) movement took off. Nonetheless, we shared a communal sense of "If we don't do this, no one else will, or worse, the stupid people will do it and then we'll really be screwed." We'd heard about scenes in other places, like London, New York, even Minneapolis. Those scenes all had various problems, mostly because they were poisoned by posers, wannabes, and yuppie-turned-rocker schmoes. It was imperative that we take action to promote a local scene that was of our design, representing our politics and tastes. We also felt the local scene needed some cohesion and a better way to communicate; alternative music radio was disappearing.[22] Posters on telephone poles were not sufficient to communicate the nuances of our philosophy. In a drunken spasm of creativity my friends Dennis White and Diana Darzin and I decided to publish a music newspaper, and before we knew it, we were pasting up the first issue of *Desperate Times* in our friend Billy Shaffer's kitchen.

We chain smoked cigarettes, drank cheap beer and swore a lot while putting together that first issue. There were assorted problems along the way. No one knew the name of the guitarist for the Rats, so the photo caption was incomplete. We didn't have enough press-type for the page numbers. The paper's last page was half empty. We all began to wonder why we were even doing

---

[21] Waldorf Education is based on the philosophy of Rudolf Steiner, and stresses the importance of imagination, analysis, and social responsibility.

[22] See "A Few Words About Radio."

what we were doing, and an argument broke out. But we finally decided that we had to publish at least one issue — we'd already told so many people about our new project. Besides, we giggled, if we did this darn thing we were sure to get passes to all the clubs and receive tons of review copies of records and tapes. Right?

God forbid there be any consistency in our efforts! In general, a band was considered good if: (A) you knew someone in the band; (B) it was fast; (C) it was loud; or (D) it had a compelling message — regardless of what that message actually was. Reading the reviews published in *Desperate Times* can be hilarious, sometimes embarrassing, and often rather charming. One local band was encouraged because they were playing faster than they had the previous month. Undistributed demo tapes were critiqued along with major record releases, fashion shows, movies, and whatever else we thought was interesting. Performance art was — well, let's just say the reviews were as confusing as the performances. There was even a review of earplugs, with the (perhaps surprising) admonishment that it was OK to wear them.

The ironic aspect of our DIY venture was that we were actually quite professional about our vision and execution. Before releasing the first issue we had agreements with local records stores and the newsstand at the Pike Place Market to sell the newspaper. That fact alone moved *Desperate Times* into a different league from the 'zines that were making the rounds in the Pacific Northwest. Wilum Pugmire's *Punk Lust* and Dawn Anderson's *Backfire* were well known, but you had to get copies from Wilum or Dawn, or read a friend's copy. In contrast, you could easily pick up an issue of *Desperate Times* at Cellophane Square Records (though it would cost you a quarter).

WAS DESPERATE TIMES A FANZINE?

According to the psychiatrist Frederic Wertham[23] , the most salient feature of a 'zine is its autonomy: "Perhaps its outstanding facet is that it exists without an outside interference, without any control from above, without any censorship, without any supervision or manipulation."[24] But

---

[23] Fredric Wertham was born in Germany in 1895. He wrote on the dangerous influence of violent images in the media on children. His writings led to the implementation of the Comics Code Authority which effectively censored comics of indecent or morally corrupt content, even though he abhorred censorship. Wertham died in November 1981 in Pennsylvania, at the age of 86.

[24] Fredric Wertham, *The World of Fanzines: A Special Form of Communication.* (Southern Illinois University Press, 1973), 71.

I'd rather not define things in the negative. Yes, independence was a critical characteristic, but we intentionally broke with the format of 'zines. We sold ads. We hired a commercial printer to print and fold the newspaper on an offset press. We distributed the newspaper to local stores. This was quite different from the Xeroxed 'zines that were traded at shows or exchanged through the mail like fan mail and autographed pictures.

I prefer to use the graphic arts historian Teal Triggs as a reference point for the definition of a 'zine. For her, fanzines exist "beneath the radar."[25] In 1981, Seattle had two popular culture magazines, the *Seattle Weekly* and *The Rocket*. We didn't want to be like them. There was also a socialist newspaper that was considered underground (it was sold on the street by people wearing Mao hats). We didn't want to do that, either; it sounded like too much work, and also too dangerous. So we found the middle way, a printed paper that looked legitimate enough to pass for a neighborhood newspaper on the outside, was formatted enough to be readable, yet also carried our own distinct voice to our friends without phones.[26] We wrote about things that were important to us, but not part of the popular culture of the time.

PRODUCTION NOTES

The production of *Desperate Times* was primitive, but we used all the resources available to us. Today, people use computers to design layouts and send copy to professional printers via e-mail.[27] Back in the '80s it was paste-up and hand delivery. For *Desperate Times* we used blue-line paste-up board snagged from another local paper (I believe we stole the blue-line boards from *The Rocket*, but I clearly remember they weren't the right size, so we had to cut them down and the printer laughed at us when we delivered them the first time). We used wax to secure the typewritten columns of copy and photocopied pictures to the paste-up boards. When we didn't have wax we used glue, which was a real drag because it tended to smear. Graphics were hand-cut to fit the available space. We used press-type for the headlines and zip-a-tone tape and patterns to make it look "edgy." Our X-ACTO® blades were second-hand and dull.[28]

---

[25] Roger Sabin and Teal Triggs, eds., *Below Critical Radar: Fanzines and Alternative Comics From 1976 to Now*, illustrated ed. (Codex Books, 2002); Teal Triggs, Fanzines (Chronicle Books, 2010).

[26] Telephones were expensive and it was not uncommon for people not to have access to a phone.

[27] In comparison, this book was produced on a computer, and the super clean PDF files were sent to the printer over the internet to the printer and distributor. The book is printed on big super-sized inkjet printers, or bypassing paper products completely, you can download the e-book to your smart phone.

[28] M. Bruno, *Pocket Pal: a Graphic Arts Production* (International Paper Co., 1973). The pre–1987 editions will have definitions for any of the production terms that you may be unfamiliar with.

If an article didn't fit, it would be edited and retyped on the electric typewriter. There was only one typeface and one font size, and we'd cross our fingers that the number of lines in the newly typed article would not fall off the edge. Otherwise we'd have to re-edit and retype and reposition all or a portion of the article. Another vexing problem was extra space on a page. Sometimes we would create "filler" to plug a gap. The biggest challenge was that it wouldn't be apparent that a page was too long or too short until way into the production process. By that time, we were usually pretty rummy and it was hard to make decisions. Billy, the art director, became brilliant at solving spacing problems. Dennis was a whiz at writing up blurbs. My skill was in making last-minute headlines fit with Letraset® press-type.

We printed *Desperate Times* as cheaply as possible. We used the lowest grade pulp paper and leftover ink. The newspaper was printed during the day, when the most inexperienced apprentices worked; in those days, professional newspapers were printed at night by the master pressmen for distribution in the early morning. The printers, bless their hearts, did their best, but frankly we gave them the most horrible paste-ups imaginable.

Once the paper was printed, it was time to get it out to the stores. Our friend Perry McIntyre had a car, so he was our point man for picking up the bundles and driving to the outlying distribution points. I also remember using the bus to deliver papers. All of our sales outlets were so kind. We started out asking twenty-five cents, and I think they all paid us the full cover price; in other words, they did not charge for selling the paper for us, and they didn't take a commission. A businessperson might call this crazy, but the stores knew the value of supporting the scene — people would come in for the paper, and end up buying other items. Also, there was a kind of prestige in carrying *Desperate Times*. I didn't understand this until one issue was distributed a few days late, and storeowners complained about our missing the delivery date. Delivery date? Hey, Perry didn't have money for gas, and I was riding the bus! "You mean people were looking forward to the next issue?"

ZOOMING IN

But the purpose of this book is to document *Desperate Times*. There were a lot of people who put the rag together; consider this book the documentation of a family project. Hey! We put this together! We created this! Here are a few of the key players:

Diana Darzan served as editor. A troublesome gal, we drank a lot together. After 30 years, I'm still not far enough away from *Desperate Times* to fairly and honestly assess her contribution. I'm trying to be kind, but she did empty the checking account and leave me in the lurch when she skipped town. *Desperate Times* was a lot of work, and we were smashed half the time, but we did good. Thanks, DD.

Dennis White was my partner in crime. We ran Pravda Productions as well as *Desperate Times*. He also made sure the newspaper was cool. He did so much, which is why he had the title of "Milk and Cookies Guy" on the masthead.

Billy Shaffer was the art director and a really good guy. He made all the ragged copy and images come together. He donated a lot of supplies, and we used his apartment for the production facilities. He now is an accomplished artist and teacher, as well as a recording artist.[29] I still sing his song sometimes:

> "I once had me a girlfriend, she was so kind and so pretty.
> But now she's gone New Wave and I think that's lousy.
> Whatever happened to my blond beauty queen?
> Why, why, yippy-ai-ai did you dye your hair green?"

Perry McIntyre is my hero. Not only did he provide transportation, he also served as bodyguard and best buddy. He was also gracious and honest. Many a time he saved me from making a complete fool of myself. You are the best, Perry.

MY CONTRIBUTIONS

I somehow managed to retain a full set of *Desperate Times*. My portfolio of posters and press releases was lost over the years, thanks to nomadism and hateful boyfriends. I've been told that I am famous, or should be, because of the concerts I produced in Seattle, and the connections local people were able to make because of those visits. (I call the concerts "visits" because I didn't make any money, I paid the bands so I know they didn't

---

[29] *Pravda Productions Volume I*, released as a cassette in 1982, reissued online and CD in 2012 by the Seattle Syndrome.

make much money, and they often ended up sleeping on my floor.) But when I remember the early '80s I don't think about bringing Husker Dü, Sonic Youth, Really Red, TSOL, the Minutemen, the Butthole Surfers, and many more great bands to town. I remember hanging out with friends. I didn't play in any bands, but *Desperate Times* was in a way "my band," and I am proud of it.

Desperate Times was critical in establishing the local scene and encouraging the local bands that played here. It let people in other parts of the country know that there was indeed an audience and a place to play in Seattle. *Desperate Times* sometimes felt a little like a Judy Garland and Mickey Rooney movie: "Hey! Let's put on a show in the barn!" It took an incredible amount of effort to create an eight-page newspaper. We had to beg and coddle people to write articles. We didn't know how to suck up to advertisers, and it felt a little creepy to sell anything. And of course after we had the contents, we still had to do the production. By the time it got to distribution, we were exhausted. After six issues, the gang called it quits. We couldn't cover the costs, and like with any "band," eventually the fun ran out. The summer of 1981 was over, but it was a great summer.

Maire M. Masco

August 2012

Tacoma, WA.

DESPERATE
TIMES

THE COMPLETE ISSUES

Issue #1

John Cale and X-15 are chosen for the cover of the debut issue to demonstrate the commitment of the newspaper to cover and support local bands as well as noncommercial touring bands.

The two-page spread on hardcore bands lists all the prominent players in the scene. The Showbox Theater was managed by a character named Space Muffin, and his ad hoc advertisement conveys his typical style of humor. The Vancouver Report lists the many venues in Vancouver, BC, but two issues later the same reporter complains there are no venues. This is very typical of the time, when venues appeared and disappeared almost weekly.

Two regular features have titles that show off our clever literary skills. "Moving Violations" reviews touring concerts, particularly independent bands that travel around the country in vans. Like modern gypsies, these traveling musicians often had to deal with flashing lights (that is, the police) and traffic citations. "Drunk and Disorderly" refers to the perceived glory and glamour of going out to clubs and getting plastered.

The publisher of *Desperate Times* is listed as "On the Edge Press," and the address is that of DT House.

DESPERATE TIMES

$.25 JULY 8 VOL.1 NO.1

ADOLESCENTS
CLASSIX
NOUVEAUX
DTZ
EQUATORS
EXPLOITED
FAGS
FARTZ
HOLLY & THE
ITALIANS
MAGAZINE
MAGGOT
BRAINS
PLASMATICS
PSYCHEDELIC
FURS
RAPID-I
RATS
RED DRESS
REJECTORS
SHATTERBOX
URBAN VERBS
VAPORS
VISIBLE
TARGETS

VANCOUVER REPORT ● HARDCORE NORTHWEST

HÜSKER DÜ

IN SEATTLE

JULY 9th 10th...GORILLA ROOM

610 2nd Ave.

JULY 11th...WREX

2018 1st Ave.

BUY:STATUES/AMUSEMENT SINGLE ON REFLEX RECORDS

CONTACT:HUSKER DU P.O.BOX 4596 ST.PAUL,MN.55104

Live it up!

Live it down.
Clothe it at
kitchy koo

6522 15th NE
522 4694

ПАРВДА
pravda productions

634·0303
booking, promotion and management

DESPERATE TIMES

Editor:
Daina Darzin

Associate Editor:
Captive

Manager:
Maire M. Masco

Art Director:
Billy Shaffer

Milk & Cookies:
Dennis White

Contributing Writers:

Bria Conradus, Erica,
Gregor Gayden,
Clark Humphrey,
Corinne Mah, Wilum
Pugmyr

Contributing
Photographers/Artists:

Skip Beattie, James
Carbo, Cam Garrett,
Michele Gianelli,
Kelly Gordon.

Special thanks to the
Gorilla Room, X-15,
Idiot Culture, The
Visible Targets, and
Rapid-i for their
support. Also, thank
you, David Goldberg,
(wherever you are),
for the name.

Desperate Times is
published bi-monthly
by On The Edge Press,
4525 9th N.E., Seattle,
Washington 98105.
(206)-634-0303.

EDITORIAL

"Life is being on the high wire. Everything else is just waiting".

-one of the Flying Wallendas
(or somebody like that)

"Anybody who doesn't use art as a weapon is not an artist."

-Jello Biafra

This magazine is dedicated to everybody who agrees with those two statements. "Desperate" is not about despair, necessarily. One of the dictionary definitions is "involving or employing extreme measures, of extreme intensity, in an attempt to escape defeat or frustration". And the thing is, defeat and frustration are all around us, so it's time to get good and desperate, so maybe things will get better.

What we are not, we are not music critics. We are not saying our opinions are any more valid than yours. They may be different. If they are, write and tell us yours, we'll be glad to print them. We want to work in a supportive rather than judgmental way with bands, clubs, and audience members who are keeping music going in the Northwest, by providing and exchanging information.

What we are: we are definitely desperate. We are completely out of our minds for doing a paper when we have no money and don't know what the fuck we're doing half the time. But, being that the best part of life is the one that's lived on the edge, it's kind of fun this way. We've been hearing all these swell quotes lately, so we'll close with one more:

"We're desperate. Get used to it."
- Exene

D.D.

IN THIS ISSUE

LETTERS

we were going to do this blurb about not having any letters, and please send us some, but then we got this letter, but we still want you to send us some. If you feel like writing but have no idea what you feel like writing about, we have included the first Capt. Clark's Reader Participation Question for, as they say, your convenience.

June 25, 1981

Fraternal greetings and best wishes for the launching of DESPERATE TIMES. Please keep NEW YORK ROCKER on your mailing list--we don't want to miss a single issue!

Best wishes,
ANDY SCHWARTZ/NYR

CAPTAIN CLARK'S Q?

CAPTAIN CLARK'S READER PARTICIPATION QUESTION

Seems all I've been hearing these days is fans bitching about some band or another they just can't stand. They're talking loudly about these bands, so loudly it's almost as if they're trying to be overheard by the right people saying the right thing.

That's no way to form your musical tastes, even in an age of cool cynicism. Examine your true feelings. Most of the bands that it's hip to hate today are just four-song power pop or show bands that were lucky enough to draw large promotional budgets. There are many other outfits who deserve your contempt far more.

READER PARTICIPATION QUESTION #1:

What act do you hate the most that it's all right to like, at least in your own circle of scenemakers?

READER PARTICIPATION QUESTION #2:

Is the opposite: Your favorite "sinful pleasure" band that would get you kicked out of the social scene if anyone knew you liked it. Dare to bare your lusts, and prepare to give good reasons for your responses. Then send them to Desperate Times and we'll print as many answers as we want to and if anyone tells you you're a jerk because you said you liked Those Dumbshits, hold your head high and walk on by.

MOVING!

JOHN CALE AND X-15

The Showbox

Ordinarily, concert reviews do not begin with the lowdown on the opening band. However, John Cale is no ordinary man, and the only way to avoid stinting on X-15 is to begin at the beginning. So here goes:

After an awfully long wait, X-15 came on and proved they were worth waiting for. They stretched it a little. People weren't dancing as much or as hard as they might have been. Waiting is an exhausting process. But by the time the band swung into the third song, "Necessary Evil", the audience was behind them. The military drumming cut with a straight punk beat suited the ominous lyrics perfectly, and it was only one of several numbers that showed the band's versatility. It's nice to see a local band that knows having a 'sound' doesn't mean it all has to sound the same.

Other highpoints were "Mad Again", "Dance or Die", and a sort of Lou Reed talk-thru with an 'oo-lah' chorus that I didn't catch the name of. Kelly Mitchell gripped the microphone like a drowning man, but he wasn't trying to climb to safety. He looked like he was going to take it down with him at one point, screaming "this world's an open sore!" When he wasn't arched dripping over the audience, he was skittering across the stage or into fellow band members. The whole set was fun to watch, but the hit of the evening was the last song, "I Wanna Be Vaporized". This one included all the people who could be dragged on stage. (Well, it didn't take a lot of armtwisting.) The group was fairly recognizable: they're the people who are always in the front row. And that special touch of reality was added by a kid whose bloody nose turned his face into a rust-colored mess as he pogoed triumphantly to the end.

X-15 is a tight band. Their lyrics are political enough, and their music is hard enough, to be classified as punk. The difference is that they're more deliberately likeable than most punk bands. Whatever distinction you want to make, they were hot that night and the crowd let them know it.

OK. John Cale; now we get to the serious part.

First, some background. John Cale is still this side of 40, but only just. He's a classically trained musician who plays a wide range of instruments, and worked with avant-garde musician LaMonte Young in the mid-60's. After that, he joined the Velvet Underground, part of a show Andy Warhol took on tour as The Plastic Exploding Inevitable. The group included Lou Reed and Nico, and had an incalculable effect on the pre-'77 'proto-punks', people like the Stooges, Patti Smith and Richard Hell.

In 1968 he left the Velvets, coming out a year later with Vintage Violence (a cut-out by the way, and worth it), and in 1970 producing and playing back-up for Nico's underground classic Desertshore. Since then he's put out nearly an album a year, none of which ever made it into the mainstream of record buyers.

Honi Soit . . ., the latest, is somewhat different musically but contains the same preoccupations Cale has been writing about for years. Which is fine, because war, death, religion, love, and literature are fairly inexhaustible subjects. Still, above all Cale writes about time: its destruction, and its implacability. From "Half-Past France" on Paris 1919, where time is distance and tradition and he muses: "back in Berlin they're all well fed/I don't care/People always bored me anyway," to "Wilson Joliet", on Honi Soit, where time is a tangible presence that has to be bought or borrowed: "before the clock slammed another door/Of the weary hours we were facing a second hand shylock."

This time the price is not a pound of flesh, but a way of life--or death. You can measure time, spend it, kill it, look at it historically or wear it on your wrist; you can't change it. And no contemporary musician has brought this closer or more precisely to our attention than John Cale.

With all this in mind, we come to the concert itself. Cale came on looking tired, dressed down, with lines in his face and a beergut edging its way over his jeans. But from the first eerie strains of "Streets of Laredo" to the last quiet bars of the encore, he put on one hell of a show. The band played to kill, particularly Sturgis Nikides whose fine guitar work put a sharp edge on lyrics that were already so far from innocuous you could cut yourself if you got too close.

Along with favorites like "Dr. Mudd" (about bombed people in Hiroshima and Nagasaki, with a bounce-along chorus of "what you gonna do?") and "Pablo Picasso"; he played a lot off the new album. "Riverbank" was appropriately intense and well paced, his voice winding over the music to bring the imagery together. "Dead or Alive" sounded much better in concert; the studio version is tame in comparison, and "Fighter Pilot" had to fight its way through a desperate grimace that stayed on Cale's face for a good part of the show.

Of all the songs, "Wilson Joliet" was the most amazing. It ended with an impassioned shriek into a countdown, leaving in its wake a haze of bullets and burntout streets in a foreign time. The crown was

PHOTO: Kelly Gordon

clotted around the stage like blood, and believe it or not, some people were slamdancing. Why, god knows. It certainly didn't sound like that kind of music.

Except, possibly, for the first encore "Mercenaries (Ready for War)". The song itself is so good, it can't be done without a certain amount of explosive shoving. When everyone else was writing songs about not fighting other people's wars, or going to war because they're such mean motherfuckers, Cale put out a single about soldiers of fortune. And if you think these people don't exist anymore, you should go to your local newsstand and pick up a copy of Soldier of Fortune magazine.

The second encore was the notorious version of "Heartbreak Hotel". It ended with the singularly appealing line, "We feel so lonely, we could DIE!" It didn't look like there was going to be anything else, since Cale had crawled offstage after hitting the floor on that number. But the audience screamed itself hoarse, and he came on alone and played a short, reminiscent "I keep a Close Watch".

"What a boring song to end with", someone said behind me as the crown thinned. This sort of reaction wasn't widespread, but it was definitely there. Some people can't seem to realize that a song doesn't have to be loud and fast to have guts--it just has to have them in the first place. Most of the audience thought John Cale was great. Some were bored to tears.

It's hard to understand how a man who drips charisma like most people sweat can be boring at all. And that's what this article is about. Because, despite appearances, this is not a rave review. Cale has put on much better shows. At the Showbox, it took him a while to warm up, he played only guitar and keyboards, and the whole show came in just over an hour, even including three encores. The fact is, John Cale on a mediocre night is better than most people at their best. And you can put me on the witness stand about that one anytime.

—Captive

THE VAPORS
THE IMPACTS
& DONUTS

Showbox

Isn't this the band that wrote a hit song, about masturbation? (I'm Turning Japanese). Well, at least that's what everyone told me. Fearing the worst, and with little expectations of fun, I slithered into the Showbox and met up face to face with . . . . living personifications of that hideous, meaningless term, NEW WAVE. A local band, The Impacts, were playing to a dancing, slamming crowd of stripes, striped skinny ties, striped skinny tie pins, and everything you've always wanted at Baby & Co. but couldn't afford. The Impacts play fast, decent vocals, some good Ramones covers and surfin' tunes, but so predictable and boring. I guess the crowd didn't notice much, but what could they notice wearing those cool Ray Charles specs? Outside, waiting for the Vapors' set, I had an interesting chat with some of my friends and yours, the infamous yet lovable donut holers. Yup, those same people (?) who manically stalk the Donut Shop Corner uttering useless splab and just giving shit in general to anyone walking by. Well, the source of their hostility has finally been revealed - I was informed that anyone writing or hanging chains on leather jackets is guilty of possessing a sick mind and should be killed on sight. "We wore leathers first and we don't like seeing them messed up by disgusting punk rockers." Now the hassles seem so much more relevant.

OK, enough stalling. The Vapors. Tight, good energy, very British sounding, songs about society, bureaucracy. After two songs, my main impression was, these guys sound like, or are trying to sound like, The Jam, but failing miserably. What do you know, Bruce Foxton produced their album. The Jam are great, and these guys were only depressing me. One song, "Turning Japanese", which gets occasional airplay, was alright, but they just weren't rocking' enough for me. I gotta admit I didn't even stay long enough to really think so.

—Erica

2

VIOLATIONS

THE EQUATORS
Showbox

Another ironic twist; the
Equators roll into town the
other night, to do install-
ment number two of the Showbox's "Cheap Thrills" concert
series. "Power Pop From
England" say the flyposters.
Power what? Well...if it
gets 'em in off the streets,
y'know. (Would've been nice to
have let the masses know what
they were plopping three
smackers down for, eh, Muffin?
Might've brought a few more in
as well).

The Equators are, in fact
from England — . .England
with a capital Jamacold.
Definitely not steeped in
that culture's flamoyant and
long history of pop-o-philia,
however. I take that back a
little: the Equators, for
all their good intentions,
tend to tip their hat a wee
bit too low toward fellow
birminghemites Steel Pulse.
A regional sound; trend in
musical direction? Somehow
I doubt it. Talented? No
question about it.

None the less...ahem... the
Equators' Seattle gig (ill-
attended for whatever reason)
had the aura of a very good act
on a very mediocre evening.
Yeah, I know, they tried real
hard, danced about through most
of the set. What few folks
showed up gathered just
below center stage, doing
Seattle's ill-interpreted
version of the skank.

What ensued (on both the
part of the band and the
audience) was a rather long
and tedious attempt to create
"atmosphere". Unfortunately,
creation never lives up to
sponaneaity.

Given the general feel of
the evening, a smaller,
sweatier venue would have
been more appropriate.
Still, no use wishing for
the past to change itself,
so only two pressing questions remain: Was it worth
it? For less than three
bucks, you bet! Would I
see'em 'gin? Shit yeah! I
know they got it in 'em
somewhere.
                — Dennis White

'KISS IN MOHAWKS'

THE PLASMATICS
Showbox

The Plasmatics are the American
Dream: they combine violence,
sex, and excessive, spectacular
gimmicks in a clever Media
Event package that's probably
going to get them a place in
Billboard history as the
first "punk" band to crack
the Top 40. And that's ok,
I guess. This country will
always buy hyped up, laugh-all-
the-way-to-the-bank performers
over real talent, so it might
as well be Wendy. I respect
her gutsiness and energy. I
probably would have liked
the Plasmatics a lot better
when they were an unknown band
playing CBGB's on slow Tues-
days. I was bored to death at
the Showbox. Slick, big-
money production doesn't
work with bamalama metal/
punk: it destroys the gritty,
anarchist edge that makes good
hardcore bands so powerful and
interesting. Without that, all
you got is Kiss in mohawks.

As to what went on: they
had a video of a car being
blown up, in lieu of an opening
band. Wendy actually did a
costume change. Most of her
performance consisted of an
expanded, more graphic version
of Tina Turner's microphone
blowjob routine. (Tina's was
much sexier.) She also sledge-
hammered a TV, which was cool,
and chainsawed a guitar, which
was not. I realize that
destroying instruments is a
rock tradition, but it's always
pissed me off. What is the
point of smashing the symbol of
one's creative expression/
rebellion?

And then there was the Patrick
McDonald Incident. Wendy
dedicated "A Pig Is A Pig" to
him, and had a banner expressing similar sentiments.
McDonald was not supposed to
have been admitted to the show,

and at one point was asked
to leave. There were several
versions of what caused all
this: the one I tend to
believe is that, during an
interview that afternoon, Wendy
was telling McDonald about
getting beat up by the police,
and McDonald suggested she
enjoyed the experience.
Real charming of him, huh.

The audience was strange.
Wendy incited very little
slamdancing that I could see;
I noticed some couples necking,
though. Hmm. The evening
was best exemplified by my
two favorite punks-for-a-day:
a really straight looking
middle-class guy who exited
yelling "Hey, let's go kill
the donut gang!",and a tan,
muscular guy in a torn pink
t-shirt with PUDZ RULE on the
back. Lettsee, Showbox capacity
= 800 x $10.50 = $8,400.00 not
counting over-capacity admis-
nions and factoring in the
$12.50 tickets sold at the
door. But then, those big Van
Halen-style tour busses use up
a shitload of gas.

                —Daina Darzin

PHOTO: Cam Garrett

PHOTO: Cam Garrett

3

H(A)RDCORE

DAINA DARZIN
photographs by
SKIP BEATTIE

PART 2 IS GOING TO HAPPEN WHEN RPA e

① No Prisoners ② Loud Fart ③ Mike Refuzor, DTz ④ Blaine Fart ⑤ Rejectors & guest vocalists ⑥ Jane, DTz

No, it's not something stupidly grabbed on to by kids who are too young to have fully experienced 1977. And no, it's not the nostalgia of people who, like hippies do with 1966, have decided that '77 was the best year of their lives and they're going to stay there forever. Anyone who thinks punk is dead should have been at the Steve Fart/Mike Refuzor birthday party at the Gorilla Room June 29th. It incorporated the best of punk--killer sets by some very talented bands--with a little of the worst of punk--playful fighting which finally turned into something heavier, and trashing of stuff that's hard to repair. That's the way the package comes, I guess. The real destructive shit is always done by a few people who are using punk as an excuse to act like assholes. But not to dwell on that: too much has been said already by the establishment press, ever ready to point out the evils of another Subversive Element threatening our great society. This column is about why punk is terrific, and important.
There is nothing like the furious energy of good hardcore to get you in touch with your own anger, and that's really necessary today. The impulse is to New Romanticize out, and pretend you don't see the shit going on around you. That's easy, but it's not right. Punk is about reality, and will stay current and valid for as long as the world stays as fucked up as it is. This ends today's lecture.
There's some hot bands playing the Northwest, a report from numerous evenings at the Gorilla Room:

The Fartz are a great band. Seeing them is like watching war footage: the camera angles leave something to be desired, but the scene is so overwhelmingly real and intense (and you know the photographer could have gotten killed shooting it) that it's more powerful than the best movie could ever

be. The Fartz do classic, no-frills hardcore, and pull it off without the benefit of leather jackets, mohawks, or a put-on, Kottener-than-thou stage attitude. I don't know how well their stuff will translate onto a record (we'll see real soon), but I'd see them live any time.

I hate writing about the last gig of a really good group: The DTz broke up, all parties plan to get new bands together. The DTz improved tremendously in the short time they were together, from being really awful when I saw them a couple of months ago, to becoming one of the most

4.

NORTH WEST PART II

THE SUBHUMANS & SOME OTHER BANDS PLAY SOMEPLACE AROUND HERE

⑥ ⑩

⑦

⑪

⑨

⑧

The Maggot Brains. We were supposed to have a photo of the Maggot brains (out Skin had to work late + the MBs came out first (sorry about that).

② Tom Fart ⑩

Ro XS ⑩

① Steve Fart ⑧ _____ *insert names of players , Rats ⑨* Ro xs

thick guitar/bass drone with a frenetic, high-speed rock beat. I can't wait to see them with a new front person.

The Rats, from Port-land, must keep coming up to Seattle on a regular basis. They can't really be classified as hardcore musically, they're in the same ballpark as X-15. As with X-15, they come off as punks at heart, though: the Rats have a dark, mean sound and project a lot of sweat and passion on stage. They have a really great song (the title of which I was suppo-sed to get and didn't) whose hook goes "You're getting restless/you're just an animal" over and over, it's the perfect musical embodiment of the urban-night crazies that hit you when the moon is full. The Rats' stuff gets into your head, real eerie and moving.

The Rejectors have potential; they do L.A.-sound slambang hardcore with a lot of pissed-off energy. The group hasn't been together very long, and still lacks the cohesive stage pre-sence one gets by playing a lot. Should be real good in a couple of months, though.

Last, and least, there's the fabulous Maggot Brains. The Maggot Brains are strong contenders, along with Rox Off, Fred, and the Correc-tive Lenses, for being the worst band in Seattle. They look heavy hardcore but can't play anywhere near fast enough. At one point, they asked if the audience wanted to hear some jokes, and proceeded to tell some in Henny-Youngman-gone-wrong fashion. Finally, they gave up all pretenses and played "Louie Louie". Sort of. I take it back, the Maggot Brains are great. I hadn't laughed that hard in weeks.

impressive bands in town. The DTz start with a hardcore beat and do somewhat more melodic guitar/vocal lines on top of it. Their stuff is origi-nal and intelligent: "Jim Jones" and "Nobody" particularly stand out. Mike Refuzor has a lot of talent; he takes over a stage, and manages to come off threatening

and entertaining at the same time. The DTz closed their June 29 set with a cover of my favorite song of all time: Lou Reed's "Heroin", and actually got away with it (Reed's version is a very hard act to follow). Anyway, watch for bands with ex-DTz in them: they'll be real special.

No Prisoners (formerly Slaughter Squad, from Vancouver) have been operating without a lead singer lately, but their instrumen-tals are good enough to get away with it. They probably have the best chops of any hardcore band around. They have an intense, army-approaching sound, incorporating

5

DRUNK AND DISORDERLY

HELLO, BLACKOUTS...

Photo: Skip Beattie

The Blackouts have the philosophy of not performing live very often and "over-exposing" themselves, or at least not playing live untill they're "ready". I don't get it. If you're ambitious enough to run a big ad in the NYRocker, why not try it out on some people first? At any rate, the anticipation level was sufficiently high for the return of Seattle's best-known unknown band. Great atmosphere at Kosco Louie, too. It's fun to be able to drink illegally whn you're 26.

Anyway, the crowd was looking forward to Blackingout, but their vision got blurred by some very exciting Rapid-i movement (eye'm sorry, no more REM puns). This band is hot.

It was one of those rare occasions where they enjoyed what they were doing and you enjoyed what they were doing. Not to be missed, especially the lead guitarist, if he can keep it up.

Sorry, Blackouts, but maybe I understand your theory now. You are one of the few groups I've ever heard that sound better on record than in performance. Love your records, though.

—Billy Shaffer

GOODBYE, FAGS

PHOTO: Michele Gianelli

The Fags' May 30 set at Danceland had the audience buzz of an important event because it was supposedly the band's very last gig. That's really too bad, if it's true: their show was one of the most interesting, inventive pieces of theater I'd seen in a long time. I call it theater as opposed to a concert because the Fags were much more about performance than music, and that's ok, the performance was great. Upchuck looked terrifically weird in his Nosferatu makeup, he has a stage presence that makes just about everything he does interesting. Circus-y craziness abounded; the Fags switched off on instruments, threw real, raw squid into the audience, and had mystery-guest vocals. They did a lot of classic covers, including the Velvet Underground's "White Light/White Heat"; Barbara Ireland did a heat Siouxie and the Banshees-style "White Rabbit". Hopefully, the Fags will reincarnate as a different band immediately: psychotic creativity should not go to waste.

— Daina Darzin

and then there's...
SLEAZY COVER BANDS

RED DRESS

I'm supposed to write something about Red Dress. Right now. Didn't know I was to do this, but here goes:

Red Dress is cool. Why? For starters, there's leader Gary Minkler. You just have to see this short, skinny, bald guy, stiffen his spine into a rigidity that increases his stature by at least three inches and tilt his head up so high that he has to hold the microphone down to it at all times, except when he bends over like--well, like a robot. And sounds come out of his mouth. Primeval R & R, R & b, or whatever you choose to call it, he delivers it with so much energy and intensity that only his jerky motions give away his roots as an art-noise performer.

Well, maybe you can. He does have more Captain Beefheart-type vocal inflections than any of the national acts that are supposed to be "Beefheart-inspired". But there's also a touch or two of Ray Charles, Stevie Wonder, maybe even Jerry Lee Lewis?

The guitarists, Pete Pendras and John Olufs, create a rich blend of licks that keep Minkler's monster relatively chained. Add the dance rhythms of drummer Greg Keplinger and bassist, sometime organist bill bagley, and you've got yourself the electricity that R&R is really about.

"We're working towards getting out (of Seattle)," Minkler told me a few months back. The other week he updated that: "At least Portland and Vancouver". He was slightly understating things, as he sometimes does offstage. The band has made one New York trek, one professional demo tape, and is working to woo a Major Label Contract. See them now while you can department. Already, you don't see too much of what used to be Red Dress's "second-set" material anymore. That was when the beast was unleashed, when the boys would venture into the nether regions of art-blues. It didn't really go over in tavs; I once heard Minkler at the old buffalo going through a five-minute rhapsody of angst, my mind trying to stay within the delicate moods he was establishing, my ears trying not to hear the bloated customer in the back repeatedly yelling "Play some Allman brothers".

— Clark Humphrey

SHATTERBOX

Shatterbox is the Gorilla Room version of Van Halen. They did a star entrance, complete with girlfriends, took forever to test their mikes and astounding set of lights. The girlfriends yelled "Shatterbox ROCKS!!". "With our cocks out" the lead singer added, put on his shades, and launched into a bunch of 60's mamalama rock covers. The lights flashed in a variety of colors, really cute stuff. For the first 10 minutes, I thought all this was really obnoxious, around the time they got to the theme from Secret Agent and the Sex Pistols' Seventeen, though, their sleazy energy started to grow on me. By the end of the set, I loved them. These guys are the ultimate parody of the decadent-rock-star syndrome: like the food you get at a truckstop diner, Shatterbox is so totally greasy and disgusting they're wonderful.

—Daina Darzin

6

.....THE VISIBLE TARGETS
MAKING IT IN THE MODERN WORLD

Let me put the nail in the coffin once and for all. The Visible Targets are an all-girl band, with a male drummer from Yakima (ha ha) and they play great dance music like the B-52s.

Now I can't be accused of writing about the Targets without mentioning any of the above (which seem to get repeated every time the VTs appear in print). Didn't want to disappoint you, I guess.

So the VTs are more then a novelty band, eh? They are sisters, Pamela, Laura and Rebecca Johnson on guitar, vocal, and bass respectively (they all take turns on vocals), and Ronnie Simmons on funny-shaped drums.

I have no idea how long and hard Mr. & Mrs. Johnson & Simmons pushed their proteges into musical careers, and for that matter, it probably doesn't matter. What does matter, however, is they seem to have been supportive. Yakima might not be histori-cally noted as one of the hotbeds of creative musical talent, but it is nonetheless a very typical, average Ame-rican town, one from scores of bands as sensitive, talented and receptive could only have come. That their drummer is a male should come as no sur-prise. The VTs are not an all-girl band with a drummer. If someone more suited than Simmons to sit in had arrived, complete with regulation physio-genital prerequisites, we mith well label the VTs "all girls with . . ." however, that's not the case, so let's drop it, snail we? Now about this B-52's thing: what the hell do the VTs and B-52s have in common? The Visible Targets are a 3-piece, sans keyboards, synths and male

vocals. The harmonies set directly up front, and there is far less over-reliance on lyrical cuteness. If one must compare bands, draw parallels to the Mo-dettes. They seem to be aiming closer, although not directly, toward similar musical goals as the Targets. Better yet, don't draw any parallels.

Last, who in God's name ever said dance music should be dismissed as a mindless excuse to fart about on the dance floor, and not take anything further than back to the bar.

What the Visible Targets do best is deliver tight, rhythmic vignettes stolen directly from a lot of their own perceptions. No warbled nonsense, none of the smarmy cuteness of your typical new-wave glot. In fact, one of the most impres-sive assets of the VTs is their sincere, professional approach to what they do. when they smile onstage, it's because they're pleased, not because they've devised an image to lead audiences astray.

They are a very visual band, and have exploited the fact that there are three women in the band by making use of their collective experience in the music biz. Simmons claims his bass drum (looking as if it were in the process of melting)

doesn't really sound any better than a conventional rig, but it does provide more than a little curiosity. "My most often-asked question is: 'How do you get heads for it? I tell them they're specially made at the Ludwig Factory in California. I have to get 5 or 6 of them at a time".

Other comments are directed toward Rebecca's clear, tight, yet innovative bass lines. It's no wonder. One night I saw Rebecca onstage, fingers bleeding and bandaged, dili-gently attempting to master a particular technique. Or Pam laboriously picking out simple yet effective leads that demanded precision over flash. They may be women, but they're selling music, not sex.

I spoke recently with The Visible Targets. I was curious about their pasts, and how they ended up doing what they're doing today.

"when I was 15, I was playing in bands" says Ronnie. "I've ben working ever since". It was only natural that in a small town like Yakima, all four would eventually get together. The other three went to Europe in 1977, which is where the idea of forming a band took hold. "We met in Amsterdam and hooked up with another American woman, Suki McLaughen. We played around with things from the Beatles to Gershwin." In London, Laura and Rebecca recorded at Snob Studios ("cheap, about $100.") with an English drummer.

Equipped with acoustic guitars they'd brought from home, Rebecca soon found herself learning bass in the studio.

When all three had arrived back in the states, then ran into Simmons, and decided to try something. "It wasn't really serious at that point" says Laura. Eventually, it did get serious, and some time later the band was forced into a decision: to stay on in Yakima or move to Seattle? The chose Seattle, "musically, to have someone to play to". Their first gig was opening for the Cowboys and the Enemy.

When all three had arrived back in the states, then ran into Simmons, and decided to try something. "It wasn't really serious at that point" says Laura. Eventually, it did get serious, and some time later the band was forced into a decision: stay on in Yakima or move to Seattle? They chose Seattle, "musically, to have someone to play to". Their first gig was opening for the Cowboys and the Enemy at the Gorilla Room's opening, under the moniker Wreckless. Since then, about 16 months ago, The Targets have steadily built up a style, repertoire and following.

"We want to record, to draw crowds, and fill places" says Simmons. With their ability and determination, it appears The Visible Targets will soon reach that goal.

"we've been at it for years" recalled Pam. we always got support, but we had to go out and earn our own money. $30 guitars are a lot at 50 cents a lawn."

Right now, the VTs are facing the same old problem.

"We're searching for the right studio. The only thing that has kept us from doing a record is that we're broke", they told me. "For the time being, they're working on a film titled, ironically, Just For Money. Bruce Vecchito is producing. And as always, each gig debuts a new song. Success can't be too far away, they've come too far to turn back now. Ever optimistic, the Visible Targets know where they're going.

we've got a future/'Cause we're living in a modern world/Coins are flipping/ Heads are turning. . .

c We Like It Johnson/Johnson/ Johnson 1981

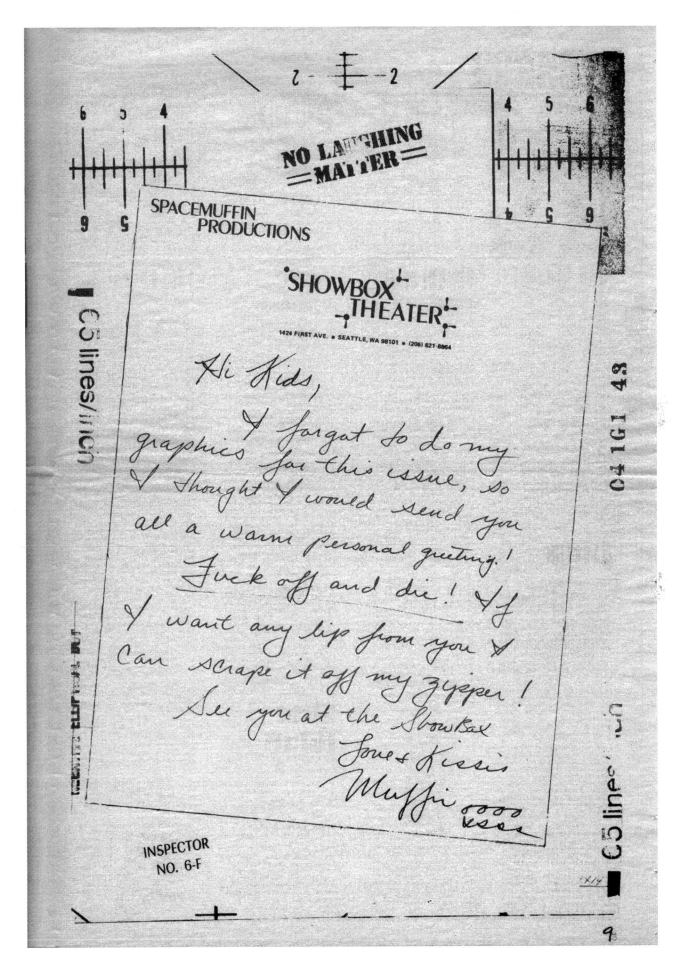

SPACEMUFFIN
PRODUCTIONS

'SHOWBOX'
THEATER

1424 FIRST AVE. • SEATTLE, WA 98101 • (206) 621-8864

Hi Kids,
 I forgot to do my
graphics for this issue, so
I thought I would send you
all a warm personal greeting!
Fuck off and die! If
I want any lip from you I
can scrape it off my zipper!
 See you at the Showbox
 Love & Kisses
 Muffin oooo
 xsxx

INSPECTOR
NO. 6-F

RECORDS

DEAD KENNEDYS
Too Drunk To Fuck/Prey

IRS

Suffice it to say that I taped "Too Drunk To Fuck" 10 times in a row 'cause I got tired of starting the 45 over. TDTF replaces the Gang of Four's "What We All Want" as the hottest single of '81: punky-sleazy, frantic instrumentals similar to the intro of "Chemical Warfare" on Fresh Fruit For Rotting Vegetables, very, very funny lyrics. An absolute must for anyone who has ever been TDTF (a tacky scene) or been with anyone who was TDTF (much worse).

The B-side, "Prey", is a sweet little ballad about a tourist about to be mugged, sung, of course, from the standpoint of the mugger. More than anybody else, the Dead Kennedys know which spots to hit to make people really nervous. That's one of the main reasons they're so fucking brilliant, my absolutely favorite band right now.

–D.D.

MAGAZINE
Magic, Murder and the Weather

Virgin SP 70020

The rumour was confirmed this past week; Magazine, who first opened my ears with the amazing debut of Real Life, and continued to see me through the last three years with very little complaint, have decided to end the affair. Sad as that may be, they have not gone with a whimper, but have left us this fine and, alas, final parting gift.

Magic, Murder, and the Weather, being three topics currently on the mind of Mr. Howard Devoto, continues in much the same vein as The Correct Use of Soap, leaving the gothic gloom of the first two albums far behind.

Opening with About The Weather, we hear the band pumping out a thoroughly danceable interpretation of sixties' Motown. "So Lucky", "Come Alive", and "Naked Eye", continue the soul theme, Dave Formula's Keyboards providing a reference point, his synthesizer updating the overall sound. As usual, Barry Adamson's fluid bass lines babble, churn, and pull everything through as drummer John Doyle supports in his very proper, restrained fashion.

Not that this is one big party. The mysterious story of "The honeymoon Killers" and the slower insistence of "The Great Man's Secrets" take a different tact. The introspective "Vigilance" allows new guitarist Ben Manderlson a chance to show what he can do, although he is mixed rather low through the entire album. Lyrically, Devoto confirms his standing as one of the best. Vocally, he is better than ever, with Laura Teresa once again adding her wonderful breathy backups as counterpoint to his somewhat droll delivery. Producer Martin Hannett deserves credit for keeping a light hand on the sound; Magazine are no Joy Division, and he knows it.

Yes, it is sad that this is the last, but five albums are no small mark. As Howard says in So Lucky: "I think it will turn out rather well . . ."

– Gregor Gayden

PSYCHEDELIC FURS
Talk Talk Talk

CBS 37339

Prior to the release of the Psychedelic Furs' second album, Talk Talk Talk, I firmly doubted their ability to follow up their brilliant debut lp. The Furs, for quite a while, could have easily qualified as the worst band in London, so the strength of The Psychedelic Furs came as a cold slap in the face to those who had followed the band during their early career. The big question was "can they do it again?"

Initial reaction to their latest album is somewhat of a dilema. It seems to be less accesible, not as bright or well-arranged as the first; yet it has brought them not only musical acclaim, but a certain amount of commercial success as well. If the Furs have been accused of formulizing their sound, this disc can only serve to fuel those arguments. There are no "Sister Europe"s here, nor any of the brilliance of "We Love You".

What is offered in their place are the rythmic intrigues of "Dumb Waiters" and churning drone of "Mr. Jones". (In this case, a re-mix of their superior single release.) More of the usual Furs musical themes and progressions, and fewer hooks seem to be the order of Talk Talk Talk.

What is most interesting about this album is a sudden obsession with Freudian gimmickry. A cheap shot, or another example of the Furs over-extending a good thing? (listen to their debut; how many times do they use the word "stupid") I'm not talking about the obvious attempt at psychedelic sex sonnets ("Into You Like A Train"), but the fact that everything here revolves around Mrs. Jones, Mrs. London, Mrs. Jones. . ."or Mrs. anyone", lots of trashy vaudevillian phrases like "I just wanna sleep with you" or "I don't wanna take you down", et al.

I sometimes wonder if the joke's on me. Am I supposed to accept the Furs as satire or take them as thelogicalextension of a brilliant musical genre? I leave the argument open. I guess it's cooler that way. If psychedelia is/was/will be basically an absurdist mode, then Talk Talk Talk soars brilliantly above the rest. Secretly, in my heart of hearts I'll take any amount of shit the Furs dole out.

–D.N.

ADOLESCENTS
The Adolescents

Frontier Records

For some reason, I haven't listened to this album for a couple of weeks. So it was a shock when, having been asked to write this review, I put it on today––and was blown away with its power all over again.

Everything about this hardcore punk band is exceptional. The lyrics are superb. Check this out:

> "Messages and slogans are the primary decor/history's recorded in a clutter on the floor"

("Kids of the black Hole")

Now that's poetry, and emotions well-expressed. Each set of lyrics stand on their own as exquisite examples of superbly put thoughts concerning the struggles of being young, an outsider, a punk.

But just as exciting as the words is the noise. The songs are quite well-structured, at one moment slow and moody, then suddenly loud and fast. Tony Cadena, on vocals, lives on this piece of plastic. His anger, his pissed-off snarls, his subtle voice when the music is slow, is a pleasure to listen to. On most of the songs he is very easily understood (they have, however, included a lyric sheet).

The drums and guitars are so well played that every time I play this I find myself listening, amazed, to something else. I cannot express myself in musical terms. At one moment I am aware of the high wailing of a guitar, then I find myself nodding to the bass guitar, then the drumming floods me with a wave of fury. This is the kind of record that captures in a studio the intense power that most punk bands can capture only in concert, or on a live album.

The packaging, containing a number of photos, and a striking cover design, is attractive. I am certain that, if I had to recommend one album to someone who was interested in punk but didn't know who to buy, that this is the album that would first come to mind. It kicks with the power of life that makes punk rock the most exciting of today's new music.

–Wilum Pugmyr

CLASSIX NOUVEAUX
Guilty b/w Night People

Liberty Records

"Guilty" is a pretty usual new wave song. It boasts clean, danceable production, one catchy hook, and a singer who sounds enough like a number of other people to capture your attention for 3 minutes. Luckily, that's how long the song is.

When I put on the other side, a friend said it sounded like 'The Cramps meet Bryan Ferry and get their balls cut off'. Don't buy it unless the idea intrigues you, because that about says it all.

– Captive

THE AU PAIRS
Playing With a Different Sex

The Au Pairs are hot and cold. Their music gets you moving, repetitive licks get you singing, and even before the intensity hits, there is an involvement with the songs that only rarely comes with vinyl.

The Au Pairs have two strengths: the first is the basic arrangement of their music. Good musicians, good producers (the Au Pairs, Martin and Ken) plus just the right amount of studio gimmickry prove to me that perfection is nearly possible. The second force being the Au Pairs wonder is Leslie Wood. She knows how to use her voice, a good jazz background, I would guess (in "Unfinished Business", she sounds very much like Sarah Vaughn). In "Come Again", her jeering intonation alone brings the message across.

Which brings me to another aspect of this "English band". What is the Au Pairs' message? The title reveals a lot. The Au Pairs show through their songs that they know the plays in the game. Their lyrics deal directly with the sexual politics that go on between men and women. The Au Pairs breach every gender-related interaction from the still holy institution of marriage in Love Song:

> Take out the ring/two fates sealed/ negotiated a business deal/Is this true romance?

to the acknowledgement of female political prisoners in "Armagh":

> American hostages in Iran/heard daily on the news/you can ignore the 32 women/in Armagh jail

but the Au Pairs are far from being plaintive about the female condition. There is no guilt to be found here. Playing With A Different Sex is a report on the state of affairs (in "Dear John", the woman encourages "it will help you with your fantasy"), and the difficulties of the contemporary life style (in "Come Again"):

> It's your turn now/but do you want to?/I don't know if you want to/It's inhibiting/restricting/so confusing.

The songs are as diversified as situations, going from the jazzy, driving "We're So Cool" through the whole spectrum to the dreamy, utopian "It's Obvious". The Au Pairs are intelligent and sexy. "Playing With A Different Sex" proves it:

> touch/glance/it's a romance

–M.M.M.

10

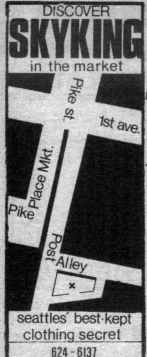
ACCESSORIES

BYE BYE ROCK DISCO

WREX is undergoing a bunch of changes. Wes Bradley is no longer involved in managing the club; booking will now be done by Bev Williams in conjunction with Steve Pritchard. They hope to have national acts and bands from out of town as well as a lot of local bands who haven't played WREX previously. Steve also wants to go on record as saying he did not say that Wes was an asshole who alienated most of the music community. Some upcoming acts: Veil of Tears, The Room, RPA, The Pudz, No Alternative, Lenny Kaye, The Blackouts.   D.D.

CONSUMER REPORT: EARPLUGS

To get one thing out of the way right off, EARPLUGS ARE NOT AN INDICATION OF WIMPINESS. Incipient or otherwise. If you play in a high decibel band, they are an invaluable aid after the fact. You don't have to read lips in the course of normal conversation. If you make it a habit to listen to high dB music, earplugs can prevent that buzzing hangover along with general tympanic deterioration. And if you've woken up once or twice with blood coming out of your ears, you'd be a jerk not to at least consider them.

Most people who own earplugs don't use them all the time, but they're nice to have around on the fifth clubnight in a row. There are a lot of different kinds, the most popular for music being Sonic II by Norton. Sonics are designed to filter out only high-level noise, leaving your ears free to hear all the music. They range in price from a whopping $10 at Friar Tucks to $5 at Kenelly Keys on 8th and 45th. If you're downtown, Myer's Music is next in line at $5.88.

Willett Maico in the Medical/ Dental building downtown has earplugs in three sizes for $1.95 a pair, and most local drugstores carry a few brands. The cheapest kind are about 19¢ at industrial places such as Safety & Supply or gun stores. They're disposable foam, and have a noise reduction rating of 29 decibels. These occasionally work too well, but are the most comfortable (aside from the custom jobs at $25 and up.)

Even if you're not too keen on the idea, 19¢ is a minor investment. Anyway they're worth having around. Because if you're too old to die young anymore, you might be well on your way to dying deaf.

                                                        - Captive

IN A CONFUSED FASHION

I was asked to say a few words about the Kitchy Koo fashion show on July 8 at Sundays, for the Alternative Arts Association committee. I've tried to write about the process of giving a show, and the dedication of the people involved, etc. etc., but we've all read enough about TV shows, and bands and backyard puppet carnivals and Watergate to know what can happen to the best of intentions in the worst of circumstances.

Instead, there follows a how-to-lose-control list, in case you'd like to do a similar show--to create a suitable vacuum in which to do your best:

1.   Do it at Sundays. This ex-church is so full of wierd vibes and cranky people that it makes me believe in curses. The first time I did a show there, I was forcibly ejected by a drunken owner. I swore I'd never return. First impulses are often correct.

2.   Have lots of room. Put 15 models and 5 dressers in a room no larger that 8'x10'. Add 45 costumes and enough food and drink for everybody, and realize that, amid all that sweat and makeup and motion, you are to emerge looking cool, calm and spectacular.

3.   Get rid of 1/2 of the show before it starts. Having been assured we could use models who were under 21, we were surprised (my goodness!) when the ever-friendly and ever-helpful management ejected 1/3-1/2 of our models, forcing a total change of show plans 1-1/2 hours before the show was to start.

4.   Keep the audience out. Sundays has a doorman and a dress code and if your jeans aren't cool, you aren't allowed. The paid audience (at a stagger-in $2 a head) was less than 20.

5.   Be unyielding in your expectations. Kitchy Koo made a mistake. We went ahead and did the show we had promised to do: three sets of 2 songs each, which was all we could do with the backbone of the show on its way home.

We learned some lessons about promises and co-operation; it will be a long time before the next show. Watch for it.

                                                        -Ralph Becker

THE FALL

Slates

Rough Trade America

I know I'm fucking crazy; I really take the Fall seriously. From their early work down to totally Wired, I've always admired them, not so much for some cynical disrespect for music industry standards, but for the sheer expressionist beauty/non-beauty of their work. With that said, I'm almost alarmed at Slates' "almost produced" sound. What's more, The Fall have never sounded better.

Basically, Slates conjures up the same sort of vision The Fall are notorious for, the kind of atmosphere that scares sleeping cats out of the room, the pasty-faced terror the thought of having them stay at your house for the weekend might bring.

Their work on Slates, as elsewhere, is the direct descendent of traditional Anglo/Gaelic morbidity, with a sense of humor. The message is obscure unless, of course, you believe there really is something to proletariat rhetoric and imagery. This record, as usual, can't be described as much as experienced; like some dark spectre of hell on earth, not glorifying man's decadence, but pointing a knarled finger at it, The Fall act as somewhat of a modern-day Mephistopheles. The poetry reverberates, the melodies drone, seemingly without direction. Slates takes us one step further down their self-serving apocalyptic route; and scaring the shit out of everyone in their path.

— D.W.

GERMS

LP Whiskey '77
Mohawk Records (Bomb)

Hey! First performance ever after being together 2 weeks. This record is living testimony that anyone can do it! My favorite song is Forming:

"Let me be your gun/
pull my trigger/
I am bigger than..."

It shows real intelligence and Darby (or at this time Bobby Pyn) is real abrasive toward the audience and continuously begs for more trash to be thrown, etc. There's even a Rodney intro. (Oh boy!) Buy or die!

FLUX OF PINK INDIANS

CRASS Records

I got good news and bad news! Flux is really great musically and theme wise. The record cover is the usual slick CRASS exitstencial stuff with a pork butcherhouse on the inside and a live pig and some bacon on either sides of the outside sleeve. Cute? The first listening had me buying so I would recommend it to anyone who like or liked CRASS. Now for the bad news. This record is produced by Penny Rimtshud. Too those not informed Penny sold out CRASS on a national British pop show. She illigitamized the whole CRASS theme by saying it was just a gimmick used to get their records out to the younger kids. As everyone knows no one likes to be taken for a fool. It doesn't matter how big a fool you are! Bye.

—Catalyst

RENALDO & THE LOAF

Songs For Swinging Larvae
Ralph

If you're tired of trying to figure out who the Residents are, now you can ponder whether Renaldo and the Loaf are really the Residents. Like these other Ralph Records anonymous, this act trades in electronic novelties. A Ralph press release says R&L are two English guys, and the 17 melodies do take more than a little inspiration from English music-hall numbers. A disc with vaudevillian joys added to your basic Residential quirks and ploys.

—Clark Humphrey

ZOUNDS

Demystification

More music, less political drivel. Sorry to say I prefer the drivel. Dymystification shows us Zounds are above-all chameleon-like. It's like they've cleaned up their act, y'know? Gone are the pedestrian social commentaries of the Crass influenced War/Subvert stuff. In fact, the looks of the sleeve take the Crass-like hippiness a step further, is it looks tacky...by accident. The song itself? Almost forgetable, and probably would be lost in the anus of time (sorry) if it had been done by anyone else. As a social document it's got to be noticed; it's sure to confuse folks; like what the hell are these guys up to? I don't know...sounds like they don't either. Guess what? I like it.

—D.W.

TOMITA

A Voyage Through His Greatest Hits, Vol. II

RCA Red Seal

This is the most erotic record of the year, possibly of all time (sorry, Johnny Mathis' Greatest Hits fans). Walter-now-Wendy Carlos was too sexually confused to synthesize the classics in the way that Isao Tomita has been doing it. What he does, on this compilation of cuts from the past seven years or so, to Stravinsky, Bach, Debussy, Mussorgsky's "Pictures at an Exhibition", and Holst's "The Planets" would convert any Eno fan, would turn any Eurodisco "new romantic" into a true romantic, will lower your pulse and release those passions that lie repressed beneath your cool poses. It also contains references to space-pop which make it ultimately accessible. That other Japanese techno act, Yellow Magic Orchestra, seems to have borrowed a lot from this man. At 57 minutes to the disc, you get galaxies of beautiful music for stimulation and mutual enjoyment.

P.S. It's also got the only version of "Bolero" I would romance to.

—Clark Humphrey

CLASSIFIEDS

Descendants - anti-everything single, unnational anthem/ facelift. Available in U-District, through Systematic, or send $1.50 to A.O.M. 7124 156th S.W. Edmonds 98020

Seattle Rehearsal studio. Reasonable monthly and hourly room rentals for bands. Special introductory rates. 1615 34th North, Seattle 634-1082

Rehearsal Studio: 4 track studio available, call Don 621-9487

Entertainment Plus Recording: 8 track studio recording special, only $15 per hour. 775-9223

Rock Guitar taught. Dan Christopherson (U2) beg/adv. $5.50 1/2 hr. 232-3223.

Custom & Unique musical promotion. Creative photography. 983-7563

Young Female Rock Star desires tanning companion call Ronnie, 322-9018

Acrylic Waves: new wave, rap, punk, funk, new music and lots more. New releases and cool old records too. Every Wednesday night on KRAB radio 107.7 fm.

The Enemy plays Danceland with Pop Defect July 11, 1981

Just Espresso ☕

6810 Greenlake Way, Seattle

OPEN 6 AM-3 AM Mon.-Mon.

Professional Pie Thrower: Kelly Pie, 625-1867

Prepare Yourself! Cuts & color at George's place. 1900 E. Aloha, 324-4760

The Features will play at the Jigsaw Tavern July 17 & 18; Dez's 400 July 19

Hungry people eat more than all their friends do/Hungry people eat more than they could need to/ Hungry people eat like a vacuum cleaner/Hungry people suck it up; Rapid-i is watching u.

NORMAN'S TOP 10

1. Killing Joke - Whats this for? (L.P.)
2. Au Pairs - Playing with a different sex (L.P.)
3. Black Uhuru - Red (L.P.)
4. Tom Tom Club - Wordy Rappinghood (12" 45)
5. Pink Military - I Cry (L.P. Do animals believe in God?)
6. Bauhaus - Bela Lugosi is Dead (12" 45)
7. Scritti Politti - (Rough Trade/NME cassette)
8. Eyeless in Gaza - Kodak Ghosts run amok (7" E.P.)
9. Gregory Isaacs - Sunday Morning (12" 45)
10. Orange Soul - Poor old soul (Part 1 & 2) (7" 45)

JIM'S TOP TEN

1. Der Plan - Whats dat?
2. Minimal Man (cassette)
3. Der Plan - Geri Reig (L.P.)
4. Discharge - Why? (12" 45)
5. Solger - (7" e.p.)
6. Kraftwerk - Computer World (L.P.)
7. DAF - Alles ist Gut (L.P.)
8. Prince Jammy - Kamikaze Dub (L.P.)
9. Siouxie & The Banshees - Kaleidoscope
10. Joy Division - Unknown Pleasures

CORPORATE RECORDS CHARTS

STOP PRESS

-Student Nurse reforming. Gone are Joe Harris, Al Evans, remaining, John and Helena Rogers. Look for them soon with new bass & rhythm (at the Gorilla Room in July).

-New M. Refuzor band debut July 9, Gorilla Room as openers for Husker Du.

-Close call for X-15 on return from Vancouver: car totalled, Doug Maya, Rick Wallace hospitalized. X-15 gig in "2-3 weeks" after songwriting hiatus.

-Terry Morgan & Co. on the road soon with 3 Swimmers. Pritchard to produce 999: Alley Cats, Pudz opening.

PHOTO: Skip Beattie

ALMOST VAPORISED: X-15's TODD FUHS PONDERS THE ETHICS OF PRACTICING WHAT ONE PREACHES.

-Danceland changes hands: Steve Pritchard opens Aug. 1 with The Room, (neo-psychedelia from England). Aug. 8: DOA, Fartz opening. Mark Brewster looking for another all-ages space.

-Contractions return, possibly in July (24/25?).

-Vancouver's E. Van Halen, Scissors due on vinyl soon.

-"The sky is falling. . .the sky. . .!" Another bombs away through ceiling at G.Room. This time not Xan Johnson.

-Time to wear something else. Jay Jacobs now stocking leopard print tops w/ bondage zippers.

-Spectators'/Idiot Culture's Byron Duff teaching new son ace guitar action. Congrats.

MORE STOP PRESS

AS WE GO TO PRESS, REPORTS OF GANG OF 4 CANCELLATION. MODERN HAVE DENIED CANCELLATION ALTHOUGH SHOWBOX CONFIRMS THEY HAVE RELEASED MODERNS DATE (10, JULY) EARLY REPORTS BLAME-ILLNESS AS CAUSE, ALTHOUGH NO CONFIRMATION. FULL REPORT IN NEXT ISSUE.

NEXT ISSUE DEAD KENNEDYS, HÜSKER DÜ, MOTORHEAD, PORTLAND REPORT, PSYCHEDELIC FURS, MORE...

there is something of great size out of control in the head of an insect.

the spectators are

idiot culture
call P avda for info   634-0303

Those OUTLANDISH Andersons!

MOTHER, I THINK ITS TIME I GOT MY OWN APARTMENT! I THINK I'M MOVING OUT!

DO WHAT YOU THINK IS RIGHT, SON.

ANDY.. MY SON.. .gone...

I CALL IT 'HIGH-TECH-WITH-PLANTS? YOU LIKE?

13

SEATTLE'S FIRST ANNUAL BAND MAG

fifty bucks a page   Free Listings

322-2795

DEADLINE: JULY 31

Issue #2

This is clearly the most historic issue of *Desperate Times*, because it contains the first in-print use of the word "grunge" to describe a Seattle band. Ironically, it was a fake band that didn't really exist. To continue the motif, this issue features a concert review of the imaginary band the Hertz, from Boston. A local promoter tried to book the Hertz after reading the phony review.

Jello Biafra is interviewed and gives his assessment of the Seattle scene: "Nationwide, Seattle never had a reputation in the punk and new wave area." There is a confused discussion about punk and post-punk, and whether the LA band "X" is loved or hated. The illustration is the actual set list from the Dead Kennedys' Seattle concert. You don't have to know the songs to enjoy their titles.

An example of self-aggrandizement is having a promoter review his own show, or in this case, a fashion show. DT's Art Director, Billy Shaffer, created a classic piece of zip-a-tone art to accompany an article about the band Bauhaus. Part of the "filler" for this issue is the news that the liquor board has recently been cracking down on clubs; readers are cautioned to make sure they have good fake IDs before going out.

DESPERATE TIMES

$.25
JULY 22
VOL.1 NO. 2

bush tetras
d.o.a.
enemy
gang of four
germs
husker dü
kraftwerk
little bears
from bangkok
minor threat
motorhead
pere ubu
split enz
stiff little fingers
three swimmers
t.s.o.l.
untouchables
vancouver report
& more

DEAD KENNEDYS INTERVIEW

Maggot Brains
HÜSKER DÜ

FARTZ

SECOND ISSUE ANNIVERSARY!

BAUHAUS

DESPERATE TIMES

IN THIS ISSUE

Editor:
Daina Darzin

Associate Editor:
Captive

B.M. and D.B.:
Maire Masco

Art Director:
Billy Shaffer

Milk & Cookies:
Dennis White

Contributing Writers:
Ralph Becker, Catalyst,
Bria Conradus, Verna
Doherty, Erica, Gregor
Gayden, Jeff Greenwood,
Clark Humphrey, Corinne
Mah, Wilum Pugmyr, Johnny
Rubato

Contributing Photographers
Skip Beattie, Bria
Conradus, Kelly Gordon,
Rich Refvem

The terrific cover photos
for this as well as the
last issue are by Skip
Beattie

This week's special thanks
goes to Veronica: we could
have never made it through
the first paste-up without
you!

DESPERATE TIMES is
published bi-monthly
by On The Edge Press,
4525 9th N.E., Seattle
Washington, 98105
(206)-634-0303

EDITORIAL

"I have excellent news for the
world. There is no such thing
as new wave. It does not exist.
It's the figment of a lame cunt's
imagination. There never was any
such thing as new wave. It's the
polite thing to say when you're
trying to explain you're not into
boring old rock and roll, but you
didn't want to say punk because
you were afraid to get kicked out
of the party and they wouldn't
give you coke any more. There's
new music, there's new underground
sound, there's noise, there's
punk, there's power pop, there's
ska, there's rockabilly, but new
wave doesn't mean shit."

—Claude, lead singer
Catholic Discipline

Thank you. Any definition that
manages to lump Spandau Ballet
and Killing Joke into the same
catagory has got to go. Not all
non-hardcore new music deserves
to be identified with ex-disco
twinkies in $140 Baby & Co.
jumpsuits bopping to the strains
of Antmusic. So if we call the
Blondie/Devo crap "new wave",
what's the good stuff? Where do
you put PiL, attitudinally punk,
musically not? What's X?
What's X-15? Where's the
dividing line between punk and
the amorphous Other? What about
bands with a sound I find real
interesting: punk loud- n-fast-
ness and attitude with melodic
guitar riffs reminiscent of hard
rock/heavy metal? If you're
thinking I'm gonna answer these
questions, forget it. (If you
have answers, do write in!)

Also, fuck the attitude of "Oh-
God- don't-say-punk-it's-mean-
and violent". Music is the only
real revolutionary force in this
country--in terms of affecting
the thought of masses of people--
and punk is the only musical
form to really hook into that
potential power since the days
of ol' Country Joe doing be-
the-first-one-on-your-block-to-
have-your-boy-come-home-in- a-
box. So say punk. If they kick
you out of the party and don't
give you coke anymore, fuck'em.

It was probably a lousy party
anyway.
P.S. It's becoming obvious that
the punk/donuthead thing is
getting out of hand. We're
hearing reports of stabbings,
smashed car windows, and guns.
There is no reason for this.
There is no reason for us to be
enemies. The real enemies are
elsewhere. If this shit keeps
happening, the police will crack
down, and that's not going to do
anybody any good. DT will be
doing a full report on the situation in the next issue. If you
have any information , please
talk to somebody on our staff.
We'll keep your name out of it
if you want.

D.D.

LETTERS

Dear DT,
I am thoroughly im-
pressed! Why don't you
charge 50¢? DT is well
worth it. I've been crazy
about the Visible Targets
since I f irst heard them
at WREX, now I even know
their names, thanks to you.
The whole first issue is
just fine. I wish the G.
Room benefit had gotten
out louder, but that's
what you're for, I guess.

Captain Clark's ques-
tions are downright scary
to answer. Way to go
Capt.! Here goes:
Band I don't like
(hate is a little more than
what I really feel) that is
ok to like: X-15.
Now, I only saw 'em
once, at the G. Room benefit for DT, so this is a
snap judgement, but any
band that takes 45 min. to
an hour to set up, begin-
ning after 1 am, had better
be a whole lot hotter than
thy were. Especially if
they seriously expect: to
follow Rapid-i and the
Visible Targets! Looks to
me like their rep is get-
ting ahead of 'em, but
being in that car crash
couldn't have helped any
either.
Band I like that I
shouldn't: Adam Ant.

I know. Monotonous
fluff. But the guy can
really dance and I like
the double drums. It's
too bad all his "fans" are
waiting so eagerly to de-
stroy him. I give him six
months before they decide
he's got enough money and
turn away like they never
cared in the first place.
So, DT, I really hope
you make it. You can count
on my quarter everytime
you get an issue out any-
way. Please keep rockin'
and writin' --anybody
who says punk is dead
never got the music in
their blood, andbody who
did knows --punk can't die!

Carole Pearsal

Dear Captain Clark:

I hate Mr. Epp & the Calculations! Pure grunge! Pure
noise! Pure shit! Everyone
I know loves them, I don't
know why. They don't even wear
chains and mohawks! They all
look different, yuk! And they
have no sense of humor. In
fact, they have no sense.
They're all pretentious, older
than the Grateful Dead, and
love Emerson Lake & Palmer
(my mother's fave).

I love Phillip Glass! While
my friends listen to Mr. Epp &
the Calculations, I listen to
Mr. Glass. His music is
repetitious, redundant, and
repetitive. Pure art! It's
soooooooo intellectual, like
me. I love to listen to
Phillip Glass over and over
and over and over again etc.
ad infinitum.

Mark McLaughlin
Mark McLaughlin
Mark McLaughlin
Mark McLaughlin

(Ed. Note) Mark McLaughlin
does guitar & vocals in Mr.
Epp and the Calculations)

Dear DT,
Thanx. Your magazine
made my week. Hope you can
make it larger, as when I
got to the last page I had
the old feeling of "it's
2:30 am and I've just drunk
my last beer and I want
more!!"
I especially appreciated
your attitude (expressed in
your Ed.) about valid opinions and musical tastes. Who
cares (I do) what anyone
thinks of my favorite music?
I just get annoyed when my
straight friends ask me
(seriously) did I see the
Plasmatics!! Or when strange
young women ask me in a club
to teach them "to dance like
a punk".
Now...in answer to
Captain Clark's Q.:

1) I like Rapid-i, X,
the Furs, Moving Targets,
X-Ray Specs, the Angry Samo-
ans, Buzzcocks, Romeo Void,
etc.
But: (now this is like
publicly admitting to beating off in private--nothing
unusual, sordid or wierd,
you just don't talk about
it, even with friends...)
I sometimes get this
sick urge to dance. Really
dance and sweat. I go and
see the Cowboys. They make
me sweat on the dance floor.
I'm really fucked-up, aren't
I? Even though there are all
these creepy women who like
to touch my black-leather
jacket and ask: "Aren't you
hot dancing in that?" or
"Do you go to the 'U'?" It's
delicious! Never thought you
could "slum" with the middle
-class? Thankx for hearing
my confession.

I'm looking forward to
the day when everyone stops
trying to be "cool" or "with
it", and just "be themselves".
Because we're all worthwhile
in our maggoty own way. None
of us need someone to tell us
who we are. Just need support as the changes occur
within and around us.
Take care -Rick Dempsey

JELLO BIAFRA

DAINA DARZIN

Sitting on the floor of a very dusty back room at the Showbox, leaning up close to the tape recorder so as to be audible above the strains of soundcheck floating up from the stage. Joined by a reporter from KCMU, whose name—sorry about that—escapes me:

DESPERATE TIMES: About that quote in NY Rocker, about using art as a weapon: Does that get easier or harder as you get more successful?

JELLO BIAFRA: It gets both easier and harder; you're much more open to the charge that because a lot of people appreciate what you're doing, therefore you're a commercial entity and no longer dangerous; but by the same token, if you pull out something that comes straight from your gut that's made to force people to think and you can affect that many more people with it, then the weapon is more effective than before.

DT: Is that the ultimate aim of the weapon, to make people think?

JB: It's the basic aim, because that's sort of the key to anything else, getting people out of these school-damaged thought patterns, like just refusing to think,they're taught not to think in this country from day one, that's why you have jock worship, that's why people automatically believe businessmen when they're trying to rip them off, they're people trained to be rodents, so we try to do our part to de-rodentize them.

DT: Who else is doing a good job in that department, in music? music?

JB: Flipper, DOA, TSOL, 1/2 Japanese, Gaza X, Crass, of course, Crass being one of the

THE BASIC AIM IS GETTING PEOPLE OUT OF SCHOOL-DAMAGED THOUGHT PATTERNS. . . .

main ones, although they're in danger with some of their younger fans treating them as a religious cult these days, which I don't think was their aim at all.

DT: Any of the other California bands, Black Flag, etc.?

JB: To a degree.

KCMU: I guess my first question should be why your record company doesn't send us anything.

JB: Because there are only a handful of people working out of an office, and also we're not their top-priority act because we don't kiss their ass in any way. We license our records out, we record them, we produce them, we do the cover art work and people are told they can either take it as is or they can leave it. Which

means total artistic control is thereby in the contract, rather than just writing "artistic control" in the contract ahead of time and then the record company sends in some jerk off producer to turn you into shit. And, like, we didn't work, we've never worked with FBI, and of course FBI and IRS are very closely knit, and they expect you to work within their organization and be part of their corporation, and we haven't done that.

DT: Really, even with an independent label—

JB: IRS is not an independent label. They're the closest thing America has right now to an independent label with big-time record company distribution, but they're still going through growing pains, and I do hope they can improve themselves; they definitely are making efforts in that area.

DT: Is there anything you'd like to be doing that you're not doing?

JB: I don't know, it would be nice to be able to work more on a record label and put out more bands that deserve to be recorded, but none of us have the business sense to do it.

KCMU: Are you sorry you don't get more airplay?

JB: No, the less airplay good bands get, the more likely people are to boycott the radio. Radio is completely irrelevant these days, anyway. Generally, people at radio stations are just record company stooges, if you start out being real enthusiastic and playing what you actually like, you get complaints from people who want to hear the same heavy metal song over and over again, or you get some program director who's already a corporate pawn telling you no, you can't play that, you have to play Martha and the Muffins instead.

DT: Somebody told me you were getting involved in movies in some way or another, is that—

JB: That was a joke we played on Damage magazine because the editor was a fraudulent gossip monger so we figured we'd pick on him and it worked very well. We made up a lie so outrageous only he would believe it.

DT: That's great, what was the lie?

JB: Tha that I quit the band in England to go off and make movies with Hazel O'Connor. I was very bitter towards the magazine because they completely turned their back on the scene in the interest of making more money and just did record company bands. The only thing they'd say about local bands was who was sticking whose prick up whose butt, which is not what I call responsible journalism.

DT: How do you feel about "rock journalism" in general? Do you think some people are doing valid stuff?

JB: I think a lot of people, especially with the smaller magazines, mean well; the most intelligent questions I get asked usually come from younger kids who are just doing fanzines themselves, they tend to be a lot more into it, and put a lot more thought into it than the people who are paid to be rock journalists, who, by that time—it's a job to them and they really don't give a shit any more.

DT: What do you think is the best thing rock journalism can do?

JB: It can use music as a tool to promote social change, not just music as entertainment. That's why my favorite fanzines are the ones that not only write about bands, but go after the Moral Majority, go after Reagan, go after jocks creeping into punk gigs.

∗×∗×∗×∗×∘×∗×∗×∗×∗

JB: The thing that does disappoint me is how many people, after you give them a really provocative interview, they edit out all the political thought and insight and just keep the basic history of the band, when your next album is coming out, it never ceases to disappoint me how many people do that after promising not to do that.

DT: When is your next album coming out? Just to get that in—

JB: Before the end of the year, I have no idea. We also have a 12" EP in the works: it'll be a violently anti-church and anti-fascist record. It'll have "Religious Vomit", "Moral Majority", "Nazi Punks Fuck Off", "Keep Home Factory" a new version of "California Uber Alles" with lyrics about Reagan, and the theme from "Rawhide". We're probably going to be doing it on an independent San Francisco label called Subterranean, who also puts out Flipper, among other people, in connection with IRS, in order to force both parties to know each other.

NEW ROMANTIC . . . . IS CORPORATE HYPE , A CELEBRATION OF WEALTH AND SNOOTERY . . .

DT: The New Romantic shit that's happening right now, is that making you crazy, being that it's the exact opposite of what you're doing? Do you think it's going to go anywhere?

JB: It's a corporate hype that is created by corporations to turn electronic music into disco shit, it's a celebration of wealth and snootery, meaning it'll die a deserved death very quickly. It's not on a street level at all, it's just a bunch of snotty rich kids being ripped off by record companies. Remember the big power pop craze a while back? It's like every six to nine months, they try to cook up a new way to prove to people that punk is dead cause they are so scared of it.

DT: You think punk's dead?

JB: I don't think so at all, I think anyone with half a brain realizes that it's very much alive, it's very dangerous and because it's dangerous and provocative is why record companies and rock journalists and the media in general do as much as they can to get rid of it, as in like the L.A. Times inflating stories of violence at Black Flag shows, thereby attracting more redneck jocks than before in order to split apart the movement before they unite and start trashing banks instead of each other.

∗∗∗∗∗∗∗∗∗∗∗

DT: There's been hassles here too, with kind of a mini-West Side Story between punks and heavy metal street kids, which

2

44 | DESPERATE TIMES

VERBATIM

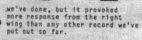

I've never understood, being that the real enemies are in Lake Washington mansions and we're all on the corner of First and Pike--

JB: The problem in SF is that heavy metal people have cut their hair, and are calling themselves punks, but keeping the same mentality that they've always had. They rarely take over an entire gig, but it has happened. Generally, the way to combat that is to channel it into a more positive direction, and by positive I mean, go straight into the bank and beat up the president rather than wait to jump a bunch of punks. The key is activity, not just trying to entertain and make money.

*****

THE KEY IS ACTIVITY, NOT JUST TRYING TO ENTERTAIN AND MAKE MONEY.

JB: Do you know anybody who taped the live Screamers broad-

calculated plan on and, yeah, there's a show I help work on called Maximum Rock n Roll out of KPFA in Berkeley, that's looking for syndication. It covers punk rock around America, the more obscure English things, and it has a political slant to it, like if we see a trend towards Vince Lombardi bullshit jock violence at punk gigs we'll say something. We've also taken on local rock promoters for jacking up ticket prices; there may be a seminar on the epidemic of speed and junk use. There's about 10-15 shows in SF, not just new wave but punk: new wave is a very dirty word to a lot of people now--

DT: Yes: it's like that Catholic Discipline rap, there is no such thing. There's also an area of music that's real hard t..o define- -starting with a hardcore base and going beyond that into other things, musically, I'd include you, X's first album (Jello makes a face) you hate X's first album a lot, huh.

JB: I used to love X, until I heard that album and then I saw them and they sounded just like the album so I never felt motivated to see them again.

THE MEDIA WANTS TO SPLIT UP PUNKS AND JOCKS BEFORE THEY UNITE AND START TRASHING BANKS INSTEAD OF EACH OTHER.

JB: Which is coming back again,

DT: Yes.

JB: And at the moment is a lot more exciting than anything else because all the other movements have spread out and painted themselves into corners. The new psychedelia thing, it's going to be sad to see some really good bands go down with that sinking ship. I mean, how many bad imitations of Joy Division can a record company dream up before somebody catches on? New Order is included in that category, by the way.

KCMU: Has Seattle's reputation kind of gone down in the punk and new wave area since KZAM went off the air?

we've done, but it provoked more response from the right wing than any other record we've put out so far.

KCMU: Does it bother you that it's not getting any airplay?

I DON'T GIVE A SHIT ABOUT AIRPLAY. WE REACH PEOPLE IN OTHER WAYS.

JB: Why do I care about air-play? Generally, radio has killed itself. Progressiv ra-dio has nobody to blame but themselves for that. If the FCC takes you off the air for playing naughty records or being too political, what you do is broadcast a letter on the air, saying let's fight it, you don't have to just sit and take it. Too many stations have done the opposite: KSAN in San Francisco, once the leading progressive radio station in the country, if not the world, allowed Metromedia to buy them out, and now they're a boring station that's losing money. What we're build-ing is a cult following, which is much more healthy, because cult followings stick with you a lot longer through ups and downs, that's what's keeping people like Captain Beefheart and Iggy Pop alive at this point. I don't give a shit about airplay. We reach people in other ways.

Photo: Skip Beattle

cast? They've kind of dissap-peared, and I was a big Scream-ers fan: if anybody has one, the post office box on the back of our album is my mailbox, try and get a hold of me, I'll trade something--

DT: I don't know how import-ant a radio station is, it seems all the valid stuff is done outside--

JB: It can be, actually, in SF, there are radio stations that play valid stuff in defi-ance of the FCC and the Reagan administration's push to get radio to move exclusively to country and western and get rock n roll completely off the air, which there is a

DT: Ok, the question still stands--

JB: What do you mean by beyond punk? You have the "punk is dead" disease now--

DT: No--

JB: You're saying it has to go beyond punk- -

QT: No, that's not what I meant--

(ED. NOTE: Not expressing myself well, for what I meant, see editorial.)

DT: Ok, what I'm saying is there is a basic no-frills hard-core sound, ok--

JB: I never heard of KZAM in my life. Nationwide, Seattle never had a reputation in the punk and new wave area.

KCMU: Since they went off the air our station is the only one that plays new music at all.

*****

KCMU: How's your new single doing?

JB: It's selling really well in England, it was a chart hit over there, mainly because of the free publicity provided by right-wing newspapers and church groups complaining about the contents of the record. It's like the least political song

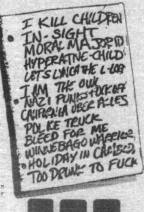

- I KILL CHILDREN
- IN-SIGHT
- MORAL MAJORID
- HYPERATNE-CHILD
- LET'S LYNCH THE L-LOB
- I AM THE OWL
- NAZI PUNIS+FUCK OFF
- CALIFORNIA UBER A-LES
- POLICE TRUCK
- BLEED FOR ME
- WINNEBAGO WARRIOR
- HOLIDAY IN CALBED,
- TOO DRUNK TO FUCK

3

GANG OF FOUR
3 SWIMMERS, LITTLE BEARS FROM BANGKOK
Showbox, July 10

DEAD KENNEDYS
Showbox July 12

photo: Kelly Gordon

簡化兩地來往手續深圳擬與港府商

Let me set the scene for you: there's this band, see? And they've been going for about four years now, ever since art school in Leeds. They're on their third major tour, and they've finally made the charts in a big way despite censorship and crossover problems.
They're in New York getting ready to hit the Northwest, when their bass player goes under. A combination of chronic kidney trouble and tour pressure puts him on a plane towards home and some much needed rest.

So they grab this funky bass player with a list of credits that includes Parliament Funkadelic and the Talking Heads. They practice hard for one day in New York, and then they practice like hell the afternoon before the show. They come on a few hours later to a packed house, half of the audience not knowing what to expect because they heard the news, the other half probably expecting perfection. And they don't disappoint a single soul.

If you were there, I guess you know what I'm talking about. If you weren't, I guess you don't. Explanations are possible. I could tell you about the disco music that was played between sets, driving the audience wild with irritation. Or about the looks exchanged onstage when the people chanting "Gang of Four!" got drowned out by the people chanting "Gang of Three!" I could even attempt to discuss the way the group has created a kind of 'anti-rhetoric' through their lyrics, while retaining an ultimately danceable beat.

But none of that is going to tell you anything about the show. It's impossible to recreate music on paper; it would be stupid to even try. And the whole show was music. One song after another, they

played nearly everything they knew, then came back for a final encore of their own accord: "Sweet Jane". There was no grandstanding, nothing to describe. Or, at least, it continued in the same way: Jon King singing and dancing his way across the stage, Andy Gill taking alternate leaps and stances with guitar, Hugo Burnham pounding out a rock-reggae beat, and Buster "Cherry" Jones bent grooving over his bass, head shaking from side to side.

The high points were purely personal, because the whole thing was great. I mean, I liked "Damaged Goods" a little more than the rest, but then I really like that song. To return to the game of writing a review of an indescribable event, I guess this is really for all you people who weren't there. You should have been, and I hope you are the next time. As for all you people who were . . . Great show, huh?

—Captive

Little Bears From Bangkok is pleasantly difficult to describe. Coming from "art" band roots, (Jim Anderson with The Beakers, Tracy Rowland and Danielle Eliott briefly with Audio Letter), they have tightened up their sound considerably in the last few months, without losing that edge that keeps the listener on his toes and typifies the best of "art" bnads. Their sound is unique. It lies somewhere between a garage band rehearsal jam and the experimental bands on Subterranean and Crass records. Anderson's manic vocals contrast nicely with Ms. Rowland's more sedate "bitch-from-New-York" monotone.

Their lyrics are political, with songs like "White Hand" (about the white hand print left on the doors of murdered El Salvadorians by the army)

and "Chevrolet": "We'll buy a car/we'll buy estates/we'll buy a baseball club/or something elite"—but luckily the politics never get in the way of the music. If the unusually polite (for a warm-up band) crowd at the Showbox is any indication, LBFB could become that rare treat: a local band with a distinctively unique sound and enough following to support them as explore and improve. I hope so. A LBFB performance is sort of like being seduced by your sexy aunt from Las Vegas: some of it's great, some of it's gross, and some of it you'll never quite understand.

Three Swimmers is vastly different in approach to Little Bears From Bangkok. Whereas the LBFB discard any song they write that sounds too much like someone else, Three Swimmers proudly admits their allegiance to their influences. Those are, in their words, David Byrne, Gang of Four, disco, funk, and rap music. It shows, especially the David Byrne/Gang of Four part. Three Swimmers know what sound they want and their challenge is to implant their own individual stamp on it. LBFB's desire is to create something unlike the listener's usual preferences. But enough of this competitive crap.

About Three Swimmers: forget that they are going on tour with Gang of Four. Forget that a few record companies are ready to pounce on these boys. Forget that their sound is derivative and that they have political undertones (that will sink in later) Forget all that. Just go to see a Three Swimmers performance and move your body into different positions in a way that relates to the polyrhythms you hear. You will feel better for it. I did.

—Billy Shaffer

The Dead Kennedys concert was the best thing I've seen since coming back to Seattle.

First, very briefly about the opening bands:

The Maggot Brains, now more than ever. I said I'd say that. The MBs have improved: bass and drums are now (mostly) on the same beat. There is no guitar player, which may be a first. I hate to admit it, but the MBs are growing on me. Anyone who has the balls to do "Louie Louie" at the Showbox after having been together for two weeks can't be all bad.

Hüsker Dü: Wilem said it perfectly in his review of their WREX show. See "Moving Violations". At the Showbox, Joey Shithead of DOA joined in for an impromptu "Taking Care of Business". Hot set.

The Fartz: I said it in the last issue. They're great, and sounded better at the DK gig than any other time I've seen them.

Ok, the Dead Kennedys:

Most bands' concert performances are somewhat grittier, more energetic versions of their albums. The Dead Kennedys show was a total entity, an animal to itself. I've never seen another band that integrates the audience so completely: beer, water, funeral flower pots flew back and forth, people climbed on to the stage and dove into the audience, the slamdancing was intense; and yet, I didn't see one piece of truly destructive violence, maybe because Jello Biafra, by himself throwing things and leaping off the stage, made what the audience was doing a part of the show instead of a disruption of it.

The Dead Kennedys sound different live than on their records, much faster and more hardcore. They included some of their new material, "Nazi Punks Fuck Off" and the Reagan version of "California Uber Alles", and did a really intense version of "Too Drunk To Fuck". All in all, it was one of those concerts where you leave thinking, if I die tomorrow and never go to another concert, it's ok, because I went to this one. Interestingly, the P-I spent most of their review talking about why the DKs and the Gang of Four were better then the Plasmatics (with not word one about any of the opening bands) and the almighty Times chose to say nothing about the Kennedys show whatsoever, doing their Monday column about how great the Gang of Four were now that they had transcended punk. Good, Pat. At least you didn't compare anybody to Bruce Springsteen.

— D.D.

VIOLATIONS

STIFF LITTLE FINGERS
JULY 1
Commodore, Vancouver B.C.

A whole mess of us invaded Vancouver July 1 (Canada Day!) for the Stiff Little Fingers gig at the Commodore. The Commodore's a really cool ball-room-type hall with a really uncool two-buck charge on a bottle of beer. I didn't mind cuz it is stronger stuff and some-how I managed to confuse the heavies at the door out of their $9.50 admission. (remember: never show money unless you're asked!) Well since this is a review and not Heloise hints --D.O.A. were supposed to open but were axed in fear of violence. The band that did open, Secret V's, suffice to say they should remain as se-cret as possible and play only deserted fallout shelters.

I could hardly wait to see SLF. I had seen them once before, a year ago at the Rainbow in Lon-don --one of the great shows recorded live on the Hanx album. This time I was right up front as the band fired out opening with "Go For It", the title track from their latest LP. Next they launched into "No-body's Hero" --
   "get up, get out,
    be what you are."
I was going crazy half-dancing and avoiding being crushed by this drunk 200-pound skinhead with tattoos of chopped-off heads. The band was in perfect form--Jake Burns ferociously spitting out "Wasted Life", "Barbed Wire Love", "Gotta Get Away" and "Tin Soldier" while bassist Ali McMordie rocked all around stage laugh-ing and teasing the crowd. Somehow SLF manage to incorpo-rate a serious military steadfast beat with appealing happy-go-lucky charm in all their songs. "Johnny Was" slowed the pace for a while -- one of my favorite modern-day ballads. Then the guys informed us they would play a special Irish folksong --none other than the Undertones' "Teenage Kicks". The encore provided the final frenzies --"Suspect Device" and "Alternative Ulster"

A few people that I talked to after the show felt SLF were too slimey cold professional. Bite your tongues serpents, any fan couldn't have been more thrilled. I won't forget the choke in Burn's voice as he de-dicated a new song, "Piccadilly Circus", to a friend who had died one night in Piccadilly, victim of a brutal stabbing. The last moment saw drummer Jim Reilly attack his kit, as snares and cymbals hit the stage, the sweat dancing and electricity filled the aftermath of a real fun night.

One last word --the Vancouver crowd seemed a lot more musical-ly informed and 'hip' than most of our Showbox tourist types. If you can handle the border ordeal ("got any weapons besides your costumes" snicker snicker), then by all means go up and catch some 'foreign' culture. See ya there.

--Erica

HÜSKER DÜ

photo: Skip Beattie

Wow. I had heard that this was a great band, but of course that can never prepare one when a band is this great. They are the kind of band that makes you move, and when you see people sitting down you want to kick them in the ass and wake them up. Founded in May, 1979, this Minneapolis band consists of Bob Mould on guitar, Greg Norton on bass, and Greg Hart on drums, with all three sharing vocals.

Although they did a few slower numbers, most of their music is loud and fast--and powerful. Even the slower songs, including the two on their single from last year, have lots of guts, proving that pop songs don't have to be wimpy.

There's nothing wimpy about Hüsker Dü. They come on with such force and energy, energy that builds with each song, that I felt as though the bar would explode at any moment. Their stage presence is infec-tious, because they move, the sweat raining from them, and only idiots would want to sit down during their sets. Bob Mould rarely stood still; he would edge to the front of the stage and grimace with emotion, then suddenly jump and crash into the wall. Greg Norton became more and more active, and at the end of second set he was never still, always jump-ing into the air, doing a cool war-dance, jerking his body all over. Grant Hart was furious as he pounded his drums, getting these great looks on his face. His vocals were the most impressive to me, at times sung in a clear voice, at times growled and spat out, dripping with feeling.

These three men keep the music coming without breaking between songs. I've seldom seen such energy in a band. I loved it when Greg and Bob jumped into the air at the same time, and after the set Grant pushed the drums out of his way and stal-ked off stage. After the set, the audience was smiling, their eyes were wide, and they were soaking with sweat and spilt beer.

The single sells for $1.25, which is very cool indeed. Of the two songs, "Statues" is my favorite, a great song that always gets me moving. If you cannot find it in a local shop or bar, send for it at Reflex Records, P.O. Box 4596, St Pau Minnessota 55104. Hopefully it won't be too long before we are treated with a live album. Wow!

--Wilum Pugmyr

WREX, July 11

motörhead
Paramount,   July 12

Motorhead is not really a well-known band. Especially among those who are not devoted to heavy metal. This is not suprising. It seems that most of the American press will only cover a band if they are pretty or make mega-bucks. Motorhead is "not pretty".

Created by vocalist and bassist Lemmy Kilmister, Motorhead has under gone a few changes since 1975. The present band, with Fast Eddy Clarke on guitar and Philthy Animal Taylor on drums, are a huge success in England. I hear they have quite the reputation as partyers. So... What first caught my attention was that Motorhead would be playing the Paramount (where I work) with Ozzy Ozbourne on July 12. To introduce myself to this heavy metal wonder, I picked up a copy of their first American release, the Ace of Spades. This album is fast and raw! Motorhead also has two other English releases, Overkill (supposedly the best heavy metal album ever) and Bomber. These aren't available in the states, (yet?).

The day of the show I raced from my day job with only an hour to spare before I'd have to check in at the Paramount. I had to find out as much as possible about Motorhead before the show started. Some how, I got in touch with Motorhead's road manager and asked him over the phone at the Camlin Hotel if I could take pictures for the paper I was met with a polite, crisp "no". Can't really blame him though. After cups on cups of coffee, I was babbling like some hyped up groupie. I was later informed it's a road manager's job to be an asshole. (I actually got a picture later but it didn't turn out, shhh...)

Slowed down but not stopped by an offical "no", I hung around outside the hotel with some adolescent boys who were avid Motorhead fans. They didn't have tickets for the show but wanted to get a glimpse of their idol, Lemmy. I asked Weber, 15, what he thought of Motorhead. Taking time to say something cool he replied, "they're the most raunchiest, heaviest, extremest metal around."

With little time to spare I decided to take some pictures of the huge crowd lined up to see the show. I ended up leading the front of the line in a rousing chorus of "punk rock sucks". It was almost sad. If those people can't see past my black leather jacket they deserve to be submitted to the blow-dry images of the likes of Styx. As far as I'm concerned, hardcore is hardcore no matter what it's labeled. Yeah that's right, Motorhead's sound could be called punk. It's hard, driving, repetitious, and LOUD. And yet, they certainly don't suck.

Anyway...when the doors opened I took up my position as a frisker...after running my hands up and down at least a thousand legs, (cheap thrills for weak minds), I got three minutes to see the show. In "the pit" feet away from Lemmy, I watched the band crank up with "Jailbait". Lemmy man-handled his bass like it was raw meat. The guitar was screaming and the drums rolled like thunder. The volume was so loud it felt as if I had two hearts in my chest. If it weren't for those peices of sponge rubber in my ears I'd probably be deaf. I wish I could have seen the whole show but a job's a job.

photo: Bria Conradus

After the show was over I heard comments like "it grunts". One girl complained "it was too unstructured". Hell yeah! But thats what makes it fun. After only three minutes, I thought Motorhead was the best heavy metal I've ever seen. They aren't pretentious. There are no gimmicks. Just seamless rock and roll. The most important thing about Motorhead is they love their fans and know how to show it. This show they were only allowed 40mins. to play. I hope next time they can play for hours. How about the Showbox guys?

--Bria Conradus

5

DRUNK AND DISORDERLY

THE UNTOUCHABLES

photo: Rick Refvem

The Untouchables generally have a lot of fierce rock n roll energy, as well as an on-the-road grittiness that you only see in national acts that have been around for a while. "Rock n Roll Hell" is like a stampede coming towards you, or a tidal wave, punk-edged drone guitar over a hard rock beat. July 15 at WREX was not a particularly good show for them. The sound mix was off, and the Untouchables seemed kind of tired. Or maybe it was just me. I wish Bev all the luck in the world doing a new & improved number on WREX, cause, well-- shit, it's hard to be there on a day when the plasma donor joint turns you down because there's not enough protein in your blood. You know what I mean? I also had a very odd conversation with a guy who asked me if the Dead Kennedys were a "four piece band". Anyway, back to the Untouchables. The end of the set was better then the beginning. I'm a sucker for Lou Reed covers, and the Untouchables do a hot version of "Waiting For The Man". They come up from Portland a lot; check them out. On a good night, they're a killer band.

D.D.

FUCK DANCE LET'S ART

Tim Ray was the token artist in Vancouver's 1977-8 scene. Then he split to join European bohemia. Now he's back with a new band, apparently to capitalize on the success of U2 and Bunnymen who are doing something similar to what he did, but without his boyish good looks or his beat.

He's combined Byrne-ish, abstract imagery with fast, paranoiac music. Portland's Wipers do the same thing, but Seattle's art-rock scene has been influenced always by visual performance art more than by poetry or Patti Smith. (exception: the Blackouts).

The Pre-Fabs, who opened both nights for Ray, represent the aesthetics of the Seattle (read Capitol Hill) style of art-rocking. Their basic set reveals a current dilemma for this style: how to deliver political messages in hard, driving music that sounds good to a modern-art community grown weary of rock n roll formulas. The Pre-Fabs' current solution, as heard July 7 at the Gorilla Room, was to follow the white-funk lead of the Gang of Four. That doesn't really work in their case: the good messages the Fabs have to make get lost beneath the theorizing. They're far better at making straight art music (i.e. a co-performance with Audio Letter last month) than in no-wave song structures. With encouragement, they will probably get better, learn their own rhythms and tones.

The new Tim Ray Band was beset by mechanical problems on the 7th, so best to judge them by their work at WREX on the 8th.

Ray is a good vocalist who can become a great one. The slide guitar and electric violin on some tunes were added attractions, the synthesizer was flavoring, guitar and rhythm sections stuck to the groove. Ray's singing was fine, but something was missing: the Bowie-Ferry pop of Ray's old band, AV, to be precise. Still, the Tim Ray Band is a potential Next Big Thing, if it can live up to the demands of his vocal style and the slick arrangements.

-Clark Humphrey

SIX DOZEN ESKIMO PIES

Danceland USA is my favorite club. It's cheap enough, sporting two bands for the price of one, and the bands are usually billed so that if one doesn't satisfy you the other one will. And, if you don't like the band you can leave and come back unnoticed. (It's also fun to yell out the windows to the "Scary Monsters" and "Super Creeps" that roam First Avenue at night).

But last night, the night before Danceland closes for two weeks, made me nervous, bored, and extremely pissed. I went to the can five times more than usual and left twice.

Yeehaw? It looked like Urban-Cowboy-takeover and I prayed to the aliens that they wouldn't be dragging in a mechanical bull! The sound guy took off London Calling to play Cattle Calling or something that sounded like southern-wailing. Soon, a ha-ha band called The Cowbirds (which looked like The Enemy dressed as The Cowbirds) took to the stage and played something I couldn't stand (nor understand), or was it the way they looked, like the Lone Ranger, that made me want to leave? Anyway, my friend and I took off in two minutes.

Ten minutes later we came back. It looked better. The band had stopped, The Clash was back on, and my expectations rose for Pop Defect. How long the bad joke played I did not know, nor did I really care.

Pop Defect satisfied my need for something wonderfully tight and fast. They were more fun than your average pissed-off band and easy to dance to. They were energetic, the kind of band that gets you "up"

That's the impression I got, anyhow. They played a short fifteen minutes and then The Enemy attacked.

Boring. They didn't open with "I'm Only Five Foot One" and I was dissappointed. I couldn't dance to this. It was bland and all the songs sounded alike. Either that or I couldn't distinguish one from another. Same difference. I left when one of the players pounced on a guy for saying they write bad songs. The musician knocked him on the ground and threw a few punches. It was over when a screen fell on top of the guy.

I was pissed then. Can't he take a joke? Bands don't have to act like "we're-so-cool-we're John McEnroe" just because of a little insult. Couldn't he have just said "Fuck off, buddy"? Didn't they know that beating up your audience is uncool?

The whole evening, except for a certain Defect, was a disaster.

-Verna Doherty

6

THE HERTZ

Despite practically no advance word (don't you guys flyposter in Boston?), the Hertz arrived in Seattle for the first gig of their current west coast tour. This highly touted N.E. techno-B & D outfit proved well worth it for those who got the word. The lead singer, She Bernstein, came on strong, tough and sweaty. She resembled a female Elvis Costello, right down to the horn rims , and her guitarist It Hertz played lounge rhythms at 80 rpm while ramming his guitar between She's legs The near capacity crowd at the newly renovated Soames-Dunn building went wild, imitating the newest dance craze from tea town, slam-writhing. It fit in nicely with their highly touted rendition of "The Match Game Theme" (available on Hertz Records, P.O. Box 93412 Boston Mass. 02138). The performance was cut short when drummer Fey Doneaway was hit in the head by a Chivas Regal bottle thrown by an overzealous fan during the Hertz' third number, "Ever Seen A Grown Man Cry?" The opening band, Tacoma's Famous Potatoes, did not live up to their highly touted advance press, even though lead singer Alan "Mr." Potatohead worked strenuously through some engaging covers of early Fugs and Van Morrison songs. Their encore, "(Mah) Tupelo Honey", nearly cleared the hall. Better luck next time, guys
                    —Jeff Greenwood

COLORPLATES

It seems funny to call a group that's been playing for a year and a half a "new band" in this day of bands hitting the Showbox after two weeks in existence, but the Colorplates are a new band. New because, as yet, few people have seen them. Their music is eclectic and intense, from a revved-up rendition of Sinatra's "It Has A Very Good Year", to a harmalodic instrumental rocker called "Ornette", as in Coleman. To me they sound "Punkadelic": Psychedelic (13th Floor Elevators) instrumental textures with usually inaudible lyrics sung with conviction. Played with a hyped-off modern intensity/desperation.

So why aren't they a staple on the Seattle performance curcuit?

The music is admittedly different, but I think the big problem many people (including club owners and bookers) have with the Colorplates is the way they look. Harvey Tawney (guitar, clarinet, theremin synthesizer, and vocals) has longish hair and is balding. Tom Dyer has long hair and is built like a wrestler. Deane Tawney (a wild and innovative drummer) is tall and thin with very long blonde hair and large glasses. Bob Blackburn (bass and vocals) has long straight hair and a Captain America vibe. None of them dresses "New Wave". Trivial? For better or worse fashion has always been an important part of of rock and roll, making progress slow for groups who don't fit in the"kind of now, kind of wow" catagory. But such bands outlast the latest trend. The Colorplates (formerly the Adults) are definitely rock and roll, and deserve to be heard. The only place open minded enough to hire them on a regular basis is the Gorilla Room, the venerable bastion of original music and downtown sleaze—my favorit club! Look for the Colorplates there August 9th. See you there.

                    —J. Rubato

BAUHAUS

SHAFFER

by GREGOR GAYDEN

Bauhaus are a band that defies being categorized, and I love them for that. I'd just as soon leave it at that and let the rest of the world find out about them in a couple of years; they give me that warm cultish feeling that hurts so much to lose. But that just wouldn't be fair, because Peter Murphy, Kevin Haskins, Daniel Ash and David Jay have created one of the most essential bands of our time and they deserve recognition.

It's too bad some critics have lumped them in with the so called futurist bands, ie. Spandau, Duran Duran, etc., and their disco historical fashion flash. I would like to put a stop to this nonsense once and for all. Bauhaus stands apart from such trendy goings on, and they'll be around long after the gilt has worn off Adam's hollywood pirate jacket.

Now with six singles and an album under their belts, and a new album on the way, the group is definitely staking itself as a potent force for the eighties. Formed in Jan. 79, in Northhampton, England, Bauhaus only six weeks later recorded their first single, Bela Lugosis Dead. Released on a tiny independent label, Small Wonder, it is a fitting tribute to the best vampire that ever ruled the silver screen, and established the band's fascination with the things on the dark side of life. Musically it is quite sparse but the promise of greater things is evident, as the short, rough snatch of Dark Entries at the end of the flip side bears' witness.

Dark Entries became their second single, and began their association with 4AD records, a larger independent that has released very good products by such obscure bands as Dance Chapter and the Past Seven Days. It is one of my favorite Bauhaus songs, hard and fast Peter Murphy's dominating vocals telling the tale of a sleazy prostitute over a gut punch chord progression. Go ahead and hit me, you can't do it any harder than this single. Murphy is an incredibly strong singer, with the kind of range and emotion usually associated with Bowie. That is as close as I want to get to a comparison, though; he stands on his own. Terror Couple Kills Colonel, their third release, is harder to pin down. It has an obvious political bend lyrically, but the music is not as powerful as the previous single. Still, it is an effective experiment from a band that is still young, and determined not to fall into an easily recognizable formula.

That determination shows on their debut album, In The Flat Field. This is truly a record for the modern age, sucking and dragging the listener into a neo-psychedelic underworld that is frightening, forbidding, and fascinating. The rock solid rhythm section of Haskins' drums and Jay's bass produces a furious footing for Daniel Ash's mind ripping guitar attack as Murphy confronts the world with unerring assurance. There is no grey here, all is black and white.
   "I dare you to speak of your despair/ for bureaucracy, hypocrisy, all liars/ I dare you."

he screams in the opening track. From there on there is no doubt that this is a band with conviction and integrity in every note, as we are swept into the eye of the storm, then set down none too gently.

Since the album they have released three singles. The first of these is a very credible remake of Marc Bolan's Telegram Sam, backed with a dangerous version of John Cale's Rosegarden of Funeral Sores. It seemed odd for a band to release a single of back to back covers, but both songs come off very well. As a bonus, the 12 inch contains an agonizingly beautiful original, Crowds, about the relationship between artist and audience. Next was Kick In The Eye, another surprise as the emphasis is on a funky rhythmic repetition, a new direction for Bauhaus. It's a good dance song, which I think they were consciously trying for, but none of the bite was lost. The latest, The Passion Of Lovers, seems to be as romantic as the title suggests, but I can't say too much about it because I haven't got it yet.

Hopefully, a new album will be out soon to add to their already impressive output. But above quantity, what I expect from Bauhaus is quality Quality in musicianship, quality in lyrics, quality period. Unfortunately, I cannot remark on a live performance. Although the band has been to the States twice they have never made it to the west coast. But judging from written reports they are as exciting visually as their records are to the ear.
   "What do you want of me/ what do you long from me/ a slim pixie, thin and forlorn/ a count, white and drawn?"
Pete Murphy asks in Crowds. Take your pick, but do it soon.

7

RECORDS

PICK HIT 45

BUSH TETRAS
Boom b/w Das Ah Riot

Here it is;the new Bush
Tetras single. This outing
the Tetras have chosen a
tighter, more produced sound
than before. All the trade-
marks are still there,
though; heavy bass, slacked
-back drums, vitamin-defi-
cient vocals, and of course
Pat Place's sharp-edged
guitar. The hit here is
Boom; no slam-dance this
one. In the tradition of
their "lower-east-side-pa-
ranoid" sound the Tetras instead go for polyrhythmic,
almost chanting instrumen-
tation.

The sound is fuller, but
doesn't seem to have lost
its immediacy, and the
lyrics are about as silly as
ever. C'mon, songs with
names like Das Ah Riot
aren't exactly expected to
be anything besides street
poetry; in fact, that's
sort of what this record's
all about. Urban, paranoid
throbbing, whatever; The
Tetras are in the forefront
of the post-no-New-York
movement coming out of the
big apple these days. This
little piece of that sound
funks along with the same
kind of headlong intuition
one might expect from any
other element as dangerous
as the Bush Tetras. Play
it over and over. If it
doesn't grow on you it'll
hypnotize you with its
sensuality.
                    D.W.

BOW WOW WOW
W.O.R.K.

If you've seen their video, you
already know that this group
doesn't look or sound like
anyone else. That's one good
reason to buy the record. The
other is that the jungle
drumbeat and rap-style lyrics
are infectious enough to get
even a confirmed introvert on
his feet and bopping. So what
if it all sounds the same. I
like it.
                - Captive

THE FARTZ ☠

A Nine song EP produced by
Neil Hubbard and the Fartz.

Usually when I first play a
record, I compare the sound to
something else. "Ah, this
sounds a bit like PiL..." With
the Fartz, this is impossible,
because they are incomparable.
The Fartz are Seattle's most
hardcore punk band. Their
sound is ominous, and to
attend their gigs is to risk
loss of safety and sanity.

One of their greatest assets
is their stage presence. The
first five times I saw them,
I could do nothing but stand
in awe, nigh and then shaking
my body to the dynamic beat of
their noise. They command
one's attention, and it was
only among a crowd at The Showbox, who were gathered to see
Dead Kennedys, that I finally
let myself go and slammed to
the Fartz
When people see "The Fartz"
written on the back of my
jackets, the usual reaction
is to laugh. But this band
is no laughing matter, because they are deadly serious
about the themes screamed
about in the songs on this
single. Many of these songs
are already favorites of mine
particularly Got A Brain. I
love the intro to How Long,
with Steve Fart's bass beginning, joined soon by the
wailing of Tom Fart's guitar.
Then Loud Fart enters with
the drums, and finally Blaine
Fart begins to scream intelligent and important lyrics.
Similar to seeing them on stage,
this record gives one lots of
energy. I cannot imagine anyone
listening to this record and
not feeling something, for the
fartz murder apathy. They
are so fast, so tight--hell,
I've had to take the record
off as I typed this, because
listening to it always makes
me type real fast and I make
typos every other word.

The quality of sound is
superb. You've got a brain,
so use it: buy this single
or be an idiot. If you cannot
find it, send for info to-
The Gas Chamber c/o Steve Fart
3915 W. Lander, Seattle WA
98116.

            -Wilum Pugmyr

(Ed. note: this was reviewed
from a test pressing. Delayed
by a hassle with Rainier Press
(who refused to print the record
on the grounds that it was
obscene), the single should
finally be available in about
three weeks.)

KRAFTWERK 🎵🎵🎵
Computer World
Warner Bros.

It has been three years since
the release of Man Machine,
Kraftwerk's electropop classic.
They haven't changed very
much. Their latest LP, Computer World, has an occasional
return to their pre-"Autobahn"
days of abstraction, but
features mostly simple melodies
with a touch of Berlin melan-
cholia, discoish electronic
rhythm (surprisingly funky
at times), and deadpan vocals
which function as another
machine. Lyrically, this is
pretty dumb and/or funny
stuff--all about calculators
and computers. We aren't
supposed to ponder too deeply.
The single from the LP, an
obvious choice, is "Pocket
Calculator", a diabolically
catchy dance tune. It is
funky and mechanized, sad but
funny, intelligent but mindless . . . the group in a nut
shell. A potential smash
single that won't get any air
play. Sigh. None the less,
these robots got soul.

                -Johnny Rubato

TSOL

12" 45 Posh Boy

Side 1, "Superficial Love"
is a great song, really
rips out at your throat.
"Property is Theft": this
one should have been
more like, "Poverty is
Theft" (crap), "No Way
Out", nice try but it's
too pretentious. Side 2,
"Abolish Government/Si-
lent Majority" are the
greatest songs on the EP.
Abolish government is
my top standing favorite
at the moment. "World
War III" (yes, it's
another attempt at every-
one's favorite topic.)
Personally, I'm tired of
World War II's. Well,
anyhow, this EP is well
worth buying. -Catalyst

DURAN DURAN 👤
Harvest

This is a disco nostalgia
record. Not authentic disco,
but a wish to return to a
simpler time when, I think they
think, you could spend all
night in mindless dance, and
endless cocaine, while tuning
your synthesizers to automatically keep up with the rhythm
machine. The chief cut here is
"Planet Earth", but down-to-
earth it is not. If these guys
could come up with such a great
band name, they still might one
day have some musical ideas.

                -Clark Humphrey

PICK HIT LP

ECHO & THE BUNNYMEN
Heaven Up Here
(Sire/Korova SRK 3569)

Initial reaction to this album
was just on the optimistic
side of lukewarm. With repeated listenings, the Bunnymen's
2nd album does what few of
their so-called noe-psychede-
lic contemporaries have been
able to pull off: turn out a
second LP that lives up to the
promise of their debut. Because the absence of an obvious
7" hit (such as Rescue) Echo &
The Bunnymen have done one
better on Crocodiles: they've
put out a consistent album.
Don't be led astray, however,
there are plenty of immediately recognizable riffs and melodies. As usual, the rhythm
section puts out a highly
crafted performance that
sounds more reliant on intuition than classicism. Ian
McCulloch's vocals soare to
great heights, plummet earth-
bound, and just before they
crash, glide, saftely back
up, and away.
"We're all groovy people. . .
groovy, groovy people", he
almost laments in the title
track. Instead of coming off
as an insipid parody, it becomes anthemic, with McCull-
oghs' eerie intonations. Pete
de Freitas' big drum sound is
mixed well up front,
providing a behemoth murky
ambience to the overall
sound, while Will Sergeants'
guitar cuts and gnaws its
way through most of the material, or as in No Dark
Things fights its way like a
bandsaw through knotted wood,
sporadically breaking to bits
flying into any face with the
guts to stand nearby.
For those that like their
music in sproradic methedrinic
doses Heaven Up Here will be
a disappointment. This stuff
is far more consuming, opiated
perhaps. It's been a long
time since I've wasted myself
in an evening's abuse, in
aticipation of only one goal;
finding myself at home with
the lights out, about 4 am,
listening to something as
moody as Heaven Up Here.
                              D.W.

8

RECORDS

BOWLING BALLS FROM HELL, VOL. II

Clone

Either there's no great talents in Akron anymore, or they've all become jaded bar bands, or whatever: the best thing on this collection is an early 1978 slice of Tin Huey, and the second best is a punk rhumba by a Japanese band, Totsuzen Danball.

The others are attempts to find whatever fun is left in pop, a disgraced genre in this age of polarized harcore and rock-disco camps. I wish there were things here that were really great, being a pop afficionado frustrated by the lack of any good recent releases of that type. Susan Schmidt and Debbie Smith almost make it with two rather stoic ditties on the failure to find instant sex ("once they get to know me they don't like me"), served up in a decidedly nonmechanical dance beat. Fun stuff if you don't look at their rather stupid back cover photo.

The Waitresses also appear here, in a pre-"No Guilt" demo made before they became minor NY scenemakers. Other bands here (Hammer Damage, Unit 5, and the Bizarros) must have something better to do. Here, they sound like they've inserted their most expendable cuts while waiting for an import-only record contract.

– Clark Humphrey

SPLIT ENZ

Waiata

A & M

Every time I think about this new Split Enz album, I can't analyze it. I have to dance to it. It's virtually flawless! Waiata represents songwriting genius.

"Hard act to Follow" is an excellent cut to begin with. Note the great lyrics:
"whenever you come on I light up, everything you do goes down well –I can tell, after you it's all downhill..."

Are they singing in praise of True Colours, their first album? Waiata is one better than that. After this it's all uphill.

"One Step Ahead" reminds me of the Beatles for a hidden reason I don't quite know. The throbbing bass at the beginning and throughout the song is as catchy as the lyric:

"If I stop I could lose my head, so I'm losing you instead --either way I'm confused --you slow me down. What can I do?"

Energetic and contagious, the album's best cut, "I Don't Wanna Dance", comes next. It's sure to be a hit if ever released. The most danceable tune!

Iris is a pretty melody about a guy's hidden sexual desires for a girl he watches out of the "--safety of his room." After a strong cut like I Don't Wanna Dance, it's a nice rest.

Wail, an instrumental, is a terrific traveling-along song. It comes on strong. It's great, although I usually don't like instrumentals.

Clumsy has an intro that sounds like Japanese falling music. What should be a very interesting word developement, is too unclear to be understood. (Good song anyway.)

Side two is self-explanatory. Besides, this is getting to be too long to be a review anyway. The good cuts are "History Never Repeats", "Ghost Girl", and "Ships".

Don't wait to get this exceptional vinyl!

–Verna Doherty

MINOR THREAT

Discord Records

Every time Daina asks me to review something, it turns out to be something I like a lot; so now everyone thinks I'm a real mellow guy who likes everything. Hey, I'm getting hate mail from Fastbacks fans because I slammed their record in Punk Lust #3, so get off my back.

I've been getting some records sent to me from people who have heard about my fanzine, but most of what has been sent has been boring dance music-- until now. Minor Threat is a tight, fast punk band, and their single is a fucking great eight-song seven inch e.p. with a lyrics page included.

Some of the lyrics are so right-on that I want to quote them. But instead, you should just send for the album and read them for yourself. All of the songs are serious, political gems. Iam MacKaye, on vocals, has a lot of power. I can imagine what he is like on stage.

They didn't send any info regarding price, so I suggest you send the guys a self-addressed stamped envelope and get the needed info. Write to Minor Threat c/o Ian MacKaye, 3819 Beecher Street N.W. Washington DC 20007. This is the third record released by Discord Records, so you might ask Ian for info on the other records as well.

–Wilum Pugmyr

FASTBACKS

The Fastbacks' first single is now on the shelf at your favorite record stores. For those who don't know, the Fastbacks are a local band who've been working the Gorilla Room and other dance joints a lot in the past six months. It's good to see their sweat on vinyl for a change. For some reason, the more I hear this record the less I like it. The two cuts featured on this single, 'It's Your Birthday', and 'You Can't Be Happy', are fast and driving with hyper guitar. The vocals are clear and strong. Unfortunately, the words are boring. The Fastbacks' sound comes off fun and energetic but seems to lack the conviction that could make it great.

– Bria Conradus

D.O.A.

Hardcore '81

Friends

This disappointed on first listening. A few more spins and "Slumlord" and "Communication Breakdown" emerged as powerful little cuts. A few more spins after that and the rest of the tracks sounded like poor fake-punk. It's a shame that Joey Shithead, Randy Kampage, Chuck Biscuits and Dave Gregg would wind up proving that a song can be very short and still be aimless.

What went wrong? Did DOA decide to penetrate the L.A. punk market by making their own Circle Jerks-like licks? Were they afraid of running out of energy? Did they run out of ideas of their own? Have they, as one of the Vancouver scene commented to me, "a commercial punk band"?

I hope it's just a case of the second-album blahs, of material written hastily to follow a set that had three years of cooking behind it.

–Clark Humphrey

DELTA 5

Shado/Leaving

Pre Records

These are the most straight ahead songs by the Delta 5 yet. Fuller guitar and some very nice vocals make for a solid A side (Shadow). But the real gem here is Leaving. Jules' beautiful, ethereal voice glides over fluid instrument action, set against a very bright rhytm section. The chorus gives way to their hallmark, the so-called "school girl chant" that made all of their previous stuff so great. Sparse yet effective drumming sums it all up.
–D.W.

PERE UBU

Not Happy b/w
Lonesome Cowboy Dave

Rough Trade

This is a multi-purpose record; you can either dance to it in your saner moments, or giggle to it in the ominous middle stages of manic-depression. The A-side consists of Dave Thomas alternately moaning, squealing, grunting and gibbering the words "Can't we be happy? . . .I am happy when you are happy!" There are also references to various insects, animals, and South America, but all with this basic idea in mind. The music is a clean, repetitive drum beat under an equally clean and repetitive guitar lick. It is quite pleasant to listen to when you are wondering what to do with yourself, or have already done it and now wonder why you did.

The B-side is a fast hysterical treatise on the Lonesome Cowboy himself. There's no point in describing the music, it sounds like the back of the picture sleeve looks. A must for all Ubu fans.

– Captive

(continued page 11.)

VANCOUVER REPORT

CORINNE MAH

Howdy neighbours! Well this kid has been on a harangue about the lack of new and exciting local happenings in Vancouver these days. It certainly has been slow since the beginning of the year. Aside from the "fuck band phenomenon" carried over from last year, the only groups that perform to any extent are the more established acts of (predominently) seasoned and commercial musicians. Most new bands are coming out in the R&B or pop-rock Top 40 vein. I suppose I should reserve judgement until the summer touring season is over and relitive stability returns.

Speaking of summer, our Annual Sea Festival is under way with a musical feature of jazz under the stars at the roundhouse by the beach.

The 5th Annual Folk Music Festival, a three day affair, was held last weekend at Jericho Beach Park, with international, national, and local performers along with workshops.

My favorite Vancouver singer-songwriter is Ferron. Formerly slotted as simply a gay-movement performer; most people have come to realize that she's an artist whose sensitive songs cut deep and whose live shows(solo

or with a band of the best session players around) are often stunning.

Dinosaur rock returns to crunch Empire Stadium this year. Heart, Ted Nugent, Loverboy, Blue Oyster Cult, and The Rockets will be pounding out cock-rock to 10s of thousands of fans who've paid $25 each. Nothing more need be said except that I pass.

Another Vancouver summer event happening is the numerous Boogie Boat, Booze Cruise,and Dance & Drown boat cruises at night with a band on English Bay.

Back to the fuck bands...Los Popularos were one of these part time, get-together-for-a-party bands, until they decided to break from The Modernettes. Young Canadians, Pointed Sticks, Active Dogs, and the Dills, in order to go full-tilt as a "pop" band last January. Their single,"Working Girls/Mystery to Myself", has just been released on Puerco-Maria Records. A recent outdoor show drew over 300 people, and a recording-performing tour back east to Toronto is in the works. Will they succeed or will new fuck bands emerge and tear up the band? (Stay tuned for more.)

Los Popularos' single was produced by Andy Grafitti. Formerly of A.K.A., then the wonderful funk-punk Obelenskys, Andy's now drumming with the Questionaires, a safe yet fun R&B band that's doing very well at the clubs and is doing the final mix on their single at Ocean Sound.

All bands thinking of recording take note: Vancouver has an abundabce of studios in every quality and price range. Also keep in mind that whatever you want to spend on recording, your American moolah is worth 20% more up here.

The ska sensation in Vancouver has reached a plateau. The talented bands have risen to the top, and the b-sides and The Villains rule. The b-sides single "Bedtime for Bonzo", (should be an American hit-it's a comment on 'Raygun'), is doing well. Onstage is where the b-sides really kick out and move. Led by blonde Bobby Herron, their

main goal of every set is to get the crowds to go wild and dance on the tables. Snappy delivery, constant motion, fun on stage,

and hot material have more than once worn my feet out. They're a "must-not-miss" band.

While the b-sides play reggae-rock-ska, The Villains perform calliope British ska. They're in the midst of a cross-Canada tour and reports are that they're knocking 'em dead: three block lineups and rave reviews in Toronto. Originally from Britain, the band took Vancouver by storm last fall but were deported as illegal aliens. After marrying their pals, they returned to a sold out Commodore show in July. They have a mix down for an E.P. and on Sept 19th they'll do another Commodore 'welcome home' show.

Little known fact for the day: Before becoming big cheese of the Boomtown Rats,lead singer Bob Geldoff spent many years as a music critic for the Georgia Straight, Vancouver's weekly music rag.

Strangest match of the year: The Payola$, probably the hottest new-rock band of the 80's, will be backing up Z.Z. Top at the Coliseum.

Help! I'm being chased around the editting table by an edit pen--it appears I'm running long; so--bye now

10

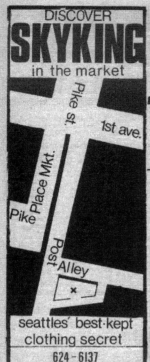
ACCESSORIES

BYE BYE ROCK DISCO

WREX is undergoing a bunch of changes. Wes Bradley is no longer involved in managing the club; booking will now be done by Bev Williams in conjunction with Steve Pritchard. They hope to have national acts and bands from out of town as well as a lot of local bands who haven't played WREX previously. Steve also wants to go on record as saying he did not say that Wes was an asshole who alienated most of the music community. Some upcoming acts: Veil of Tears, The Room, RPA, The Pudz, No Alternative, Lenny Kaye, The Blackouts.

D.D.

CONSUMER REPORT: EARPLUGS

To get one thing out of the way right off, EARPLUGS ARE NOT AN INDICATION OF WIMPINESS. Incipient or otherwise. If you play in a high decibel band, they are an invaluable aid after the fact. You don't have to read lips in the course of normal conversation. If you make it a habit to listen to high dB music, earplugs can prevent that buzzing hangover along with general tympanic deterioration. And if you've woken up once or twice with blood coming out of your ears, you'd be a jerk not to at least consider them.

Most people who own earplugs don't use them all the time, but they're nice to have around on the fifth clubnight in a row. There are a lot of different kinds, the most popular for music being Sonic II by Norton. Sonics are designed to filter out only high-level noise, leaving your ears free to hear all the music. They range in price from a whopping $10 at Friar Tucks to $5 at Kenelly Keys on 8th and 45th. If you're downtown, Myer's Music is next in line at $5.88.

Willett Maico in the Medical/Dental building downtown has earplugs in three sizes for $1.95 a pair, and most local drugstores carry a few brands. The cheapest kind are about 19¢ at industrial places such as Safety & Supply or gun stores. They're disposable foam, and have a noise reduction rating of 29 decibels. These occasionally work too well, but are the most comfortable (aside from the custom jobs at $25 and up.)

Even if you're not too keen on the idea, 19¢ is a minor investment. Any they're worth having around. Because if you're too old to die young anymore, you might be well on your way to dying deaf.

- Captive

IN A CONFUSED FASHION

I was asked to say a few words about the Kitchy Koo fashion show on July 8 at Sundays, for the Alternative Arts Association committee. I've tried to write about the process of giving a show, and the dedication of the people involved, etc. etc., but we've all read enough about TV shows, and bands and backyard puppet carnivals and Watergate to know what can happen to the best of intentions in the worst of circumstances.

Instead, there follows a how-to-lose-control list, in case you'd like to do a similar show--to create a suitable vacuum in which to do your best:

1. Do it at Sundays. This ex-church is so full of wierd vibes and cranky people that it makes me believe in curses. The first time I did a show there, I was forcibly ejected by a drunken owner. I swore I'd never return. First impulses are often correct.

2. Have lots of room. Put 15 models and 5 dressers in a room no larger that 8'x10'. Add 45 costumes and enough food and drink for everybody, and realize that, amid all that sweat and makeup and motion,

you are to emerge looking cool, calm and spectacular.

3. Get rid of 1/2 of the show before it starts. Having been assured we could use models who were under 21, we were surprised (my goodness!) when the ever-friendly and ever-helpful management ejected 1/3-1/2 of our models, forcing a total change of show plans 1-1/2 hours before the show was to start.

4. Keep the audience out. Sundays has a doorman and a dress code and if your jeans aren't cool, you aren't allowed. The paid audience (at a stagger-in $2 a head) was less than 20.

5. Be unyielding in your expectations. Kitchy Koo made a mistake. We went ahead and did the show we had promised to do: three sets of 2 songs each, which was all we could do with the backbone of the show on its way home.

We learned some lessons about promises and co-operation; it will be a long time before the next show. Watch for it.

-Ralph Becker

RECORDS (CONT.)

THE FALL

Slates

Rough Trade America

I know I'm fucking crazy, I really take the Fall seriously. From their early work down to Totally Wired, I've always admired them, not so much for some cynical disrespect for music industry standards, but for the sheer expressionist beauty/non-beauty of their work. With that said, I'm almost alarmed at Slates' "almost produced" sound. What's more, The Fall have never sounded better.

Basically, Slates conjures up the same sort of vision The Fall are notorious for; the kind of atmosphere that scares sleeping cats out of the room, the pasty-faced terror the thought of having them stay at your house for the weekend might bring.

Their work on Slates, as elsewhere, is the direct descendent of traditional Anglo/Gaelic morbidity, with a sense of humor. The message is obscure unless, of course, you belive there really is something to proletariat rhetoric and imagery. This record, as usual, can't be described as much as experienced; like some dark spectre of hell on earth, not glorifying man's decadence, but pointing a knarled finger at it, The Fall act as somewhat of a modern-day Mephistopheles. The poetry reverberates, the melodies drone, seemingly without direction, Slates takes us one step further down their self-serving apocalyptic route; and scaring the shit out of everyone in their path.

– D.W.

GERMS

LP Whiskey '77
Mohawk Records (Bomb)

Hey! first performance ever after being together 2 weeks. This record is living testimony that anyone can do it! My favorite song is Forming:
"Let me be your gun/ pull my trigger/ I am bigger than..."
It shows real intelligence and Darby (or at this time Bobby Pyn) is real abrasive toward the audience and continuously begs for more trash to be thrown, etc. There's even a Rodney intro. (Oh boy!) Buy or die!

FLUX OF PINK INDIANS

CRASS Records

I got good news and bad news! Flux is really great musically and theme wise. The record cover is the usual slick CRASS exitstenxial stuff with a pork butcherhouse on the inside and a live pig and some bacon on either sides of the outside sleeve. Cute? The first listening had me buying so I would recommend it to anyone who like or liked CRASS. Now for the bad news. This record is produced by Penny Rimtsbud. Too those not informed Penny sold out CRASS on a national British pop show. She illigitamized the whole CRASS theme by saying it was just a gimmick used to get their records out to the younger kids. As everyone knows no one likes to be taken for a fool. It doesn't matter how big a fool you are! Bye.

–Catalyst

RENALDO & THE LOAF

Songs For Swinging Larvae
Ralph

If you're tired of trying to figure out who the Residents are, now you can ponder whether Renaldo and the Loaf are really the Residents. Like these other Ralph Records anonymous, this act trades in electronic novelties. A Ralph press release says R&L are two English guys, and the 17 melodies do take more than a little inspiration from English music-hall numbers. A disc with vaudevillian joys added to your basic Residential quirks and ploys.

–Clark Humphrey

ZOUNDS

Demystification

More music, less political drivel. Sorry to say I prefer the drivel. Dymystification shows us Zounds are above-all chameleon-like. It's like they've cleaned up their act, y'know? Gone are the pedestrian social commentaries of the Crass influenced War/ Subvert stuff. In fact, the looks of the sleeve take the Crass-like hippiness a step further, ie it looks tacky...by accident. The song itself? Almost forgetable, and probably would be lost in the anus of time (sorry) if it had been done by anyone else. As a social document it's got to be noticed; it's sure to confuse folks; like what the hell are these guys up to? I don't know...sounds like they don't either. Guess what? I like it.
–D.W.

TOMITA

A Voyage Through His Greatest Hits, Vol. II

RCA Red Seal

This is the most erotic record of the year, possibly of all time (sorry, Johnny Mathis' Greatest Hits fans). Walternow-Wendy Car los was too sexually confused to synthesize the classics in the way that Isao Tomita has been doing it. What he does, on this compilation of cuts from the past seven years or so, to Stravinsky, Bach, Debussy, Mussorgsky's "Pictures at an Exhibition", and Holst's "The Planets" would convert any Eno fan, would turn any Eurodisco "new romantic" into a true romantic, will lower your pulse and release those passions that lie repressed beneath your cool poses. It also contains references to space-pop which make it ultimately accessible. That other Japanese techno act, Yellow Magic Orchestra, seems to have borrowed a lot from this man. At 57 minutes to the disc, you get galaxies of beautiful music for stimulation and mutual enjoyment.

P.S. It's also got the only version of "Bolero" I would romance to.

–Clark Humphrey

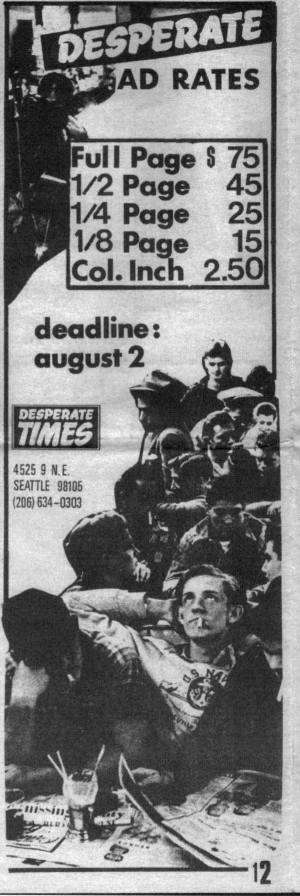
12

CLASSIFIEDS

Descendants - anti-everything single, unnational anthem/ facelift. Available in u-District. thro ugh Systematic, or send $1.50 to A.O.M. 7124 156th SW Edmonds 98020

Rehearsal Studio: 4 track available, call Don 621-9487

Acrylic Waves: new wave, rap, punk, funk, new music and lots more. New Releases and cool old records too. Every Wed. night on KRAB radio 107.7 FM

Seattle Bands Magazine has extended its deadline to August 5th. ree listings for all bands. Call 322-7955

Spectators and Rapid-i will, play at WREX's first art show, Wednesday August 12. "Paintings on Plastic"

Typist w/o typewriter?; Silver-Reed 225 C self-cor- recting for rent. Rates are CHEAP. letter gothic and orator balls. 634-0303

Cheap band equipment, call Terry (J & M Distributing and Promotions) at 746-6284

Rock Guitar taught. Dan Christopherson (Uz) beg/adv. $5.50 1/2 hr. 232-3223.

Prepare Yourself! Cuts & color at George's place. 1900 E. Aloha, 324-4760

Singer/vocalist wanted for Reggae/Rockers sounds call 622-1428

Seattle Rehearsal studio. Reasonable monthly and hourly room rentals for bands. Special introductory rates. 1615 34th North, Seattle 634-1082

Entertainment Plus Recording: 8 track studio recording special, only $15 per hour. 775-9223

just Espresso

6810 Greenlake Way, Seattle

OPEN 6 AM-3 AM Mon.-Mon.

CLASSIFIED RATES: just one green back ($1) for up to 25 words. Graphic ads are $2.50 per column inch. Call 634-0303 -best in town.

AD DEADLINE FOR NEXT ISSUE IS AUGUST 2.

CORPORATE TOP TEN

Singles

1. Dead Kennedys-
   Too Drunk to Fuck
2. Jah Wobble -12"
3. Bauhaus -Passion of Lovers
4. Joy Division -
   Love Will Tear Us Apart
5. Killing Joke -
   Follow the Leader
6. Tom Tom Club -
   Wordy Rappinghood
7. Au Pairs -It's Obvious
8. Killing Joke -Psyche
9. Bush Tetras -Boom
10. Generation X -
    Dancing With Myself

L.P.s

1. Killing Joke-What's This For
2. Au Pairs-
   Playing With A Different Sex
3. Joy Division-Unknown Pleasures
4. Der Plan-What's dat?
5. Raincoats-Odyshape
6. Siouxsie & the Banshees-Ju Ju
7. Wire-Document & Eyewitness
8. Psychedelic Furs L.P.
9. W.S. Burroughs
10. CRASS-Penis Envy

STOP PRESS

photo: Skip Beattie

IS LONG HAIR COMING BACK IN?
Mike Refuzor joins Shatterbox at the Gorilla Room

-KCMU is the victim of budget cuts. The UW School of Communications does not want to foot the bill anymore, now that the school has less state money. Volunteer staff is researching ways to keep the station going.

-Clockwork Joe's in Portland has been closed permanently because of fire code viola- tions.

-Mike Vrany taking off from these parts to manage the Dead Kennedys.

-Impromptu set of the week: Untouchables at the Gorilla Room, joined by Kevin Collins, Mike Refuzor, Loud Fart and other guest vocalist types.

-Billy Shaffer will have an art show at WREX: Idiot Culture and Rapid-i will play. August 12.

-Social Deviance, fuck band with Peter Davis, John Bigley, Steve and Loud Fart, currently practicing.

-The Untouchables are changing their name to Napalm Beach.

-Ronnie Noize,of the now- defunct Portland club Urban Noize, is now booking for Euphoria. Scheduled: Fix from Minnesota, No Alternative. Ronnie is looking for west coast hardcore bands to book.

The liquor board has really been harrassing live music clubs lately. Please don't give them the ammuni- tion to close places down: always have valid I.D. with you. If you're underage and don't have good phony I.D. please don't try to get in.

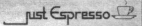

shaffer

13

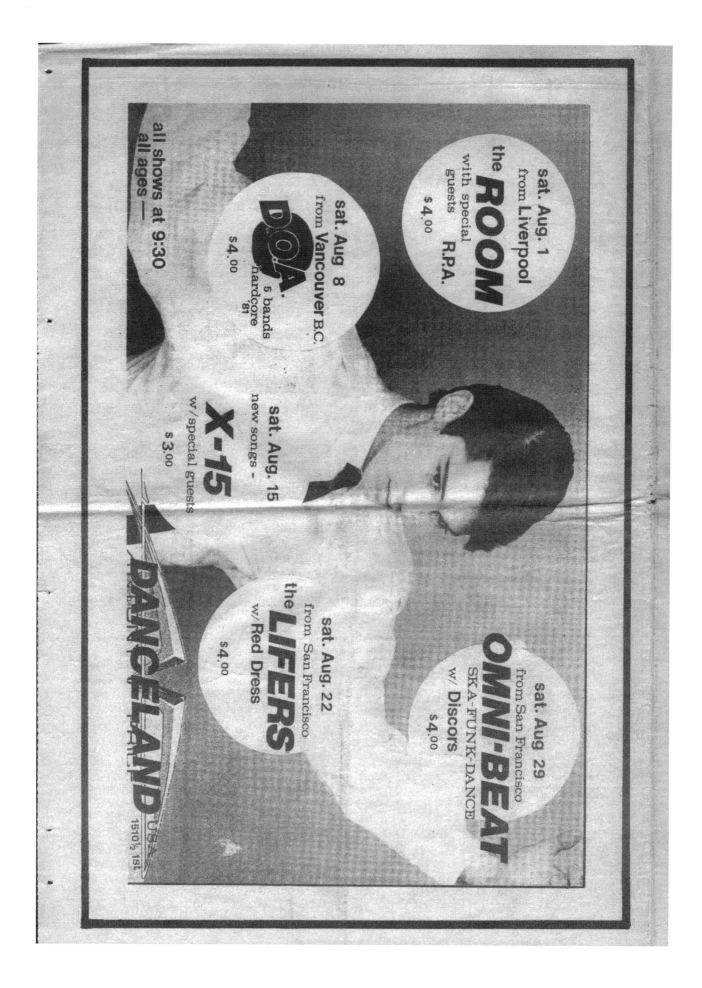

Issue #3

In the ongoing love affair with Mr. Epp & the Calculations, a letter mocking Space Muffin's ad in the first issue is printed. There are editorial complaints about local bands not getting enough stage or media time. Local bands perform at rallies to protest the draft (Selective Service Registration) and bring attention to the illegal war in El Salvador.

Neil Hubbard writes a vivid account of touring the west coast with the UK band Gang of Four.

Our first and only London report was recited over long-distance telephone by J.D. Sheppard — an expensive activity before cell phones and the internet. Riots are occurring all over England, and Sheppard specifically mentions the horrible Brixton riot of 1981. He also talks about skinheads, fascism, and racial tension. With clear insight, he calls out the royal wedding as inappropriate during a time of economic crisis.

The "Drunk and Disorderly" section features a short interview with British band the Room. Band members joke about fascism, anarchy, Barry Manilow, and the spoils of participating in riots. Their glib responses are a little hard to take, but their description of the English riots is likely accurate: "They're just people without hope that are rioting, because of the situation they're in."

DESPERATE TIMES

$.25
AUG 5
VOL.1 NO.3

on tour with the GANG OF 4

Gorilla Room

news from the EASTERN FRONT

LONDON REPORT

LAURIE ANDERSON

nine   nine   nine

china white
contractions
joe despair &
the future
flipper
go gos
mission of burma
psychedelic furs
ramones
the room
rpa
social deviates
theatre of hate
tsol
undertones
veil of tears
and more

DESPERATE TIMES

Editor:
Daina Darzin

Associate Editor:
Captive

Art Director:
Billy Shaffer

Photography Director:
Skip Beattie

B.M. and D.B.
Maire Masco

Milk and Cookies:
Dennis White

Typing:
Kathy Moschel

Contributing Writers:
Catalyst, Bria Conradus,
Verna Doherty, Gregor
Gayden, Clark Humphrey,
Neil Hubbard, Mark McLaughlin
Corinne Mah, J.D. Sheppard,
Heidi Weispfenning

Contributing Photographers:
Lou Allen, Bria Conradus.
Kelly Gordon

Special thank this week go to
MM's Mom for the credit
rating and Kathy for her
magic fingers.

DESPERATE TIMES is
published bi-monthly by
On The Edge Press,
4525 9th Ave. N.E., Seattle,
Washington, 98105
(206)-634-0303
Printing by Consolidated.

Cover Photo Credits:
Skip Beattie, Kelly Gordon

THIS ISSUE

I'M GOING TO VOMIT!

GOOD LORD, I CAN'T BELIEVE MY EYES, WE CAN'T PUBLISH THIS, IT'S FILTHY!

OPINION

It doesn't seem to be enough that state liquor and tax laws have kept local music from reaching any more than a token standing in Seattle. Aside from the obvious problems local bands have reaching a younger audience by playing what little "club scene" is left, the overhead costs of presenting hall gigs prohibits most from taking the financial risk upon themselves.

The only real crack at reaching more than a handful of people is as opener for a touring act. Here again, it seems someone's bound to get screwed; and it's hardly ever the headliner (secure with contracts) or promoter (who's business it is to take risks). No friends, it's usually the local act that takes the greatest financial burden when shows face ill attendance or miscalculation on the part of the backers.

Some of the brightest talents locally have had to pack up and leave Seattle for a more receptive, communicative atmosphere (usually SF or LA). More often than not, they pack it in. Doesn't say much for the local scene, does it?

The whole gist of this whiny little statement is that Seattle club bookers and promoters have just as often as not penalized local talent just because they are local. On the other hand, as long as Seattle bands allow themselves to be exploited, they will be fair game for the unscrupulous.

What we are suggesting, is that more lines of communication be opened between local musicians. Supporting each other can't be such a bad thing, since support from other quarters seems non-existent at this point. We hope to see a little more care and thought on the part of those who present music in this town. More than that, we hope to see an even more active part by bands themselves in the changing of some very ridiculous booking policies. Face it, it's one thing to get sold down the river; it's another to sell yourself.

- Dennis White

IN THE MAIL

WITH A FRIEND LIKE YOU...

I just want to write a brief rebuttle to Verna's comments on the Enemy which appeared last issue. I caught the Enemy twice at Baby O's. I wasn't expecting much, and so I was very happily suprised to find them a band with loads of energy and music to dance to. A lot of people dislike them because they are no longer an "angry" band. Well, they now sing songs about being happy, and there ain't nothing wrong with that. Although they sing a lot of pop songs , they do some excellent rock material, such as their cover of X's "Los Angeles". I was disappointed only in that they did not sing "I Need An Enemy", a favorite song that I would love to see live. The Enemy is a cool group, so I thought I'd give this point of view to counter all the negative shit that's been said about them.

I see, Daina, that Maggot Brains are growing on you. Yes they are a bit like fungus. They are working on a single. Sounds like our local joke band is getting serious.
—Wilum Pugmyr

STILL TEND TO BELIEVE IT

Your first issue and you've fucked up already. In your review of the Plasmatics concert, you wrote that the so-called "Patrick McDonald Incident" (its MacDonald by the way) was a result of him suggesting to Wendy O. that she enjoyed getting beat up by the cops. Or at least that was the version you "tended to believe".
Well what the hell is up your asses, anyway! The true and only version of what happened at the Wendy O. interview was printed in Pat MacDonalds article. He wouldn't say shit like that to anyone! Just because you may not like what he writes in the Times (for whatever reason you happen to have), it is no reason to print bullshit lies about him in your paper. Real charming of you, huh?
—John Steed

SOUND OF MUSIC

How many times have you played one or the other New Rock Clubs in Seattle and found that the soundman got paid more than your band? When you were quite capable of supplying not only the soundman but the PA as well. It wouldn't be so bad if you got what you apid for, GOOD SOUND!
If there's a house PA, why can't the bands have an option of hiring someone to run the board? If the house has to rent a PA, they should budget the fee in their percentage of the door or bar. Let's make it clear who is responsible for what. There is a charitable attitude in some of Seattle's promoters, expecting most bands to play for free depending on personal taste and draw. What they don't seem to realize is that people don't pay 3 bucks to see the club, they pay to see the band. It's obvious that some bands draw more of an audience than others, and Seattle's audience is minmal, therefore bookers will tend to go for a sure thing, burning out the band and the audience, which leads to little variety and no chance for a new or old band to develop an audience through exposure. Capitalism strikes again!
Both the club and the bands provide a service for the public. We depend on each other. Nobody makes enough money in this business, the issue is: will the club profit from the band or will the band profit from the club, or will the soundman take off with the loot? I say let's cooperate.
Because Seattle is such an intimate city, there's no need for the exploitation and beating around the bush when dealing with a band. Let's both be fair and frank and organize the contracts.

—Adull Thud

AN OBVIOUS HOAX......or is it?

CALCULATION PRODUCTIONS

Hi Kids,
I forgot to do any graphics for this week's promo poster, so I thought I would send you all a warm personal greeting!
Be Frogs and Fly! IP
I won't any gyp from you I can rub my lipper off!
See you at the Dico
Glance + Minus
Eppa the boyfriend by
deceased spiritual leader of
Mr. Epp
& the
CALCULATIONS

DT recieved this sophomoric piece of drivel last week. We hope our hardworking advertisers get their hands on the little pimps who plagerised a perfectly... functional,er work of...um, art.

GANG of FOUR DIARY

NEIL HUBBARD

FRIDAY, JULY 10th   Carlo Scanduizzi of Modern Productions had received word that the English members of Gang Of Four's road crew had been denied re-entrance to the United States from Canada. Apparently Phil Allen and Jol Burnham had spent too much time working in the U.S. and their visas were no longer valid. Carlo asked me if I was free for the next week, if I'd like to work for them on the last four dates of their tour. It was rather short notice and quite a surprise, but I said yes. The dates included Seattle, Vancouver, San Francisco, and L.A. Fun in the sun, I thought. I was introduced to road manager John Botting and was hired. The equipment arrived from the airport and we began to set up. The Gang did have one roadie with them - Thane Thomas, an American from San Francisco, as well as their regular soundman, Kevin. Ray Witowski was flown over from England to run the lights.

Of course by this time, I had heard that bass player Dave Allen had suddenly left the group after the last East Coast date and had been replaced temporarily by all pro bassist Buster Cherry Jones. It seemed the Gang had had enough difficulty and I was glad to be of assistance. The band was having their second rehersal with Buster, so everyone sort of hung out. Then a freak accident occured. John Botting was going to throw a bottle of beer to soundman Kevin, ya know, go for the gusto. Kevin stood with his arms out apparently ready to catch it. Instead he didn't see it at all, for some reason, and it hit him squarely in the forehead. He was wisked off to the hospital for novacaine and stitches. Before the show, I was dispatched to pick up the Ryder rental truck that had been left parked near the Edgewater Hotel. It was not there. The spot Thane had left it was a Metro bus stop and it had been dutifully towed away by Lincoln Towing. After tracking this down and getting some money from John Botting, I went to pick up the truck. Back to the Showbox in time for the first act, the Little Bears From Bankok.

Three Swimmers came on next and I stationed myself stage left, as I knew I would wind up helping them on the next three dates, which they had been scheduled to play with the Gang Of Four. The Gang had rehearsed with Buster Jones for only the second time that afternoon, but when they hit the stage at about 10:30, Buster appeared confident and fit in perfectly with the group. The show came off without any hitches and we began to pack up the gear. By the time I got home it was about 2:30 AM. I had to pack and try to get some sleep before picking up Thane and Ray at 10:00 AM at the Edgewater.

SATURDAY, JULY 11th   The trip to Vancouver was short and uneventful. We were met at the border by a represen-

tative of the Perryscope concert company, who helped make the crossing smoother. The opening band, the Punts, from San Francisco, took to the stage and were given a rather cold welcome. The girl lead singer, who is also a music teacher, writes very good pop songs, but her attitude onstage that night was snotty and sarcastic. She kept laughing like a bitch and telling the audience in a very contemptuous way what "really, really nice people" they were. They got a few beer cans tossed at them in appreciation. The Three Swimmers arrived ten minutes after the Punts had left stage, set up in a rush and began to play. Maybe their sound was too foreign for the tender ears of those in attendance. Beer cans now hit the stage with regularity. Surprisingly, the crowd called the Swimmers back for an encore. Later, the stage manager told the band it had been a very good response for an unknown act. I guess beer cans thrown are a form of applause in the Great White North.

The activity begins again when showtime finally comes around. Time to clear the beer cans off the stage, check and reset lights, amps, microphones, put some drinks out for the band, and tune the guitars. Most all headlining acts require that the equipment be left set as is after soundcheck, so it is all in place. The stage at the Commodore is rather low--about two and a half or three feet--and the audience

is right up against it. The stage moniters are in front of the stage on tables and become a major problem during the show. Fans packed up front jostle them and move them around. A slight change in their position can cause feedback or keep a singer from hearing himself.

The Gang Of Four also use floor lights placed directly upstage of the moniters, which are carefully focused. Throughout the show, we had to keep moving these back into position. Another disadvantage of the low stage is that it is easy for rowdy fans to jump up on the stage. And in Vancouver, there are lots of rowdy fans. People coming up over the top, landing on their heads or back on top of the moniters

and lights, knocking front line mikes over, jumping up, dancing around. It looks bad for a group to have roadies that treat these people roughly, so I had to quickly but gently dispose of any stage leapers.

Some of them chose to leap back on top of the crowd. Fine and dandy. It's not my head they're landing on. Because of the small stage, the band did not have as much room to move around as in Seattle, but their performance was no less energetic; Buster humping up behind Andy Gill as he tried to sing, Jon King parading maniacally back and forth, pushing Buster wrecklessly out of the way. And during the encore numbers, things got real fervent. The stage was a tangle of quick movement. It is like entering a battle field when I step out to retrieve the melodica tossed on the floor by Jon. The show ends with a great finale, the audience happy, the band retreats to the dressing room, no doubt to meet girls and have a good time. Meanwhile, the lowly roadie is packing up the gear, as fast as he can with what energy he has left after a strenuous fourteen hour day of driving and lifting huge boxes of gear. We finally got the truck loaded, drove to the hotel and checked in. It seemed like they were filming a chase scene on the streets below our room early into the morning--screeching tires, racing cars, screaming sirens-- the whole bit. Sweaty and smelly, I fitfully fall asleep about 4:00 AM.

SUNDAY, JULY 12th   I'm woken up at 8:00 AM by the sound of a huge helicopter lifting some heavy equipment off the top of a skyscraper a couple of blocks away. Up for a shower and breakfast and hang out while Thane does some laundry. On the road, you've got to grab the opportunity to do laundry or you may miss it for another week.

Ray, Thane and I finally depart Vancouver in the Ryder about noon. We are able to spend about an hour at my house in Seattle relaxing before getting back on the road. Burger King dinner in Portland; we drive 'til after midnight when we hit Roseburg, Oregon and decide to get a motel for the night. Thane takes care of the room and thoughtfully books the three of us into one room with two beds. I lay my claim on one of them and the other two pull the matress onto the floor. Thane gets the box spring.

MONDAY, JULY 13th   Thane had put in a wakeup call for 8:00 AM, but Ray was clever enough to take the phone off the hook. After breakfast, we're back out on I-5. It's hot through Southern Oregon and even hotter the farther into California we get. My butt is aching from long hours in the truck. About 5:00 PM we stop in Redding, California, for dinner. The temp had been over 100 degrees a bit earlier. The waitress tells us it had been cooling off from what it was during the last two weeks.

TUESDAY, JULY 14th   Day of the show, and I have about two hours free before we have to be at the Fillmore. Wow, man! The fucking Fillmore West and Bill Graham! In my free time, I catch a bus to the Broadway district and browse at City Lights bookstore and Rough Trade. We arrive at the fabled Fillmore at about 1:30 for load in, which is up three flights of stairs. Fortunately, Bill Graham has supplied an ample team of humpers who gripe and whine as they heft the gear upstairs. Apparently, it's the first show in twelve years at the Fillmore, so the vibes are cool.

What's hard to believe is that power for the lights has to come up those three stories from a generater on the street. Like, how did the Dead and everyone do their light shows? During the soundcheck, some people from Target Video had their cameras and bright lights set up at the same time Ray was working on focusing the stage lights. He walked over and switched off their lights while they were taping and an argument ensued. He yells at them, they snivel at him, and Hugo lashes out at Ray, telling him to cool it so he doesn't make the band look like "a bunch of cunts."

We are treated to a turkey dinner upstairs while Hugo and Buster--the rhythm section--are interviewed by Target.

Shortly after that, Ray found himself in another altercation when he tried to walk backstage without a pass. The security girl stood fast while Ray protested, somehow "spilling" his cola on her. Other staff members are summoned and it is decided that Ray be ejected from the building until the Gang Of Four take to the stage. He will be allowed

CONTINUED ON PAGE 11

2

PERFORMANCE ART

LAURIE ANDERSON

Laurie Anderson makes her living as a performance artist, and she does her job well if her performance at Volunteer Park was any indication. Her popularity can be traced to the fact that she is magical without being mystical and, what is rarer in these days of hyper-art, intelligent without being obscure. Although the section she performed here was billed by other writers as being a dark and moody piece, the show itself came off as upbeat rather than depressing. Perhaps that was due to the obvious pleasure radiating from the stage: as she says, it's all in the tone of voice. She will be returning to Seattle April 10 and 11 at Washington Hall as part of their New Performance series, which will include Meredith Monk and Eiko & Koma. There she will perform United States, I-IV (Transporation, Politics, Money, and Love), the second part of which was seen on the 26th.

Her other work includes books, records, and sculpture, and a recent recording, "O Superman" b/w "Walk the Dog" is available for $3.98 on One Ten Records, 110 Chambers St., NYC 10007. I had a chance to talk with her a few days before the show, and here, in no particular order, is some of what she had to say about different things.

(confusion)

I'm trying to build a studio in my house now. Came home last week, just completely gutted my life, real satisfying. To just come in and trash your place, it's wonderful. Have you ever done that? Get a sledge-hammer and go WHOMP WHOMP. Now it's all huge piles of sheetrock and it's great because I don't have to do anything organizational anymore. If someone calls me up and says, "Listen, I have to ---", I can't even find a piece of paper, let alone _that_ piece of paper.

(records and video)

I have a complete phobia about records. I just don't like--well, I do and I don't like the idea that something's permanent. The whole thing I like about doing the work that I do (performances, pictures) is that you can't ever reconstruct them without doing them. And I like that; just erase...and to, first of all, make something without the pictures. I can't stand videotape, so that wasn't an option. Mostly cause the sound is crummy on videotape, and the picture's ugly, I think. And it's a box. It's not a way to report a real thing.

(next project)

A series of things about jobs, people's jobs.

(vienna)

I was playing in Vienna, and somebody came up and started pounding on me on the back, really hard. And I said, "May I continue?" I finally had to stop, because no one was pulling her off. She was going "Scheisse! Scheisse!", which means shit. The audience thought it was a part of the piece. It was right after this blood and guts piece, blood strewn all over the stage. Bad atmosphere. And I tried to explain it wasn't part of it. And they thought THAT was part of it.

(europe)

I spend about a third of my time in Europe. I do the pieces there in French or German or Italian. If there's a word game like mood/mode, I have to find a corresponding way of expressing it. I work with translators, it's very difficult. Sometimes I like them a lot better in other languages.

(environment)

I've been working in my hallway--you can hear the elevator in every tape I do. Many worlds, many layers: dogs, trucks passing.

(news)

News always reminds me of single's bars. You're at this big curved counter and: Joe! What's new in sports! No drinks, but the breezy attitude is there. "What's for dinner!" and "Bring a sweater!" and "They've just invaded Iran!"

(stars)

I think that people are realizing now that this whole thing about stars, movie stars and things, that it's all some kind of horrible cheap trick.

(guilt)

For a while I felt guilty about using electronics, things that used a lot of power. Till I finally realized, I don't have a toaster, I don't have a garbage disposal. I don't have a car. I don't have a lot of things that drain power. I have harmonizers, volt guards; mixers, speakers. But I don't think they quite stack up to a typical American home.

(germany)

It's a very good place for me to work. I have a problem with being there. I used to do a lot of things on the street, and Italy's the best place to do it. Germany's more like here. People in cars...I was in Germany once, doing a song about flies and the letter Z. And I heard this other sound that I KNEW was not on the tape, and it was just like this zzzzz, zzz. And I looked out, and about six rows of people were going

CONTINUED ON PAGE 12

JOHANNA WENT

"I've always wanted total control. That's the whole point of my performance. What I've done is to create a form, a collage of image and form colored with sound. It can be interpreted according to the individual any way they see fit. Above all else, I'm a surrealist."

Johanna Went is telling the truth. In fact it's pretty hard to believe otherwise, listening to her. With a vote wavering somewhere between Tiny Tim and Shirly Temple, it's easy to believe her sincerity. Far from the violent-absurdist stage persona she has projected over the last two or three years, Went is a firm, yet soft-spoken woman committed entirely to her art and opinion.

"Hey!" she says during a recent phone conversation from Los Angeles, "I got a four page spread (sic) in the latest issue of Velvet Magazine. It's got a picture of Victoria Principal on the cover with nude shots inside. She says she was drugged and blackmailed into doing it. I didn't even have to take my clothes off. The article was like the woman clipped together lots of interviews I've done before. It's horrible but the photos are great."

How did she feel about being featured in one of Southern Californias' semi-notorious soft-core porno mags?

"Well, it's just like WE or PEOPLE magazine." she explained.

"You mean like WE or PEOPLE but sort of pornographic" I ask.

"No...just like WE magazine. They've been doing a series on L.A. women in rock...The GoGos, Nina Hagen, Nita Benyaga, that sort of thing.

Looking at the article in Velvet it soon becomes apparent the angle is geared toward some of the more "purient" aspects that could be gotten through a Went performance, rather than its artistic nature. The truth is, one such performance utilizes lots of archetypical imagery. Dildos, sex dolls, the gynecologist nightmare sequence; it's all there. One of her more celebrated performances saw her suck an eyeball out of a sheeps' head. Another saw Johanna stab a frozen (obviously dead) cat to a wall, drawing shivers of both terror and glee from L.A. critics.

"My shows are more or less dreamlike. People have to be open to that. They must be interpreted on an individual level. I feel my shows ARE violent. They are also funny. Many people are frightened or upset, especially by the scatalogical elements. The whole point is the audience can manipulate their feelings any way they choose. It's like a huge canvas; here there is red and pink and

blue. Over there, green. Sometimes people cut the piece up. They only want to remember blue; the most violent, the most sensational. There may be violence but over there a baby is being born."

As in the case of many other artists' whose public grasps for their more notorious elements of their work, a lot of misunderstanding evolves. Went literally exploded onto the Los Angeles underground upon returning from a European tour in 1978.

"People thought I just popped up from nowhere."

The truth is, Johanna has been doing what she's doing (performing) in one form or another for nearly a decade. A native of Seattle, Johanna was working at the Kelly Ross drugstore downtown, when at a party one night she met a fellow by the name of Tom Murrin.

"He just walked up and said, "Hey, I'm doing Balloon Theatre", which he'd just invented two days before."

"I said, what's Balloon Theatre?" and he said, "Well, it's just going around with balloons acting silly."

"It sounded real interesting, so I joined up. We did our first real performance in Billy King's loft in Pioneer Square. It was Mothers Day and there were a couple of other people involved (including Alex now with the Theatrical Re-construction Co.). I'd never done anything free-form before, so it was really amazing."

What ensued was the formation of a loosely-knit troupe, variously titled The World's Greatest Theatre Co. and The Theatre That Doesn't Get In The Way. Murrin and Went left Seattle and toured around the country playing in anyplace that afforded them an audience: parks, streets, any space available. Eventually, they hooked up with another performer, Craig Cilander, and in 1977/78 they fled to Europe, again playing any space available to them. By this time it was becoming apparent Johanna would break out on her own, into a totally new area of performance.

"I observed the beginning of the punk thing in London. I thought it was great, but I wondered if it would ever move across the ocean to America. In London it was evolving from economic need, and middle class America was just too damn comfortable."

Returning home, Went was in for a surprise.

"It was like I saw the whole thing mutate. It came to America as a fashion. In Britain, it came out of the soul and here it was calculated; thought-out."

It's not surprising that Went felt such a strong sense

CONTINUED ON PAGE 12

3

Photo: Skip Beattie

PSYCHEDELIC FURS
VEIL OF TEARS

The Psychedelic Furs have become popular with a certain audience, an audience that usually demands contemporaneity and a kind of anger that oscillates between healthy strength and sick deliberation. Yet their songs are not paeans to alienation, degradation fantasies, or comments on the political overview. In fact, if Richard Butler's lyrics are political at all, they are political in the larger sense of individual power: how do I see/control (my) life?

Neither the first album's blatant reiteration of images (flower, ceiling, stupid, etc.) nor the self-preoccupation in the love songs on Talk Talk Talk can be classified as 'psychedelic', 'new wave', or even 'modern' (much less 'punk'). Ten years ago this would have been fairly usual. At this point, it's astounding. To add to which, the modern sound is very involved with necessity: having to play, needing a release. The energy level of a good show is one that goes beyond the individual members and becomes—to use an apt if tired phrase—more than the sum of its parts.

The Furs droned into their set with "Into You Like A Train", the light show more an expected part of the show than an addition to it. The songs were an equal mix from both albums, and they blurred together towards a basic hum of sound that varied slightly but never wavered out of range. Having seen them six times, it can only be said that they gave the sort of performance they are in the habit of giving. Whether the song was "Mr. Jones", "Pretty in Pink", "Imitation of Christ", or "Pulse", the music moved with a slow motion feeling that was echoed by the movements on stage. Richard pulled in and out of Jaggeresque positions: jacket half on and sliding, a hand sloped on the curve of his ass, knees tightly crossed in a crouch. He danced straightfaced and blank, making every smile an occasion. And though he seemed to be having a good time, and the band was tight, and the songs contained all the live potential one could ask for, the energy somehow never quite made the shift from static to kinetic.

It seemed deliberate and controlled because when the Furs came back for the encore, they turned the level up a notch. Say, if they had been going at 50 mph, they were now doing 55. Both "Fall" and "We Love You" are strong, relentless songs. So why didn't the band let loose? Because they didn't want to. This attitude kept a good show from being a lethal one. They Psychedelic Furs left the crowd with a happy feeling that dissipated,rather than anticlimactic exhaustion. They were fun. But they ought to start driving with the gas, not the brakes.

—Captive & D.W.

Veil of Tears is apparently an everchanging group that contains only one member not subject to approval: Steven Wymore. Try to recall the blond stage presence with the guitar. His associates that night included Indian on guitar, and Gregory Coruikshank as singer and lyrist, and his sound basically consisted of disorienting live additions to pre-recorded tapes. James Husted, a member of too many local bands to name, was there too, helping the system to move electronically along. Good things were said about the show afterwards at WREX, but this place and time just wasn't right for the kind of music being played,not as warmup for the Psychedelic Furs. The sound wasn't clean enough to take the audience with it, and it wasn't dirty enough to fill a large space. The only part I remember clearly is when the singer looked intensely into the microphone and said, in a mildly sinister manner, the single word "bicycle". The rest of the lyrics came off as the usual mixture of fear, reality, etc. Wymore has worked with Minimal Man, and done some things with film. Right now, Veil of Tears could be considered a work in progress. I'll wait and see what happens, because if there hadn't been something in the music, I wouldn't have stuck around for the whole set.

The mysterious lightfooted Monolith didn't appear, ostensibly due to some preshow bashfulness. Instead, we had Autosax, whose work was even less timely. The audience almost got violent on this one, but you gotta admit the guy had guts. Unfortunately, the sound didn't, and the sax wailed meaninglessly against jeers from the crowd.

—Captive

999
ALLEY CATS
PUDZ

It was the sort of night that made you wish the Showbox was airconditioned. The Pudz opened with their repertoire of mouldies like "Yummy Yummy Yummy" and "Little Willy". They had a lot of trouble with the crowd, finally leaving the stage abruptly. Trouble was, people wanted to see punk, not 60's dance music.

Next up were the Alicats from L.A., a trio consisting of Randy Stodola, guitar and voc als, Dianne Chai, bass, and John McCarthy, drums. I had gotten the impression from the advance promotion that this was to be a rockabilly band, so I was surprised to find a punk band that I'd heard on record before. They were tight, fast, and quite good, but somehow they just couldn't get much reaction from the audience. No one seemed to dislike them, but the pogoing was pretty limited. They closed with the one recorded number that I know of, "Too Much Junk", after announcing that Seattle couldn't be all bad since it had a Space NEEDLE.

Then we sat and waited for a longish while. I was supposed to interview 999 before they played, but they returned quite late from their hotel, so it had to wait. I got the impression later that they were catching a last few fish.

I positioned myself in the very front row so that I could see clearly while only getting shoved from three sides, and waited for the set to start. After a few minutes of pre-show pogoing (huh?) the lights dimmed, and the band trooped on. Instant mayhem in the front.

They played old favorites like "Emergency" and "Let's Face It" and material from their new album, like "So Greedy". Nick Cash ran around frantically, singing and bashing away at his guitar. Guy Davis kept things moving on the right with his guitar work, and John Watson, looking like a Marine sargeant this year, leapt, did jumping jacks, and drenched the front row in sweat while his bass runs kept the crowd moving. Pablo Labritais just contented himself with pounding away expertly at his drums, no flashy dramatics.

It was a hot show (in more ways than one), and Nick interrupted a few times to ask people to ease up on the slamdancing and to please quit flinging themselves off the stage, so that everyone could have a good time without injury. Many of the people I talked to later thought that it was a really nice thing for him to do; although there were a couple of injuries anyway, there easily could've been more. They closed their set with "Homicide", naturally, and came out for one encore.

Afterwards, I got to talk to Guy Days for a few minutes. Although he was a bit fuzzy from van-itis (being cooped up in a van on long drives), he was very friendly, and we covered a variety of subjects, most of which were too silly to write about.

He told me that since their last show in Seattle, they've been kept busy with tours of the U.K. and Europe, and recording their new album, Concrete.

"If we're not recording, we're usually on the road. We can't afford not to be doing anything."

They started their tour about 2 months ago in Miami, and will shortly be heading home, after a benefit gig in L.A. for the childrens' sports facilities, which are presently shut down.

His thoughts on America run like this:

"I'm fed up that none of the restaurants here serve vegetables with your meal. I hate the moronic adverts on your TV, but the all-night programming is great."

Seattle was one of the high points of the tour for him, as they stayed at the Edgewater and had great fun fishing from their rooms. Guy also liked Pioneer Square because he found some great clothing shops.

I asked him about the riots in London. He hasn't been around for most of them, but his flat is near Brixton, and that area gets a lot of action. According to him, there's no one particular cause, but he'd probably do the same thing if he was in their position.

"Last week my flat was burgled, but they only nicked my checkbook and bankcard, so it wasn't too bad."

We talked for a bit longer about nothing in particular and then it was time to leave. Say goodnight, Dick.

—Heidi Weispfenning

4

VIOLATIONS

EASTERN FRONT PART 1

notes and pictures by: BRIA CONRADUS

EASTERN FRONT was organized by Wes Robertson. In contrast to the annual Western Front, Eastern Front brought some of the best "new music" to the Aquatic Barn in Berkley. Located between a salt water inlet and some railroad tracks, the site (a dry field) resembled a country fairground. To add to the atmosphere, the stage was a flatbed truck, and a waterskiing exhibition was being held across the inlet. Hell of a place to see hardcore.

Saturday, July 25th, had probably scheduled the most hardcore line-up north of L.A. (All the bands are hardcore and fast). The first band was Anti-L.A. Unfortunately, I don't see them.

Sic Pleasure was second up. This band was real powerful, my favorite act of both days. The singer, Niki Siki, had that kind of anemic charisma that makes you want to stretch your neighbor's neck. Guitar player, Mike Fox (owner of Subterranean Records) was high energy, bringing the crowd out of their sun-induced daze for "I Want To Burn My Parents", and "Sic Pleasure".

7 Seconds, from Reno, was on at noon. (By this time about 200 people were lounging about, sitting and talking. It was

breaking into a fast paced set with flying guitar and drums in control. Still, they came off kind of "scrappy." And their stage presence was less than memorable.

War Zone's name was appropriate as far as the appearance of the whole scene. But the crowd was getting mellow: a punk Woodstock. Jeff Bale, War Zone's vocalist, tried to liven the crowd with insults and slogans (bullshit): "Some people say punk rock is

real hard to get enthused about the music in such a wholesome environment). Although they got off to a slow start, 7 Seconds showed their power. Fast and political, they knocked out songs like "Riot" and "Anti-Youth" (a song about bars that ban minors).

The Fix began their set with some kind of voodoo rhythm,

dead. Looking at this crowd, I almost believe them". As far as their music, it was speedy and a little bit sloppy. They also dedicated a song to "the new wavers who lick Bill Graham's ass": "Punk's not dead, it's the punks." (D.M.)

I was really too stoned to remember a lot about these

bands, but here's what filtered through:

The Lewd's set was great, but people were dead throughout most of it. When the crowd did get moving it was dangerous! L.A.'s violent mindless slam/skank dancing has infiltrated San Francisco.

T.S.O.L., from L.A., are really hardcore, with most of the band sporting skinheads. Once again, the dance zone was a giant mixer of human bones and flesh.

Flipper didn't really work in an outdoor setting, their hypnotic strains were lost in the dust. The encore ended abruptly with a lesson for all those over zealous teens: if you trash the band, they'll trash you. The details aren't really important.

D.O.A. got the best reception, as most headline bands do. These guys are looking real professional and sounded great

----

July 26th had a relatively calm line-up. Tanks, the first band, made an attempt at waking up the (no more than) 75 people. On an early Sunday morning. They had a great beat, but the tempo gets too slow. The female guitar player rocked, obviously influenced by Patti Smith and the Ramones.

(This audience, by the way, was real "new wave". Not so much spandex, but quite a bit of Fiorucci fashion. There was the obvious influence of New Romanticism, and the Slits were wearing makeshift Rasta gear).

The Toiling Midgets were introduced as the "Next Doors". With their checkered amps and plastic shades, they looked like twits. The attitude was "Joe Cool". They don't have a singer, but they managed to knock out some harmless R & R. It was the best time for a beer run.

The Wounds opened with an electric flute swooning into a rolling bass drum. Good music, with a loose melodic structure and heavy rhythm.

It's almost drug-like, but sleepy, like sounds from the bottom of the sea.

Middle Class was the first band on Sunday that had any volume. Kind of like a fast Blackouts, with a surfin' guitar.

Once Earl Zero hit the stage, the Rasta Love was flowing. (Quite a contrast from the day before, and not exciting when nursing a hangover). The band played a few classic Reggae numbers before Earl came on. It was too beautiful. Earl's a ham; he held the stage for about an hour and a half of rasta tunes. He was good, but in my head the sounds of Sic Pleasure still echoed off the trees.

The Offs were entertaining. They rocked, popped, and reggaed, looking like they'd been beamed over from a local night club. The Offs are a tight, swinging band with horns, and they threw in songs like "Johnny Too Bad" along with the original tunes. Real cool.

I was tuned out by the time Snakefinger appeared. It sounded ok, but it got boring. Sounds from Ralph Records weren't what was called for.

The Slits wound up the show, but at this point, all I could think of was rasta clones with fake accents. It might have been the set, or it might have just been my frazzled brain.

That's it for me, folks. Stay tuned for Part II by Erica next issue.

5

DRUNK AND DISORDERLY

CONTRACTIONS

Photo: Lou Allen

WREX
JULY 25

The CONTRACTIONS are an unpretentious all-girl 3-piece high-energy band from San Francisco. Their return to WREX provided 3 nights of exciting entertainment and, from a chat with the band Fri. night, a glimpse of the San Francisco club scene.

The Contractions consist of Mary Kelley on guitar, Kathy Peck on bass, and Debbie Hopkins on drums. Vocals are passed around between all three, and while there are no "stars" in the group, Ms. Kelley's lead guitar work and fascinating facial expressions garner most of the attention. Their presence is sensual without selling sex. Their songs more often than not deal with the denial of romance, rather than the allure of it, with songs like "Shut The Door and Slam It"(about divorce),

"Your Love Has Thrown Me a Bone", and their claim that "Breaking Up is Not Hard to Do".

Talking with the group in WREX' cramped (contracted?) band room, the girls confessed that, surprisingly enough, they make more money on the road than in the bay area. This was attributed to the monarchy Bill Graham holds in the City of the First Filmore. According to the band, his "lieutenants"are engaged in a booking war vs. independant promoters and apparently winning, in S.F.'s current dirge of "new music" clubs.

Oh well, bad news for S.F., good news for Seattle, if groups like this can find a migration northward profitable. In my book you're welcome anytime.

Billy Shaffer

RPA DTZ JOE DESPAIR

WREX JULY 30
The first night of local hardcore at WREX, a part of their new- n-improved booking policy. The audience mix didn't quite make it. WREX regulars were in sparse attendance, and the Gorilla room refugees looked homesick. The change of turf had a good effect on the bands, though: it was a hot show.

Photo: Skip Beattie

D.T.Z and guest artist

Photo: Skip Beattie

joe despair and the future

Joe Despair & the Future have been playing more lately, and have improved tremendously. JD&F combine punk loudfast with a few tricks from good ol' rock n roll, like extended guitar solos (fortunately, Ward's chops are together and flashy enough to pull it off). Their sound intersperses wall of sound with spare, inventive breaks that work as a dialogue between guitar/bass & drums.

Their focus is strongly political: Joe D. comes off as a YAF member who has been suddenly and vehemently radicalized, and feels driven to share his enlightenment with the world. The vocals have a this-shit-is-serious-you-gotta-listen-to-me urgency that intensifies the band's already-rocking high energy. All in all, impressive stuff.

THE ROOM
DANCELAND, USA   AUGUST 1

The Room is the best band I've heard in a long time. You have to witness them in action, they are terrific! Original, talented, tight, and intense, it's music at its best. Excellent vocals by Dave Jackson--whose singing reminds me a bit of Adam Ant's. Powerful and wild drumming by Clive Thomas and a great throbbing bass by Becky Stringer made up the extraordinary rythm section, while Rob Odlum played sensational guitar riffs. An overall compelling performance by an awesome band--The Room, you mustn't miss them!

Before the show I talked with the group. (Steve's Broiler, with the sound of clanking dishes.) The Room have been together for about 18 months, Clive joining 2 months later. They all write their parts individually and then work them together as a band. Different members mentioned Capt. Beefheart, Talking Heads , and Magazine as music they liked, but Dave answered the question of musical influences with, "None particularly. I mean we all come from different backgrounds I suppose." As for being political, the band made various claims.
Rob: I'm an anarchist.
Dave: In that sense we've all individualists you know. Clive's not.
Rob: He's a fascist. Yeah, we're an anarchist-fascist band. And Becky, she's into Barry Manilow.
Dave: No, some of the lyrics are political. I write all the lyrics. And you can't really have political drumbeats or guitar riffs.
Becky: You see, the main point of the band isn't to get across a political message really.
Clive: It expresses sort of a view of the social situation, rather.

How do you feel about about all the positive reaction to your group by the press?

Rob: We have ego crises all the time.
Dave: You react to what people say about you.
Clive: It's a bit pleasin'.

How does it affect your decision about signing with a major label?
Dave: It's difficult to say because we haven't had that reaction from the major ones. The press isn't a factor either way. There's interest in the band but I think major labels want people to go crawlin' to them, unless you get an incredible amount of press.
Rob: Like cardboard cutouts 6 feet high that say "Hi I'm Dave.
Dave: We've got our own label,we put out our own stuff. Our first single was recorded and mixed in 5 hours because we didn't have enough money to stay in the studio any longer.

What do you think success is?
Rob: Well, to support yourself playing.
Dave: My ambition at the moment stretch as far as the band.

Do you have any comments about the riots in England?
Dave: We live in Toxtith where the riots started, and we saw the first couple of days of it. In a way it's probably like what the punk thing was when it first started, only that was started by people who weren't as directly affected by it. They're just people without hope that are rioting because of the situation they're in.

Have you ever been in a riot?
Rob: Yep.
Clive: He was watching.
Rob: I was looting.
Becky: He was not.
Dave: He got a few packets of cigarettes.
Rob: I got 400 cigarettes.

CONTINUED ON NEXT PAGE

In the continuing story of the DTZ (Have they broken up? Are they back together?): Despite occasional weird vibes between band members, they did a terrific, outrageous set: punk with a touch of vaudeville ("You want some PUNCH?!" Mike Refuzor screeches during the intro to "Jim Jones"). The DTZ material sticks in your head; it would be nice if they came up with some new stuff, though.

Anyway: hearing RPA is like being in the direct path of a herd of psychotic dinosaurs. I think their set takes the prize for the highest decibel level ever recorded at WREX. With 2 guitars and flying hair, RPA cops some of the attitude and sound of heavy metal and combines it with the raunchiest, most intense punk. I loved them, but they're a band you gotta be in the right mood for. RPA doesn't perform, they assault.

-D.O.

Photo: Skip Beattie

R.P.A.

6

ACCESSORIES

TRAVEL CASES: $6.95; $7.65

---

the room, cont.

Do you think you'll be releasing any U.S. 45's?
Dave: We're tryin' to get a
licensin' deal so that we can
release the stuff we've already done in England over
here. We've got 2 tracks
goin' out on a compilation
album in September in England.

Your music is intense, and
contains a lot of paranoid
overtones. Where do you feel
this comes from?
Dave: The paranoid overtones
come from me because I write
the lyrics-- if they are
paranoid.
(The others agree that Dave
is paranoid.)

Describe your music in two
words.
Clive: Geometric rock.
Dave: I think it's sort of
atmospheric, you know. Atmos-
pheric impressionist.
Rob: It's ambience. Very
ambiant.
Dave: Well, no, but it's a
bit more expressionist--
Clive: Post- industrial.
Rob: 7th day evangelist.

-Verna Doherty.

SOCIAL DEVIATES
WREX   AUGUST 2

Deciding to take a break from
last-minute paste-up on the
magazine, I went to see Social Deviates at WREX. The
band consists of Peter Davis
(vocals), John Bigley (bass),
Loud Fart (guitar), and Steve
Fart (drums). A veritable
cavalcade of local talent,
no? They played. They sang.
They gestured. They fell
over. Other things fell too;
but down, not over. The other things that fell were, in
chronological order: bass
pick, bass pick, guitar strap,
guitar pick, bass strap, song
sheet, bass pick.
The band ran speedily through
their more or less unintelligible set; it couldn't have
taken more than 20-- say 22
minutes at the outside. This
I nclu des songs that started
twice. The music was fast,
earsplitting, and danceable
only in the abstract sense,
I tell ya, it's only their
second gig and already the
choreography is superb. They
were aided in this respect by
a lone Bovver Boy who divided
his time between spitting at,
kicking at, and generally
irritating Peter, and solic-
itously rearranging Loud's
scattered accoutrements. (I
won't mention his name, but
I'll give you a hint: think
about certain exhibits at the
Health Museum.)
To compliment this foray into
hardcore country, the band-
memb ers posed, grimaced, and
occasionally giggled to themselves. So did the audience
(which w as rather small when
compared to the people at the
bar).

Social Deviates were a lot of
fun. I plan to see them again
Often (if possible). No kid-
ding! They were swell.
-Captive

A VERY SUBJECTIVE COLUMN ABOUT THE GORILLA ROOM
Daina Darzin

As probably everybody knows
by now, the Gorilla Room has
been closed down for 6 weeks
by the liquor control board.
Infraction #1: one 17 year
old musician on the premises, 18 & over band members
are allowed to perform as long
as they sign a minor musicians form. The G. Room staff
wants to take this to the
ACLU on the basis that the
law discriminates against
under-18 players. Hope it
works. The penalty for this
instance (admittedly are a
number of others) was one
month closure. An extra 2
weeks was added for Infraction #2: 3 minors on the premises. In this case, the
minors were dates of the band
which was playing that night,
after the band members had
assured the door person
that everyone in their entou-
rage was over 21 and had ID.
Which brings us to the part
of this article that's going
to sound like a fucking lecture. Ok: having moved to
New York when I was 18, I never had to personally deal
with the stupid liquor laws
in this state, but I know it
must be a frustrating bitch
to be 19 here an not be able
to go see bands you want to

Photo: Skip Beattie

see. But that's the fault of
the state legislature, not the
club, and the unfortunate reality is that, by sneaking in,
it's the club that you're
fucking up. I'm not going
to say "don't try to get in",
cause that's bullshit--but,
get it together and get some
good fake ID, know how to
dissappear fast if the liquor board shows up, in short,
avoid getting the club in
trouble.
I miss the Gorilla Room tremendously. More than any
other club in town, the G.
Room gives new bands a chance
to perform, and books hardcore
and experimental groups on a
regular basis. That's essential for a music community
if it's going to stay alive
and grow. The G. Room is
run on human instinct rather
than profit margin. That
makes it a lousy business
investment and a wonderful
place to hang out. It is,
to (very loosely) quote a
testimonial offered one drunk
afternoon in the back office
'the sort of place where you
go after you've been released
from jail, where they dragged
you for some shit or other,
and you hav e 30c in your
pocket and it's the first
place you go cause you know
you'll get a pitcher of beer
and there'll be people you can
deal with, and things are
going to be ok'.
To get back to the short
informational piece I was
going to do before I got
carried away: this is not
meant to be a eulogy. The
Gorilla Room wil l reopen in
September. In the meantime,
two benefits are being planned
to cover the losses incurred
in staying closed, Aug. 15
at Freeway Hall and Aug. 30
at the Showbox. Bands will
include DOA, the Fartz, Idiot
Culture, Rapid-i, DTZ, Student
Nurse, Joe Despair & the Future,
the Untouchables, X-15, and may
be the Subhumans. Please note
that this information is
tentative. For more information,
contact Kim/Brian at 345-9393.

ROSCO LOUIE GALLERY

The Rosco Louie Gallery opened in 1978 bent
on running hell on the art front. As Seattle's
only modern art gallery, we are charged with
the responsibility to showcase the most exciting and innovative talents in the forms of visual arts,
performance art, poetry, new music, film, video, fashion, and revolution. We don't rely on fascist poten-
totas for funding, so we can get away with just about
anything.
Our fall schedule contains the best artists to be
found anywhere. We hope you appreciate it and if you
don't, well, fuck you.

INCITES '81

1
BILL WHIPPLE
9/3-9/22

3
NIRMAL KAUR
10/15-11/5

2
BETH ELLIOTT
9/24-10/15

4
CORK MARCHESCHI
11/5-11/25

5
Dikes Mentai
11/27-12/12

6
ROSCO LOUIE'S
GREATEST HITS
12/13-12/24

7
PETER SANTINO
12/31-1/15

87 S. WASHINGTON ST. SEATTLE, WA. 206-682-5228
HOURS: MON.-SAT. 11:00-6:00 (NOV. & DEC. SUNDAY NOON-5:00)

X-15 ON FILE
WHO'S NEXT IN LINE?...

Earlier this year, Registration Age People (RAP) put
on a benefit at the University of Washington featuring X-15. It was an effort
to draw young people and
students together in protest
of the draft and U. S.
intervention in El Salvador.
We hope that the secret service caught some of Kelly
Mitchell's lyrics. They
obviously got hold on one
of RAPs leaflets. Because
of their involvement, X-15
have now been filed away
in the Intelligence Office
of the Seattle Police
Department. In a binder
labeled "miscellaneous articles and relative information" lies a flyposter
announcing X-15's appearance
at the benefit. It is filed
right at the top under "anti-
draft activities".
Our informant, Liz Bouiss,
had to sign a release of
information form to inspect
these files. One point made
in the form is "No infer-
ence regarding the criminal
involvement of any persons
or organizations should be
drawn from the mere inclusion of that person or
organization in this information." Yet the "mere"
existence of these files
is just another tool for
police control over activist groups like RAP, or
musical groups with a
political base like X-15.
At this time RAP and other
anti-war groups are organ-
izing an all-day benefit
in opposition to the current
military build-up. Groups
and individuals also interested in getting their names
into police files and government dossiers should contact
Liz at 323-5345.

RECORDS

PICK HIT LP

T.S.O.L.
(True Sounds of Liberty)

Dance With Me
Frontier (1004)

If anybody heard the EP by these guys, and thought they were a great political band, you were right. What you'll be surprised to find out is that they can write about other subjects just as well, if not better. For example--

"Code Blue" deals with necrophiliacs--

And I don't even care how she died/I like it better if she smells of formaldahyde

"Sounds of laughter" deals with heavy paranoia while under the influence of LSD. I could easily continue telling you how good the lyrics are, but the music itself is just as hot! It isn't the same sound song after song, either. I've been real bored for a while and it's great to hear a new, original style and sound. This is the best headbang band to date as far as I'm concerned.

—Catalyst

EIGHT-EYED SPY

ROIR cassette

This "not available on vynil whatscover" tape arrived at DT 24 hours before deadline; not long enough to get it in the hands of my favorite Lydia Lunch expert. Truth is, though, that you've got to listen really close to hear the words she wails. That might not be advisable to all, however; at least not until after you've absorbed the sheer power of Lydia's screeching, emphatic attacks.

During that time, you'll marvel at the band's solid wall of fashionable dissonance that keeps turning into rock n roll and back into noise. Musicians include the late George Scott on bass, undermixed. They sound a bit like the X-Ray Spex scene in The Punk Rock Movie, except that 8-ES goess off the edge, into a total sensual assault. Includes a Sonics cover.

—Clark Humphrey

RAMONES

Pleasant Dreams

Sire

The cover and inner sleeve appear to be tribute to the self-released bands that have appeared under the Ramones' musical inspiration. Nice to see the guys abandon that designer T-shirt look of End of the Century. As for the noise inside, it's no return to the classic sound of the four key LP's. In retrospect, Century was just Phil Spector's superfluous overdubbing onto the basic cretin hop. This is different. Graham Gouldman of 10cc, whose last outside production was the score for a TV cartoon special, has removed the trademark big heat sound of Da Brudders. Too many cuts move within the speed limit or don't have Johnny Ramone's guitar loud enough to qualify as prime pogo pieces (exceptions: "You Didn't Mean Anything To Me", "You Sound Like You're Sick".)

"We Want the Airwaves" shows a rare serious side to Joey Ramone. You know times are desperate when Joey sings "We want in now/we're gonna take it, anyhow." "Come On Now" and "All's Quiet on the Eastern Front" make great twist songs. "Sitting In My Room" drives me mad because that's where I've been every time I've listened to it and it seems to be calling me lame for being there.

DISCUSSING RAMONES LYRICS? The guy MUST be mad! But continue I shall, because Pleasant Dreams includes not one but two star-crossed-lover novelties: "The KKK Took My Baby Away," and "7-11".

The LP doesn't hit you right away as a smash, but you still want to keep on playing it. Welcome back, guys, even if you aren't pinheads no more.

—Clark Humphrey

TUBES

The Completion Backward Principle

Capitol

Greatest back-cover notes of the year. Only a band with the Tubes' wild theatrical image could realize that what high tech really means is not Futurism but a corny-square PR language. Somebody should send a copy of this to John Fluke or the guys at Criton. Fans insist that it can't possibly be Fee Waybill in that grey flannel. Why isn't there any Re Styles sporting a dress-for-success blue blazer?

Inside: another Tubes producer, another Tubes sound. Was Tubes Group better with Rundgren at the controls? Some say yes; they also might say Principle is, in its business-like way, too dangerously close to suburban stadium rock. I don't think it's that awful; most of the fun's still there, and the band finally has a hit single, and A&M is about to capitalize on the group's Capitol success by bringing out a rehash of old stuff, to be called T.R.A.S.H., and the music is the industry of human happiness and I can't find ANY mention of the conceptual title in the lyrics, which is tasteful.

—Clark Humphrey

CHINA WHITE

China White

Frontier Records

China White's the kind of stuff that will intimidate a donut holer. This makes the best of any heavy metal band sound like meek, wimpy shit played by geriatrics. No shit! There isn't one slow song on this EP. One dose of this with heaphones on will make a Bellevue kook smash his face against a wall.

There was a tedious delay waiting for this piece of wax to get here. It seems that Posh Boy sold to Frontier (after advertising the record for at least 2 months).

This record is produced by Mike Patten of "Middle Class": There's no way I could pick a favorite cut. They all crank!

—Catalyst

PICK HIT 45

UNDERTONES

Julie Ocean b/w A Kiss in the Dark

The Undertones never cease to amaze me. For a non-political band from Northern Ireland, they're better than (their own) Teenage Kicks. Their dance music is perfect; last spring 3/4 of the band were in the hospital recuperating from various injuries (overstrained back and broken eardrums from dancing and playing too hard during a gig on their England tour). Yet they come out with this single that is so atypical, yet so...so Undertones.

Julie Ocean is a smooth gentle song about love and a typical girl. The vocals express the sound of the surf at dusk. It's not Golden Gardens with the hot-rods rearing, but more like St. Mark's at 2 AM with the vista. Julie Ocean is a typical song with the Undertones touch that makes it special.

A Kiss In The Dark is more upbeat than the A-side and just as casual as a touch in the dark on a hot summer's night. Still it is a tad more forceful, but then again it's getting late.

If you're expecting fast--fast dance songs, forget it. Both of these songs could be re-released for air-play on KIXI, but don't let that hold you back. These songs fulfill the Undertones ideal. Play this 45' and take your sweetheart out on the back porch for a slow dance.

—M.M.

RECORDS

THE CURE

Faith

This is a good album to put on when you stumble in at two or three in the morning and need to pass out gently without disturbing anyone, but you could probably do it without the record.

The Cure seem to have arrived at a formula, which was quite refreshing on last year's <u>Seventeen Seconds</u>, but I suppose I expected more from <u>Faith</u>. Not that this is a bad album, it's just that the formula, a prescription of dirges that wallows in the depths of Robert Smith's lonely soul gets to me sometimes. Yes, I know it's supposed to get to me, that means he's accomplishing his objective, but that doesn't mean I have to like it for six songs out of eight.

Gnerally, I have no argument with the Cure. I have liked everything they've done in the past with hardly an exception. Then I listen to <u>Faith</u>. Where the hell am I, in a cathedral? I like the architecture of great cathedrals, but it is quite old, and that music...

The playing on <u>Faith</u> is without a doubt superb, especially the bass. It's the songwriting that leaves me cool. When Smith whines in his plaintive English boy vocal 'there's nothing left but faith' at the end of the album, I suppose I would have to agree with him. Not from a religious standpoint, but from the standpoint of a Cure fan.

This is an escapist album. You'll never find the Cure singing about revolution or drugs, or something all too real life. No, they prefer translucent dream imagery, the kind inside your mind. It's so hard, though, to transmit such imagery from one mind to another without losing something in the process. I think the formula needs some spice.

—Gregor Gayden

MISSION OF BURMA

Signals, Calls and Marches
Ace of Hearts AHS 1006

It's been a long time since Boston rockers Mission of Burma have been heard from. 'Bout time, too! All at once sounding like some demented 1981 version of 70's rock stars, driving all the way toward a destination clearly marked "new". They are at once restrained yet disarming, using tricks you would have thought were tossed to the back of the closet long ago. Well, don't go rummaging through the back of your closet, just buy, steal, or whatever, this EP. Like their debut single <u>Academy Fight Song</u>, S, C & M's shows the band's pop sensibilities in full splendor, while managing to catch the listener off guard by changing tired-old-riff horses midstream, galloping away on something that doesn't sound...quite

right. It's perfect for annoying drunks and morons. Here they are joined by old buddy Martin Swope, ostensibly on "tapes", whatever that means. People who frequently use hard drugs are not advised to study the insert, lest they infer some sort of "message" from it. B+, guys, hope to see you back in Seattle soon.

—D.W.

FLIPPER

Love Canal b/w Ha Ha

Subterranean/Thermidor Records 912 Bancroft Way Berkley, CA 94710

This is very intriguing music. Both songs begin with a Jah Wobbleish bass riff which is soon joined by a heavily distorted, often feedbacking, out-of-tune guitar. The drums set a pace that is too slow for pogo (intentionally done, I am told, to annoy punks) but danceable (for those who actually care about the danceability of a song).

Bruce Lose's voice is plain bot forceful. It is sometimes tampered with neat little studio effects causing it to reach extremely high notes and enabling Bruce to sing at tremendous speeds (without, incidentally, sounding remotely like the Chipmunks). The lyrics are grotesque and humorous. The first side is about New York's infamous Love Canal and the slow death and generic mutation it is causing. The second song "Ha Ha" is about the absurditiy of life (or something like that).

Flipper's music is quite psychedelic. It is not like the Jefferson Airplane or the Doors, it is closer to some of the songs on the first two Velvet Underground LPs. The guitar goes beyond musical boundaries while the rhythm section keeps the listener in touch with reality. The surprising thing is that both songs are very catchy.

—Mark McLaughlin

GO-GO'S

Beauty and the Beat

IRS

Five women who sing with harmonies about being slaves to their hormones, BUT write all their own material and play all their own instruments, are not the creation of producers or managers, and are emphatically not a gimmick outfit. It could only happen today.

File under the "impressive debut" category. Good, could've been great except that I miss those gimmicks. If you want your women turning up the camp, head for some of those early Motown albums that have just been reissued. If you want your post-feminist discussions of romance to be more intellectual, check out the Delta 5 LP. If you are intrigued by the Go-Gos' sincere, straightforward pop

but aren't ready for eleven tunes, IRS has a popular-priced single of "Our Lips Are Sealed"

Me, I'm going to listen again to "How Much More", "Automatic", and "Lust to Love", wishing that they'd been made with more hooks, more bass, more beat.

—Clark Humphrey

THEATRE OF HATE

"He Who Dares Wins"

According to the band, this album was released to "beat the bootlegger's bootleg". Well, it looks like a bootleg, the sleeve tells us it was recorded live at the warehouse in Leeds and not to pay more than two and a half pounds. The label says one and two. It sounds like a bootleg, the pressing is absolutely horrible. But through all the crackle and hiss one can tell this is a great band.

Four of the songs we recognize from their two singles, Legion and Orginal Sin from the first, My Own Invention and Rebel Without A Brain from the second. The other titles singer Kirk Brandon graciously lets us know before they are played. They are: Wake, Freaks, Propaganda, '63', and two versions of Incinerator.

This is not music to get comfortable with. But it's not really headbanging music either. What it is is raw angry energy, channeled honestly into a perfect post '77 sound, mistakes and all. I wouldn't say there is any production at all; it was taken directly off the mixing board, and aside from the fact that you can hear all the instruments, it lacks the bottom fullness that Mick Jones got out of Stan Stammers' bass and Luke Rendall's drums on the second single, or the guitar power of Legion. You might say it sounds rather accoustic. But Kirk's wailing, high strung vocals cut through the emptiness like a jagged edge, and the sax of John Boy is right beside him, as though it needed no amplification at all. Guitarist Steve Guthrie's presence is not felt as much as it could be, but no mind, guitar seems somewhat secondary in Theatre of Hate anyway.

TOH is a modern punk band in the sense that they are not churning out regurgitated Pistols' riffs (though they owe much in that direction), but finding new and eccentric ways to express their anger and, yes, concern with THE WAY THINGS ARE. This eccentricity is what makes them great. Fury is not how fast you can bash the chords out.

Soon we should see a studio album from these boys. Good, because He Who Dares Wins is really just a benchmark, a documentary on a band less than a year old. I just hope their new product won't be too slick. But I know it can't be.

—Gregor Gayden

9

VANCOUVER REPORT

CORINNE MAH

Unfortunately, things are not pleasing me at all in the Vancouver music scene. Putting it mildly, the whole shebang is pathetic: new talent is being stifled by lack of venues and interest, and new ideas are being repressed due to the fact that it's safer and easier to make money in the Top 40 accessible market.

I'm sure this is going on in a lot of places, but having seen Vancouver burgeon into a respected place for good ideas and an expanding new music market with very close ties to England, it's really hard to just sit back and watch it wilt incredibly quickly before my eyes.

To give you an idea of how poor morale is: Gary Taylor's Rock Room brought in the Breeders from Calgary last week (quite good rock-new-pop). The sparse crowd was

alternately vindictive or apathetic to the point where the band walked off stage, disgusted, in the middle of a song - and the people didn't say boo.

The following night Virginia, the lead singer didn't even show up - and those at the club didn't even notice for an hour that Stones tapes were playing. Fortunately, most of Los Popularos were at the club and for margueritas and $100 they were talked into playing, Buck (guitar) has reportedly quit the band as they were in the studio and Tony (bass) wasn't there, so Gord Nichol (Dash Hamm) keyboard player for the Pointed Sticks played bass, and they trashed their way through a set of tunes.

Once again, the lack of response or acknowledgement of good or bad songs disgust-

ed me.

On top of that the Cave, which should have gone totally new rock and pop and lasted forever as a landmark club, is now just a pile of debris and will soon be a three-story retail center. (Appalling!)

On the good side - Radio Active Artists' B-Sides and David Raven and the Efforts have appreciative followings and are progressing and growing. Both bands are being hyped by the Villains in Toronto, so their upcoming tour together back east is bound to be successful. An album is due out any day now. The Escorts are tight, high energy and very danceable. Their music is good old rock and roll and raggae and lots of original rock too.

The Luv-A-Fair disco is a

popular and fun place. It used to be exclusively gay, now it caters to everyone - especially wild dancers. A huge dance floor and light show and (sometimes) great new music, the Luv-A-Fair is recommended. (Dress to the teeth - or not - and have a great time).

Apparently a Luv-A-Fair type club is opening on the other side of town - I guess if

I sure hope things improve though. I'm bitching about Vancouver but it's happening in Seattle too. Wake up everybody - let's see what can be done - more clubs, more bands, more chances taken, anything!

Until next time (and I'll try to find lots of up stuff to talk about) this is your northern correspondent signing off.

LONDON

reported by J.D. SHEPPARD

This column marks the debut of our London report. Our correspondent, J.D. Sheppard, should be familiar to some of our readers. J.D. was a regular fixture on the Seattle scene for the year he spent in America. He has since returned to his home in London, and will from this issue on be keeping us informed of what's

going on back in old Blighty. This report was filed via ITT/Ma Bell at no mean expense to DT, and therefore lacks some of the detail and color we can expect from Mssr. Sheppard's future reports. In this installation, J.D. fills us in on what it takes to distract an entire nation in the midst of social upheaval:

Lots of joykillers in London these days, what with massive amounts of explosives high above Hyde Park when they could have been put to much better use at the gates of Parliament. There are, as everyone knows, lots of riots these days. Dalston Junction, Wood Green and Brixton have been particularly hard hit. Shop after shop window has been boarded up. Maybe it's for the best. Those shop windows not boarded up sport the ever present, ever smiling faces of that fun couple, Chuck and Di (not particularly pretty faces, either)! It's really sickening; worse than the jubilee or the coronation. When a 32 year old man living off no more than glorified welfare marries, it's some kind of grand success. While tens of thousands of kids have neither work nor adequate lodging, and the government expects these kids to live on a handout of less than 20 dollars a week...well, you get the picture. It's not hard to see why a generation fed on radical rhetoric of pop politics are more than willing to take said politics into the streets.

Speaking of pop politics, whether rightly or wrongly, initial blame for Asian riots in Southall has been placed on the perennial antagonisr by skinheads in general and the followers of "Oi" music in particular. Under the

heading "Oi" are such popular bands as the Cockney Rejects, Splodge, and the 4-skins, among others. Skins have always had a reputation for their involvement in Britain's fascist National Front and its youth wing, the British Youth Movement. The sympathetic music rage Sounds have clearly defined themselves as a newspaper quite unwilling to temper a particularly vapid point of view, in regards to the various exponents of "Oi" music. Look for a particularly volatile late summer with Asian Defense Committee, who in at least one instance have been pegged for burning down a pub used by Skinheads.

Back to the wedding festivities. Some respite was found over the course of the dreadful week-long absurdities as the Venue in Victoria hosted the Alternative Wedding Reception, while the Delta 5 played the following night. Ian Dury and the Blockheads played the Hammersmith Odeon in honour of the horrible couple. Funk the Wedding and Rock Against Royalty did their things as well.

Note, all is not Royalty and riots these days. Of some concern is the demise (at least temporarily) of Time Out, London's comprehensive, left-leaning arts and entertainment magazine. The writers have walked out over management's apparent bid to hire more exclusive (read higher paid) journalists. The strikers immediately set out to publish their own rag during the hiatus, entitled Not Time Out. The name became shortened to Not after copyright problems surfaced. Of particular interest are Nots film listings which describe the movie, give showtimes and dates, ending with recommendations of suitable drug induced states which are most compatible

with viewing the film. Until next time chip, chip, cheerio, stiff upper lip, et al.

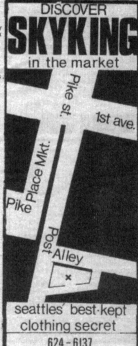
10

GANG OF 4 cont.

back only to run lights for the show, then he'll have to leave immediately by cab. Heavy vibes. And right next door to Jim Jones' Peoples Temple!

After the set, the stage goes black, which is something Ray doesn't normally do.

The band is back onstage for the encore and still no lights. Suddenly, Ray is at the stage, going for the dimmer box. "Someone's cut the control cable," he curses. He is able to control the lights from the onstage dimmer box. The band winds up the set with "Sweet Jane"; an investigation reveals not one, but three slices in the cable to the light control desk.

I lay no blame, but some malicious asshole had severed the cables which control at least twenty four separate wires inside. This is the beginning of the post-show fun.

We begin the "tear down" the equipment. A normal enough term, but Bill Graham's crew interprets it literally, as they are all over the stage dismantling things quicker than the eye can see. I'm running around trying to keep track of things so they don't get lost, when all of a sudden, the stage left lighting tower topples over and goes crashing to the floor. One of the big goons had moved a column of speakers right next to it and knocked it over. A quick electric test of the lamps shows, miraculously, no broken bulbs. I begin to worry a bit less about the effect of going over bumps in the truck on light filaments.

The stuff is hastily packed up, ready to go back into the truck, when we discover our keys missing. Thane, who last had them , frantically searches his pockets and carrying bags to no avail. One of the house crew fetches his lock picking kit (handy!) and we hope they're locked in the back of the truck. No luck with the picks, our padlock is just too damn good. A sledgehammer is brought out, and right when the guy is ready to swing—I mean he had the thing poised for the downstroke—Thane comes running out with the keys. Somehow, they had found their way under an ice tray in the coat check room. The gear is loaded and I go to start the truck. Dead battery.

The emergency flashers had been left on inadvertently, and we didn't have a Die-hard. Are we ever going to get out of San Francisco? Someone from the sound company, with a U-Haul, had jumpers and we were able to start the Ryder. We leave the Fillmore about two hours later than we should have. Some fun. Back to the hotel to fetch Ray and our luggage. It's 3:00 AM by the time we hit the road for L.A. Charged with special fuel, I drive until 8:00 AM.

WEDNESDAY, JULY 15th Thane takes over driving somewhere near Nowhere, California. I'm able to catch one or two hours of sleep before we arrive at the gig in Pasedena. Perkins Palace is the venue, and we go straight there, arriving at 12:30 PM. Perkins Palace is a real nice

theatre—air conditioned, fountains in the lobby, a nice big stage with a curtain and all. When we arrive and load in, one of the opening acts, Tonio K are already set up and doing a "soundcheck". This is unheard of! Normally, the headlining act is first to set up and check, but from what I'm told, Tonio K has some clout with the Perkins family.

By the time the Gang Of Four arrive for the soundcheck, it is 5:30 PM, and I'm running low on energy. We stay on at the gig through showtime, though. At 9:10 the Three Swimmers go on. They appear nervous, playing for the first time to a large, dark theatre, which contains record company scouts who have come specifically to see them. The audience gives a polite applause after each number, no boos are heard, but the curtain drops abruptly before the band can get back out for an encore. Tonio K followed, and their show was totally ridiculous. The band was wearing these weird flour sack costumes, and the lead singer was decked out in a chicken mask with a large beak. I watch for a few minutes, replused. They've got shovels in the guitar stands, a vacuum cleaner that really works and...they're cooking pancakes on a portable griddle! Oh God. This must be some sort of bad dream. They finish their set none too soon and the audience boos and cat calls loudly. When it is clear they won't return, the house lights come on and the crowd cheers triumphantly.

By this time, the crowd is more than ready for Gang Of Four. There is a high level of anticipation as the band comes on for the last show of their U.S. tour. Now in Seattle and Vancouver there were a few problems with people jumping on 'tage. In San Francisco the cattle catcher averted any of that. And here, I thought, with a stage that was nearly six feet off the floor, there would be no problem at all. Wrong, wrong, wrong. This is L.A., boy. The kids here love to jump up on the stage. And they managed to do it even with a real high stage.

The band was working through their set building up the intensity with every song. They played virtually the same set on all four of the dates I worked with them. It included some of my favorite Gang Of Four songs: "What We All Want", "In The Ditch", "We'd Send In The Army", and "To Hell With Poverty", their newest single. Everything hit the top when during one of the songs near the end of the set (I don't recall which), I saw another person come up out of the crowd. I went over to the edge of the stage just as he came flying over. Instantly, when he stood up, I noticed he was naked! What do you do with a nude sweaty non-skinhead? Now, if this had been a female, maybe I would have reacted differently. I grabbed his arm real hard as a huge cheer went up from the crowd. I tried to lead him off to the side of the stage, but he slipped away and went straight for the lead singer, Jon King, locking him in a full embrace. Well, Jon didn't know quite what to do, so he just sort of stood there with his mouth open and a titilated look in his eye. Someone else got there and grabbed the guy and we pulled him off Jon and got

11

him off the stage. He was thrown out the back door into the balmy Pasedena night in full birthday suit. The incident had brought the house down, and when Andrew Gill stepped to the microphone to bid his farewell, it was the most sincere thing I'd ever heard a rock performer say from the stage: "Goodnight. Thank you. And we really love you all." It turns into another line here, but he really meant it. And it showed the Gang Of Four's honesty and conviction. The audience left, doubtless of the simple greatness of the Gang Of Four. But the story does not end here.

For the band, the show is over and in two more days they'll be back in jolly old Blightey. There's this small matter of stage equipment that has to be sorted out and packed up. The crew at Perkins Place is great, sort of young college jock types but real efficient and helpful without being malicious to our equipment. We quickly are able to pack up the Rider Hotel and hit the freeways again. This time the Pasedena to the Hollywood Freeway to Santa Monica Blvd. With two not so alert navigators, I manuvered my way into the netherworld of the Los Angeles freeway system. We missed the exit to the Hollywood Freeway, took the next possible exit and promptly got lost in East L.A. Or at least I think it was East. I think it was the place where they used to film Dragnet. Or was it Emergency? California is the home of many great American Firsts: Hollywood, Disneyland, Fast Cars, Urban Sprawl, Choking Pollution—all the crass signs of a decomposing, loathing society. California Uber Alles! After cruising by City Hall and a bunch of wrong way streets, we managed to get back onto the myriad of snaking freeways. We finally made it to the legendary Tropicana Motor Hotel.

This place is the ultimate! At 2:00 AM, people hanging out around the pool, sizing up each others genitalia. Drinks, pretty girls from Huntington Beach who are so mixed up they don't know the difference between a tennis racket and a rock club. The Tropicana is the World Headquarters of sordid rock and roll jive hustler groupie scene bullshit that is so nausiating. I wonder if the pool is filled with bile. Naw, it's a real nice place. I found some Jack Daniels and went to call my sweetheart back in Seattle. It's funny, on the road, how you lose sense of where you are, what time it is, and what you would be doing if you were at home. I know loneliness can set in with ferocious intensity. But with the telephone, you're only a call away. On and on. I fell into the sack drunk and exhausted. This is rock 'n roll.

THURSDAY, JULY 16th
        I go to see the road manager, John Botting, who pays me, tells us where to take the gear to be airfreighted back to England. Originally, I was to have driven the truck all the way back to Seattle with one box of rented lighting cables I had a thousand or so miles to think about that one and was able to convince John of the excruciating absurdity of that. He sorted out airfreight for the cables and

arranged a flight for me out of San Francisco the next day, as we did have to take Thane back home. We dropped the stuff off at the airfreight, and I felt somewhat relieved to actually be on the way home. The trip north through the desert was a little less trying and we arrived in the Bay Area about midnight.

FRIDAY, JULY 17th After returning the Ryder truck, I had a couple of hours to spend in Chinatown. My flight was at 5:30 and I was back in Seattle two hours later. A very different week in my life, indeed.

It was a lot of hard work with a little rest and a lot of shitty food. But in all it was a fun experience to work for the Gang Of Four.

Z-ZZZZZZ, Z-ZZZZZ. I didn't know what it MEANT. I didn't know what to do. I pretended that it was a nightmare, and that I would soon wake up.

(haircuts)

I was in Germany. Winston Tong cut my hair. We just didn't have anything to do. And he had cut lots of hair before, and I was there: another head.

(politics)

My politics aren't terribly sophisticated, I don't have the stuff worked out. I'm really an observer, and I use it for my own purposes. And if the facts aren't quite right statistically, that really doesn't bother me. I'm more interested in rumor than fact anyway. I read a lot; I don't watch TV. And talking to people, that's probably more of a source of information to me than anything else.

(latest from new york)

There was a noise festival. This is a brand new thing. They're called the Noisemakers. The high priest of it is named Glenn Bronca. I like it pretty much. Symphonic noise, it's quite amazing. It uses just the structure of a symphony to make noise that just...knocks your socks off.

(art)

The example I used with somebody was: You're listening to a song and you love it, it's just so wonderful, but you can't quite understand the words. You hear the lyrics later, and they're just horrible words. Either they're really stupid, or they're insulting to somebody. And...it's too late. Because it's already inside of you, you've already accepted it. Not that I want to be precious, stupid, or didactic. But the whole point, to me, of making art, seems to be that that's the way that you perceive it.

(selective memory)

Things that I see that I don't like, I can't even remember seeing them. In my own life, I mean. I think I've had a fantastic life; I've probably had a shitty life, I just can't remember it—the bad parts. I think in general I tend to be fairly optimistic. I'm not out to aestheticize misery, that's not my goal.

(do you read reviews)

Not seriously. I usually read them. But the thing I like about them best, is if they're well written.

(getting started)

For a while I just did stuff with photographs on the wall and writing underneath, and then I thought that was not my real interest in language because it doesn't have a tone of voice in it. And that made all the difference. So then I decided: if that's what it is, do it as simply as possible and just talk. But I wanted a combination, too, of the other things, and it all sort of sneaked in eventually. More or less in a way paralleling the ways you get information: looking, listening, and reading.

(cigarettes)

I'm a chainsmoker.

(reactions)

People sometimes think that I'm the performer, not the artist; that someone else shot the film, composed the music, and wrote the text. It's a one woman operation in a lot of ways. It's easy to forget.

—Captive, with thanks to Steve Rabow

of betrayal. Most of her childhood had been spent in Georgetown, just south of Seattle's lengthy expanse of industrial parks. Her family had lived a fairly meager existance, her mother dying young of TB, and her brothers and sisters helping their father at his job tearing down and scrapping old houses. According to her sister, Mary Humble, another Seattle performing artist (TRC, Sister Esmereldas Church of the Devine Light and Gin Mill), "Our dad worked at tearing down and scrapping old houses. We spent a lot of time helping him; pulling down walls, salvaging windows, things like that." performing on a shoestring have left a keen awareness of the financial disparity in the world... especially in Southern California.
I asked her about L.A. these days.
"The scene is dying," she remarked, lapsing into cynicism. "L.A. is so apathetic to change. Things move so slowly. Musicians repeat the same song 20 times at least before anyone else even hears it. It's unfortunate. It's so calculated and so unnecessary to continue that same format. I guess I can respect it. I can respect Opera too, but I don't go to see any of it. I'm sick of all of it."
"Did you see the Decline (of Western Civilization). It missed the point entirely, they went for all the violence and played it up. It was not at all representative. It was purposely manipulated. In fact, it was really disgusting. The woman who made it (Penelope Spheeris) totally ignored women in L.A. There were hardly any women in the film and what were in it, they made look like fools. Alice Bag looked silly. Darby was great though. L.A. is just a lot of fancy clothes, there's no committment."
But, I ask her, isn't there anything left in Los Angeles? Aren't there people, especially the younger kids, who still believe that they can do something? Isn't There a sincere

element left?
"Sincere? Los Angeles?", she laughs. I see how wrought she is becoming in her whole frustrating mission. "There are some younger kids that are excited. I like to see that. There are some interesting things coming out of East L.A. (L.A.'s Chicano populated barrio). But I'm in a state of transience right now. I feel punk has been wiped out. I'm not connecting myself to anything now. There's no feeling of movement like there was two years ago. The whole country is more conservative now; fashions are conservative now, and L.A. is the perfect place for those two things. So where is Johanna Went now, artisticaly?
"Well, I'm working with Brock and Mark Wheaton, and Kerrie McBride now. I used to play with Zev, but he left long ago. Right now we all face all the usual stuff: problems with live sound, no money...all that. The single we put out was originally to be done as a flexi-disc for Slash Magazine, but when it folded we found Boyd Rice to help us get it out. He payed to have it (No U No b/w Slave to the Grave) pressed. We didn't go into the studio with any particular plans. We just did it and we liked it."
"We want to put out another record, but we have no money to do it. We hope the right person will come along to help us; someone we can get along with. Maybe we can make an album."
What about gigs?
"Well, I played the Fourth of July in SFO and on the 12th I played a benefit for NO magazine at the Whiskey. I'm doing about two shows a month now (Went's pre-performance collection of props and assorted garbage can take up to two weeks for a single show. I really want to go to Japan. We've been covered in the press there. We'd love to come to the Northwest if the situation were right. We've been trying to get back up there for a long time."
At this writing Johanna Went is in Los Angeles plotting (or NON-plotting) her next move in the world of high speed art and music. Up 'til now her career has been nothing if not serendipituos. Music and art critics from Paris to Tokyo have applauded her devastatingly original form; a form that can honestly be described as no ones but her own. Touring is almost unthinkable, due to the nature of her art. It must be done in a very sensitive and time consuming way, something Johanna refuses to compromise on. A visit to the NW, however, is not that unreasonable a thought, again, "If the situation was right." A summer appearance in Seattle was shattered earlier this year when Bumbershoot, under whose auspices Johanna would have come to Seattle apparently felt her act was just too wild. Shame on you, ya jerks. Especially when, as the Velvet article pointed out (the music paper BAM observed) "In a better world Johanna Went would have already graced the cover of LIFE."
Until Seattle gets another chance to see one of the most unique performing artists in the world (if we ever get a chance) the only thing left is to sit and wait; those lucky enough to have seen her in action in the past can smugly savor those few precious moments.

CLASSIFIEDS

STOP PRESS

Paintings on Plastic with
Portraits, WREY's first art
show with the Spectators and
Rapid-i on August 12.

Pritchard has announced a
few bands he is hoping to
put up in the next month:
Echo & the Bunnymen, Siouxie
and the Banshees, Romeo Void.

Rough Trade has picked up
the Fartz and Solger singles.

Mr. Epp and the Calculations
will finally show their
collective faces on August
7 with the Color Plates at
Freeway Hall. A don't miss.

Steve Pritchard and John
Bauer have gone into partnership. Few music fans,
watch those ticket prices...

The infamous Hertz band has
decided to move their roots
from Historical Boston to
Historical Seattle. Says
lead guitarist It Hertz
"The underground is where
It's at." And all this in
the midst of a libel suit
from Gene Rayburn against
their hit single "The Match
Game Theme Song"

Pravda Productions will
bring Toxic Reasons to the
Seattle area in later August.

OOPS! Mr. Epp and the
Calculations have had to
cancel their Freeway Hall
gig. Reason given; Their
bass player has been
grounded by parents.
Dave Ford of Rapid i will
be taking a well-deserved
vacation. The band will
be working on an EP after
his return.
Husker Du have returned
to Minneapolis after a
successful tour. They
send their thanks to all
who supported them here.
Upchuck will be recording
at Wave Studios in Van-
couver WA with his new
band.
Members include Gordon
Doucette, Pony Marie,
Barb and Ben Ireland,
Mike Davison and mystery
persona Dahfny Raphael.
Here's a question...Do
you sleep in the sleeping
Movement?....Donuts &
punks, Eastern Front II,
D.O.A. and all the hot
shit you'll need are in
the next issue

corporate top 10

Singles

1. Laurie Anderson-
   O Superman
2. Gang of Four-To Hell With
   Poverty
3. Dead Kennedys-Too Drunk
   To Fuck
4. Bauhaus -Passions of Lovers
5. Tom Tom Club-Wordy Rappinghood
6. Joy Division-Love Will Tear
   Us Apart
7. Ramones-We Want The Airwaves
8. Virgin Prunes-In The Grey
   Light
9. Au Pairs-Its Obvious
10. Joy Division-Transmission

L.P.'s

1. Delta Five-See The Whirl
2. Siouxie & the Banshees-
   Ju Ju
3. Killing Joke-What's This
   For?
4. Joy Division-Unknown
   Pleasures
5. Au Pairs-Playing With A
   Different Sex
6. William S. Burroughs-
   Nothing Here Now But
   Recordings
7. Wire-Document and Eye-
   witness
8. Echo & the Bunnymen-
   Heaven Up Here
9. Birthday Party-Prayers On
   Fire
10. Raincoats-Odyshape

seattle dj top 20

THIS WEEK	LAST WEEK	TITLE	ARTIST
1	5	Too Drunk to Fuck	Dead Kennedys
2	17	Boom/Das Ah Riot	Bush Tetras
3	3	Primary	The Cure
4	6	Ha-Ha-Ha	Flipper
5	1	Wanna Go Home	Holly & the Italians
6	13	Heaven Up here	Echo & the Bunnymen
7	2	Obvious (LP Edit.)	Au Pairs
8	8	Pretty in Pink	Psychedelic Furs
9	4	What We All Want	Gang of Four
10	20	Demystification	Zounds
11	18	Leaving	Delta 5
12	12	Highline/Animal	The Rats
13	7	Beat My Guest	Adam & the Ants
14	9	Can't Be Happy	Fastbacks
15	-	To Hell w/Poverty	Gang of Four
16	11	Fascist Groove Thang	Heaven 17
17	16	Tanz Mit Mir	DAF
18	-	Motion	The Room
19	-	Poppa's Got a Brand New Pigbag	Pigbag
20	-	Signals, Calls, Marches	Mission of Burma

Issue #4

The masthead gives credit to the Seattle Police Department for "contributing to the entertainment at our party." DT House had a "rent party" to raise money for house expenses. A flatbed truck served as the stage in the backyard, and any band that showed up was invited to play. By 10 pm, the police came to close it down, and there were still two bands who hadn't had their chance to play. I talked with the police and distracted them through the very short performances of the last two bands.

Desperate Times was getting real letters by the fourth issue. A punk in the US Army expresses his support for the newspaper. One letter complains about the bad sound and security at a concert.

The bylines in *Desperate Times* used a mix of full names, partial names, and initials. Some articles were group efforts and written by committee. In these cases, an imaginary persona would be created for the byline. "Jeff Greenwood" was a fictitious writer named after a north Seattle neighborhood.

Neil Hubbard narrates the wonderful story of the first time the Ramones played Seattle in 1977. The Ramones were originally booked to play at the Aquarius Tavern, but Neil was a minor and really wanted to see the band! So he re-booked the band at the Olympic Hotel for an all-ages show.

DESPERATE TIMES

25¢
AUG. 19
VOL **1** NO **4**

AUDIO LETER

AUDIO LETTER
BLACK FLAG
CHILDREN OF
KELLOGG
D.O.A.
EURYTHMICS
THE FIX
FLIPPER
FRED
THE HEATS
LITTLE BEARS
FROM BANGKOK
THE LIVING

more from the
EASTERN FRONT

POP DEFECT

REJECTORS

VANCOUVER
REPORT
SOLGER
SPLIT ENZ
X-15

LOCAL BIZ !

RAPID I

DESPERATE TIMES

Editor:
Daina Darzin

Associate Editor:
Captive

Art Director:
Billy Shaffer

Photography Director:
Skip Beattie

B.M. and D.B.
Maire Masco

Milk and Cookies:
Dennis White

Contributing Writers:
Arlene Adler, Norman Bately,
Berlin, Catalyst, Bria Con-
radus, Daniel Danelski,
Steve Fart, Jeff Greenwood,
Neil Hubbard, Clark Humphrew,
Corinne Mah, Kathy Moschel,
Heidi Weispfenning

Contributing Photographers:
Bria Conradus, Cam Garrett,
Kelly Gordon

COVER PHOTO CREDITS:
Skip Beattie (Rejectors)
Cam Garrett (Rapid-i) Kelly
Gordon (Pop Defect)
Bob Jenkins Audio Letter.

Special thanks this issue
goes to the Seattle Police
Department for their contribution to the entertainment
at our party. Two squad cars,
better than Henny Youngman.
We found the phone call to
our landlord particularly
amusing. But seriously
folks, thanks to all the
bands that played. Y'all
were terrific!

DESPERATE TIMES is
published bi-monthly by
On The Edge Press,
4525 9th Ave. N.E., Seattle,
Washington, 98105
(206)-634-0303
Printing by Consolidated.

THIS ISSUE

OPINION

This issue is dedicated to local bands, from the ones who are having little talks with record companies, to the ones whose current ambition is to play somewhere in addition to the Gorilla Room. Especially the latter, cause they--like all other artists in this country--get shit from everybody, but they're not getting any money or fringe benefits to compensate for the hassles. Last week, bands around here got together and stood up for some of their rights. Hopefully, their effort (see article, page 10) will lead to a better relation-ship between the various parties that comprise the music community. Cause, let's face it. We--bands, promoters, audience, clubs, record stores, press-are all in this together, we're stuck with each other, so we might as well get along and avoid spending time and energy on a lot of unnecessary political bullshit. Also, there's a fine line between acting to effect change and attacking people, and it should be emphasized that it was never anyone's intention to do the latter.

On a different subject; a whole bunch of people have mentioned that DT's coverage is heavy, and heavily favor-able, towards hardcore. This is probably true. We feel that one of our primary functions is to cover the stuff that is ignored by most other media. Generally, the "straight" press covers the "punk scene" without ever talking about the music. There's the Oh-God-What-Is-Happening-To-Our-Children? approach (like the infamous PI punk article) or the Isn't-This-Strange-And-Amusing?-Look-At-A-Weird-Subculture trick (like the woman from the Times who was bouncing around the DOA show, perkily trying to interview audience members for her article on slamdanc-ing, and not understanding why people didn't particularly want to talk to her). So we're going to keep talking about hardcore. The music part. A lot. However, we admit that there is a world beyond the Gorilla Room/WREX circuit, and some of it is probably real interesting and worthwhile. So we're going to start at the extreme other end and work back--this week: the Heats at Astor Park.
                    -Daina Darzin

IN THE MAIL

WITH A FRIEND LIKE YOU (PART 2)

Dear DT,

About your review of The Enemy at Danceland, we learned that your reviewer yelled out the window at "supercreeps", left the hall two times, and surpass-ed her usual number of trips to the can by five. How did she, in the midst of all this scur-rying about, ever find time to listen to the music?

In the case of The Cowbirds, of course, she didn't. Yeah, The Enemy did some country songs. Verna was offended.. OK, coun-try's not her style. But let your readers know that the music was loud. Fast. Full in your face punk stylings of some whorey old classics. And mention the costumes. And the humor. Maybe even give a nod to the band for trying to inject something new into it's Danceland gigs. It was a present, a free-bie, you goof.

These efforts are something for which this band receives precious little credit. I'll assume Verna knows about The Rird, the tours, and the BAM awards in San Francisco, and concentrate on some recent history. Like the 23-member big band (as in Glenn Miller, Verna, not Marsh-all Tucker) in the Showbox New Year's eve. Cyndi Bemel per-haps described it best as "magic". Or the Memorial Day set at the Rainbow- a dazzling array of tunes by rock's famous victims done up punk. I'll be hard pressed to say what was more fun that evening - the slack-mouthed astonishment of the Rainbow hippies - yes, there is rock beyond, way beyond, Jr. Cadillac. Or the sight of Hibbles mammoth manager pogoing on the dancefloor of a rival club. Or no less amazing scene at Hibbles recently when the Smart Set found itself pogoing to songs like "Gut Reaction" and "Undermined", having never known what hit them. Or the Cowbirds. Or the attempt to present new songs at every return engagement. This all bespeaks professionalism, Verna. Take a hint.

A final note. You certainly can dislike a group, a performance, or both. Your right, naturally. Don't slag the soundman for taking off The Clash, however. It is, after all, "London Calling" in which Joe Strummer tells us that "phony Beatlemania" is finally dead, that any knee-jerk attempt to place a band or type of music on a pedestal is dead. Less categorization, please. More listening.

Your little puddles in the john are more than we care to know about.

                    -Charlie Ernst

GIVE THIS GUY A SECTION 8

Dear DT people:

I was recently on leave in Seattle, just in time to catch your first two issues, as well as the Furs and 999 concerts. As a mem-ber of the U.S. Army at Fort Campbell, Kentucky, I am rarely able to actively participate in the punk scene, and found great relief in my humble hometown. I am wri-ting to say how much I en-joyed your first two issues, and hope you keep up the good work. Could you tell me what it will cost to subscribe for one year of your 'rno? Myself and another Army punk went to keep up on the happenings.

                    -Steve Lawrence

1

PUNK........

Dear Daina (how the fuck do you pronounce that?),

First, I'm glad to see this: the scene has needed this kind of thing. You fill the void The Rocket would fill if they didn't have to waste time with Pat Benatar. Intimate detail, you write like you're beside me at gigs, I like the things you point out that the others don't. <u>Real</u> involvement.

Second, do I <u>have</u> to wear leather to read this 'zine? I really get this impression that it's the movement, not the music, that's at issue here.

Your bias is evident - so evident you don't even realize it. Pugmyr reviews punk because he is an afficionado of the style-a hopeless fan. Then you send some girl down to the Vapors who obviously does not want to do it, abuses her press priviledges, and compares them to the Jam. Tsk, tsk, didn't the bored urban guerilla like the pop show, just wasn't cool enough for her, huh? If you wanted a real objective review, you would have sent Pugmyr, right? I'm not going to say you should send someone who likes the Vapors, 'cuz I know you probably don't <u>know</u> anybody who likes them. Remember, Capt. Clark's question? I don't like K-15 much either (singer grates)! Sometimes it appears that everybody else I go to concerts with is there just by coincidence, not because of music...but then, I walk into Cellophane and Jane restores my faith in punk. Anybody that sweet couldn't be a poser.

Please, please, <u>please</u> don't make me classify this paper, put it in a niche, and incidentally throw it in the wastebasket. Remember, you aren't writing just for your friends. This ain't England or New York, this is Seattle, and nobody <u>knows</u>, lady. It took a Vancouver band to say it: "There's nothin' to do in this damn town but drink and drink and then FALL DOWN!"

-Tom Sheehan

P.S. Check out Stereo Review. They call "Flowers of Romance" the worst psychedelic album ever made. It kind of makes sense... P.P.S. "I'm going to sacrifice something here that means a lot to me..." Jimi Hendrix, Monterey, 1967, "I was really drunk and I rammed me guitar neck into the roof, and everybody started laughing. I lost me head and smashed it to pieces. They were laughing at me...I couldn't stand it." Pete Townshend. Two of the best. Two of the best reasons. Now do you know why they smash guitars? Too bad it's a cliche now. Wendy doing it is obscene.

NEW WAVE.........

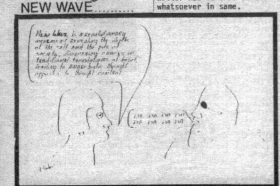

BAZOOKA?

Dear Captain Clark:

In the continuation of "groups I should like but hate", I shall submit this short spiel. I'm a girl. I'm 15 years old. 15 year old girls like Rob Morgan. They're madly in love with him! They go to all the Pudz shows.

If this is true, why do I find myself so queer as to think of Rob Morgan as a haughty asshole, and find their whole set too sweet and boring to tolerate? I must be terminally perverted.

Yes, it's the world's 8th wonder...Just thought I'd share this peculiarity with you, strictly out of interest.

sincerely,

NO-body's one's thing...

P.S. Never did like Bubble Yum....

GIVE THIS GUY A BICYCLE LANE

Dear DT,

Has Seattle become, in essence, incompatible with competent concert promotion? Last night's show at Danceland USA was a fucking disgrace. Anyone questioning the dearth of imported talent in local venues need look no further than 'the promoter'. No one in their right mind would travel across an ocean and a continent in anticipation of brutal mistreatment.

'The Room' was forced to play through a p.a. that reduced their sound to aural-mud-with-a-beat. Whoever was responsible for that atrocity deserves guest of-honor status at a necktie party.

And I hate to raise the ugly question of 'security' but some method of dealing with bipedal black leather shit-bags must be devised. Playing under constant threat of "assault with a ten-speed" is not conducive to an optimum performance in any circumstances.

What's to be done? In my opinion, if strenuous, emphatic objections do not result in improved conditions drastic action is called for. The threat of boycott would no doubt bring shoddy promoting practices to a screeching halt.

Or doesn't anyone give a shit?

-Joe Piecuch

Ed. note: this letter was received prior to any news of the boycott, and the writer has no involvement whatsoever in same.

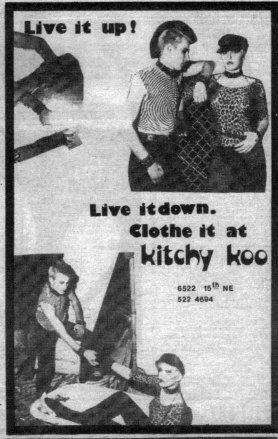

2

MOVING

D.O.A.
DANCELAND   AUGUST 8

To start off the evening, one hopped on the bus, only to be very surprised once at Danceland. I would say extreme heat was the main chemical factor. To quit beating around the bush, the evening was really pretty casual, dare I say MELLOW! Although there was a fairly large crowd, I believe the crowd was rather sussed with a few exceptions. Getting a late start I missed most of the Rejectors set which pissed me off. These guys are getting better all the time. The Rejectors are one of the few exceptional bands in Seattle and deserve far more recognition than already recieved. From what I gather their set was excellent.

Maggot Brains were OK. I can't really recognize any established set of music; it seemed to be mostly improvised. In fact, I can't even recall spotting a song sheet. That's alright tho, Maggot Brains are comedy.

Joe Despair and the Future is another local band that has not gotten the recognition it well

RANDY RAMPAGE, JOEY SHITHEAD OF DOA   Photo: Skip Beattie

deserves. As of late they have become impressionably better. The only disappointment I see is their stage presence. They seem to hold back. For some reason I think it would be more appropriate if they were more aggressive, had more movement.

OK now assholes, listen here, the Fartz shredded any hopes of DOA rousing the audience. With Fart For A Day, Criss Utting substituting for Tommy Fart, still in Norway at the time, they went through their set efficiently with the acceleration of a shotgun blast right between the eyes!! After the first three songs, the slamming slowed down, with masses of exhausted, sweaty bodies ready to collapse. They just couldn't keep up. A large contingency of folks were lounging on the sidewalk outside between sets.

At about 1:00 a.m. or so, DOA finally started. They rolled through their set, a short one at that. DOA did a professional, slick set even though I personally believe their show at the Gorilla Room last May was much better.

-Catalyst

SPLIT ENZ
SHOWBOX   AUGUST 18

Split Enz, Loose Enz, Fair-Weather Frenz, Making Amenz

The Box was not as full as the last Split Enz show, but those who did show up paid a lot more than $1.80. Can't really say that for their $6 they got a 440% better show. In fact, this one tended to drag. One slow song could have been a good Dionne Warwicke vehicle, another had a tedious blues-rock guitar solo straight out of, say, 1971. Nevertheless, the assembled throng had lots of fun at the Split Enz pop party. Ever see kids try to pogo to something at a fox-trot pace before?

The highlight of the evening came when goateed drummer, Mal Green, got out and played the spoons. Ever see kids try to pogo to a guy playing the spoons? The instrumental "Wail" also

struck. Ever thought you'd hear electric piano again?

But those things were all distractions, useful and useless, from the big beat guitar-keyboard-cute vocal sound everyone came to hear. The Enz played fast, slick arrangements, including a speeded-up "Missing Person." Everything was from the new "Waiata" and the breakout LP "True Colours", you know the one with laser etching that's mistakenly called the "first" Enz record? They did make a lot of off the wall stuff before that, which didn't sell; they got rid of the crazy outfits they wore during that period, presumably selling them to Spandau Ballet fans, and now seem content to let the earlier songs remain unheard, as they go on the path to American stardom.

No Cheese Please, back from an extended engagement at Gary Taylor's in Vancouver, played a basic hard power-pop set that brought little response, even in a Showbox where they'll dance to almost anything these days. Folks, of course, had been tired out by the week's hot weather, and the joint was still filling up while NCP were playing, and it didn't help that the band has "tightened" their music to the point of having just one basic song with slight chord variations. Still, the rhythm guitarist can coo just like McCartney.

Ruffin, how'd you get things done so efficiently? NCP starts at 8:30, Split Enz just after 9:30. I got back from the Xitelite Cafe thinking there'd be plenty of time before the set, to find that I'd missed them playing the single "Hard Act To Follow" and maybe a couple of other things. Am told that shows in NY don't even start before this one was over, in plenty of time to prepare for work the next day or parties into the night.

-Clark Humphrey

LENNY KAYE
WREX   AUGUST 14

Lenny Kaye is a good musican. Lenny Kaye is a respected musican. Unfortunately, this time around, Lenny Kaye was a boring musican. He played a mixture of pop-rock, country-rock, soft-rock, and a leetle bit of rock-n-roll. (Easy on the roll, needless to say.). I'll tell you right now, I left early. I should've known. His first night there I went by the club, and everyone was outside. Don't go in, they said. No, he gets a look. Tomorrow.

So in I go. Spend half an hour before he goes on kicking my heels to the tunes of Patti Smith, the Beatles, and (what?) the Royal Gaurdsmen playing their effervescent hit "Snoopy vs. the Red Baron." I'm sure you can understand how ready I was to like something after listening to this disgusting display of recidivism. But it was not to be.

Lenny came on with his game group of guys. One song about jealousy. One song about giving it all up. So far, it's radio rock. The next one was about asking some girl to meet him halfway. He must've meant it, he said it often enough. A semi-soft repetitive rocker, competently executed. 'Competency, ech, NOT GOOD ENOUGH. He started the next one by saying, "You ever hear of Hank Williams?" Hey, maybe some rockabilly or hard blues, I thought. Nope. Countryish rock. By the end of an interminable version of the Yardbird's "For Your Love", I was ready to go. So I did.

As one member of the audience said, "I thought he was going to be exciting, but you know, he was just regular." A lot of people liked it. A lot of people like a lot of things. I've seen Lenny

Kaye do amazing things with other people, most noteably at a murderous Cafe show on New Year's Eve at CBGB's. Apparently, when he picks his own tunes, it's just another trip back to nostalgia land.

The Enemy is another story. I never liked them, and I came ready to not like them again. Surprize: They've tightened up their sound and bled some high energy in as well. If they'd only dirty their licks a little bit. Well, it's not my kind of music; too positive and too reasonable. But it was pleasant enough, even though the effect palled after a while.

I went back and asked Suzanne Grant if they were pissed at getting slagged by an article in DT. "Ah, no," she said, "We've been slagged by SLASH. We've been slagged by DAMAGE. What do we care about a little paper like Desperate Times?" If that attitude came through in their music, The Enemy would be a band to contend with. As it is, they're fairly listenable.

-Captive

VIOLATIONS

FLIPPER

"Phenomena" is a word frequently used to describe Flipper, a squirming San Franciscan underground band. Their name derives from a passion for row boats, (among other things), not necessarily from a TV show of the same name. Albeit appropriate, they rarely if ever lapse into a rendition of the theme song "Flipper, Flipper lives in a world full of wonder..."

Emerging three years ago from the rubble of S.F. hardcore bands, Flipper's first performance was held at the Golden Gate aquatic stage opposite King Tut's treasures. Although fully licensed, the show managed to generate 15 violations in a matter of minutes, including excessive noise. Flipper has been causing (having) trouble ever since. The present band includes Bruce Loose on vocals, Will Shatter on bass, Ted Falconi on guitar, and Steve Depace on drums.

The music Flipper generates can best be described as indescribable. They don't fit into any music category but align themselves with hardcore punk. They are so different, so bizare, what they do could almost be called...choke...art. Then again, some people consider them to be just another fuck band.

It is on stage that the magic of Flipper is revealed. With a steady beat and discordant guitar the music can lead the audience into what is almost like a cult-like trance. Bruce Loose is an extremely emotional and yet obnoxious performer. Writhing on stage his energy is intense. When singing, he appears to hold back, and then explodes upon the audience shrieking. Will Shatter shares the stage with Bruce alternating between bass and vocals. The bass sets the pace with a usually slow, danceable, but neurotic beat. Ted Falconi adds mystery to the band. Hiding in the corner of the stage, he is strapped to his guitar. Expressing perhaps frustrations, perhaps joys; behaving as though in isolation, Ted's guitar song is bent, distorted, warped and drown in a sea of feedback. It is Steve Depace's drumming, steady drumming, that keeps it all together.

Now, is this all enjoyable? Yes. During a good show the audience is actually drawn in to become a part of the band. Flipper has been known to have more people on stage than on the floor during parts of a show. As for the contents of their songs, Flipper seems to have "tapped everything that is sick in America."

Besides being a popular stage act, Flipper has been very successful with their recordings. Their current single with Ha-Ha-Ha/Love Canal has been selling well nation wide, selling out recently in Seattle. Another single is in the works with a five minute version of Sex Bomb; a seven minute song cut short b/w Brainwash, a 28 second song repeated 12 times. An album is also expected to be released in October on Subterranean Records. As for touring...there is a great possibility we will be seeing Flipper in the Great Northwest.

—Bria Conradus

THE FIX
WREX   AUGUST 2

This gets the prize for best show nobody heard about. The gig was booked last-minute, not well publicized, and attended mostly

By friends of the Social Deviates (who opened; see last issue for review) and a couple of lets-hang-out-and-wait-for-the-keg WREX Sunday regulars. Too bad, particularly for afficionados of hardcore. The Fix was great. Their set started with a slow, ominous guitar-drone piece that made the monster

assault of the second number even more effective. The Fix have a Discharge-ish heavy hardcore sound and are technically together and extremely powerful. It was one of those sets where you keep watching the amps and the walls because you know something is bound to collapse from the amount of energy and movement of stage (nothing did, in this case, but it was real close). The Fix are from Lansing, Michigan. They claim they liked it here (God knows why) and are coming back. If and when they do, SHOW UP. OK?

—Daina Darzin

4

POP DEFECT, FRED & THE LIVING
I.C.T. HALL   AUGUST 18

A little hall by Seattle Center, friends, fans, and few people who haven't forgotten how fun hall shows can be. That's all you need, folks.

First up were The Living, a new band **made up of** Fastback-Zipdad people,

like Duff, and Criss Crass. It was their first gig, and as far as my own tastes were concerned, they were the best band of the evening. Good basic punk-pop with melodic vocals. They even did some (tongue-in-cheek?) Beatles.

Next on the bill was Fred. If you

haven't heard them, they're a danceable art/no wave band. They added atmosphere to their set with an electric snowman, incense (coff coff), and candles. The high point of their show was a totally perverted version of James Brown's "Sex Machine", during which most of the band stripped to their shorts, and a couple of them went briefly beyond.

Last was Pop Defect, a trio with David Scott (formerly of Psychopop) on drums. They sound like their name. They were all good on their instruments, and got the audience going. They danced, pogoed, and had a generally good time, except for a minor alarm when the cops turned up outside.

It was a pretty good night, and the price was right, $3. Let's see more of these independent hall shows, huh?

—Heidi Weispfenning

THE ROOM AND AUDIO LETTER
WREX   AUGUST 7-8

I couldn't move when The Room came on, much as their music was suited for it. The heat, the parade, and running out of money and not being able to get more because the bank machine was on the other side of the parade helped to contribute. Nevertheless, The Room put on a spectacular set. They're a great band, as was reported in the previous DT.

Audio Letter was also highly pleasant. Their sound is getting more specific, and the words of Sharon Gannon were clearer than ever. If you've read the stories about them in local art journals, you know that Audio Letter's name comes from a guy in Texas who sends mail-order cassettes where he reads his conspiracy theories; their music, which might sound like noise to the uninitiated, is really a carefully-constructed extrapolation of mathematical theories and Enoesque aural experiments; their lyrics contemplations on philosophical concepts and the Big Picture of things. Have fun; surprised? You might be if you've only read about them, as some of the details of their performances read colder than they are. Quoting Gannon's theme for the WREX evening, "A mirror is like the water," just doesn't have the impact of seeing her smile while enunciating that "A mirror is like THE water."

The point I'm trying to get to is that you don't have to drink cappucino on Capitol Hill with the Ivy League art grads discussing the limits of minimalism to enjoy Audio Letter. You can be mesmerized by Gannon's singing into tape devices, by Sue Ann Harkley's approaches to guitar, violin and sometimes drums, by the noises of an ever-changing lineup (this time Bob Jenkins, Jeff McGrath and James Husted). You might get baffled by the concepts, especially if you don't regularly hang out with the folks and aren't told

beforehand that the next performance will be dedicated to Wilhelm Reich or such. They plan to alleviate this in the future by supplying program notes.

This night found them in more lyrical moods than some of their shows. Every time they appear is at least a little different, and this was a breezy, erethreal summertime set. If you closed your eyes you could see shooting stars over a sea full of flying fish, while just over the next hill the grasshoppers are chirping away so loudly they're making you crazy, and are probably also eating all the wheat. Their second set was billed as an operetta, but I couldn't tell what the story or characters in it were.

—Clark Humphrey

THE HEATS
ASTOR PARK   AUGUST 14

"Astor Park? Where is it?" one nature lover asks. No, no, not that kind of park. It's a club. Located on the edge of scenic Belltown, decorated in late 70's Holiday Inn Modern. Astor Park caters to greater Seattle's pop afficionados. From Bothell to Ft. Lewis, they drive to Astor Park in search of R&R and all the fringe benefits.

This last weekend the Heats were gigging at the Park. This local "soon to be famous rock band" is always sure to fill a club with fans in search of...Promoted for the last two years as a punk band, the Heats are as clean and cute as they can be. No wonder they've had it rough (as far as image goes) since the beginning. The guys in the band are real nice but their love of partying overshadows their "serious" musical intentions. I chose to witness the Heats. Opening their set with a song that sounded like a Stones number, the Heats continued

on with Knack soundalikes. Nothing really reached the peak of Beatles soundalikes. It's hard to tell which of the singers looks more like Paul Mc. These guys are pretty talented but their energy is so schlocky. I found it impossible to dance without boredom. Pop, burned-out sound. The crowd of fans loved the band, and filled the dance floor. Some referred to the Heats as the best band in Seattle. Poor sheep!

—Bria Conradus

SPECTATORS, RAPID-i, PAINTINGS ON PLASTIC
WREX   AUGUST 12

Hello, what's this? A night full of twisted metaphors, non sequitors, etc. etc. etc. Walking into WREX Wednesday night, the first clue as to something gone awry hits you like a brick. The place is lit up like a fucking Christmas tree. Paintings on Plastic is ostensibly the headlining act tonight--a series of various-colored slashes, swaths and swashes on the not-so-hallowed surfaces of drop cloths, (deflated) inflatable air matresses, and the like. Oh yeah. I see...it's uhh..culture. Local artist Billy Shaffer

Photo: Skip Beattie

has assembled his latest seris of works on the red brick walls of WREX, and for the most part, cheered the place up a bit. Their artistic merits I must leave to the viewer. I particularly liked the idea, but I'm not about to critique it. I'm not sure how many actually came to view the art, and the conspicuous absence of cheese-nibbling and such lessened the shock of dealing with WREX as a club cum gallery. The free champagne

didn't hurt much, though, and a very inebriated Shaffer added to the fuck-the-festivity bullshit that could have ensued.

Oh yes...and there was music. The Spectators were up first. I'm beginning to think that the Spectators, Seattle's answer to the undefinable musical genre, are getting a bit too close to definition for comfort. It's hard for me to be objective about them, but the audience seemed to be almost respectful... patiently waiting to hear something new--more than happy to hear all the old faves, but in strained anticipation of the same energetic spark with which the Spex burst onto the Seattle scene 6 months ago. The performance wasn't particularly inspired, especially the vocals, and some of Byron Duff's flash guitar work wilted a little in the apparent over-heated drought we've been facing for the last week or so. Chalk it up to sunstroke.

After the usual WREX disco break inbetween sets, Rapid-i took the stage. It shouldn't have come as a shock, but it did; from their first note the stage exploded into one of the most energetic sets to hit WREX in ages. These guys haven't been seen much lately, and it was pretty obvious they've missed being on stage. Their almost fucked up funk rhythms kept the audience churning throughout their set, while Dave Ford's enthusiastic theatrics played a perfect foil to bassist Phil Otto's stage cool. Best of all, for one of the first times I can think of, the sound mix placed Terry's percussion work almost exactly where it should be--weaving in and out of the bass, guitar, vocals, and Jerry's rock steady drumming. These guys have got to be one of the most invigorating bands Seattle has ever had to offer. They've got an EP coming out shortly, and if its energy can live up to their live performance, look for an unqualified hit.

—Jeff Greenwood

X-15
DANCELAND   AUGUST 15

If you go out on any sort of regular basis, you've probably seen X-15. Musically, they're on the melodic end of punk; their lyrics have a hardcore political content; their following includes a lot of cute, expensively dressed punkettes; they've been around for a while; they're very good.

They're particularly a real good band to get drunk to-- preferably swigging straight from a brown-bagged pint bottle. X-15 projects the best aspects of being smashed; a fervent belief in one's opinions; a ragged loose edge around one's perceptions, which have gotten real inventive since you hit the second half of the pint...; (Ed. Note: the magazine takes no

DISORDERLY

responsibility for the incoherence of this thought pattern. DT has learned that our reporter was thoroughly inebriated during the viewing and writing of this, and we are appalled) Most important, X-15 has a drunk's willingness to go over the edge into passion, fury, emotional excess. That, in these days of colder-than-thou, is a statement as important as any this

X-15

band makes: it's ok, goddamit, get pissed, cry, throw that bottle, listen to it shatter.

Mind you, X-15 is a good band to see when you're sober, too (even though it's not as much fun that way). They're playing again after a break that did them a lot of good. Their WREX set was particularly sharp and tight,

and introduced several hot new songs (at last!) which will also appear on the EP they're currently recording (at last!).

Their Danceland show didn't go off as well, probably as a result of not-great attendance. The high' (?) point of sorts was when one of the above-mentioned punkettes demonstrated the negative aspects of being smashed by throwing up on the stage. X-15 has definitely progressed, though, since their last round of gigs. If you haven't seen them lately, it's time. Sneak in some hard stuff Bourbon is best. Watch out for Dick the security guy.

—Berlin

EXECUTIVES
HIBBLE & HYDE'S AUGUST 4

The Executives play spy music. Remember The Man From U.N.C.L.E.? Well, they could play the background track, and make it more exciting than ever before. Intricate, hazardous melodies are their calling card.

The Executives are Gregg Silagyi on bass, Randy Nealy on guitar and Mike Stein on drums. All have been in bands for years, the most mentionable being Mike, who was with The Accident.

Their show is full of restrained energy, but it is also very personal. The between-song dialogue is great. You can tell they really appreciate their audience. Each Executive has his own strong stage personality, Gregg with his sneering Iggy vocals, Randy with his extroverted and always amusing presence, like a child expecting enthusiasm from the crowd, and Mike with his very English Lydon-like vocals and bobbing head. All wear suits, the reason being that they don't want to be classified as a "punk band". Gregg admits to owning only one leather jacket, and a conservative one to boot. I think its great that the E's want to keep their own identity This gives them a broader base of style to work with - versatility is their middle name.

Their music is spy music, but it's also heart music. It makes you FEEL. I'm inclined to compare them to early Clash/Jam/Joe Jackson, but really they have a style all their own, something I've never heard before (they do all originals, no covers). The show includes lots of instrumentals,

which is unusual these days and also very refreshing. And the songs with vocals are innovative. My favorite is "Ice Age". This song is reminiscent of the Sex Pistols, and it makes you THINK. "Pornographic Thoughts" has Nick Cash-ish (999) vocals. Gregg sings exceptionally on this one, and expresses his lustful yearnings: "I've got these pornographic thoughts in my head/of

things I'd like to do to you in my bed." See, something for everybody!

They even do a token anti-Reagan song - "State of the Union".

You might think that after seeing the Executives three times in one week, I might be bored to death by them - not so - they have remained appealing each time. In fact, I bopped around the office singing "Pornographic Thoughts" (I drew some pretty strange looks let me tell you!). The E's really grow on you - they're addictive.

—Kathy Moschel

Little Bears From Bangkok
Children Of Kellogg   WREX   AUGUST 13

The Little Bears From Bangkok are a motley crew. Not ragged or loose, but definitely the assortment pack (polo shirts vying with running shorts, etc.). The songs played that night were a mixture of politics in general and society in particular. Many lists were enumerated: a particularly diverting item informed me that I had a responsibility to change my socks, sheets, and light bulbs when the necessity became evident

It wasn't the usual set, as Tracy Rowlands (bass/vocals) was not in voice that evening owing to a bad cold. The short display of her singing sounded a lot like her talking (both of which can be very nice, if you're wondering). Jim Anderson carried most of the vocals in a husky voice that squeaked at the edges. He was eminently likeable. In addition he played sax and bass, the bass line fitting into the music in the way a lot of groups generally utilize keyboards (Yes, they have two bassists). Guitarist Joan Maneri (ex-Beakers) plugged in with an alternate line of choppy chords and runs, also singing occasionally. But the most consistent thrill of the evening came from Danielle Elliott's drumming. She beat these drums. I had a momentary vision of them trooping home

sublime. Who says contemporanity is over-rated? Yeah, sure, everyone knows it's a sick society, but these people don't beat you over the head with it. They give the audience a little credit for having brains (or should I say, the benefit of the doubt). Future shows: 8/30 at the Virginia Five, 9/4 at the Bumberball.

The Children of Kellogg are Frankie Sundsten (bass, formerly with the Beakers), Annie Mulcahey (drums, formerly with the Fags), and Sue Anne Harkley (guitar, vocals, currently with Audio Letter). They were, that night, only eight rehersals away from never having existed. The music was casual but concise: start with a certain sound, take it somewhere, then stop. Just like that. There were a lot of treble-y, deliberately dis-

after her of their own accord, like little disciples.

The band played two sets, the second of which sounded remarkably like the first. Then they played "Louie Louie". (That song is turning into a local religion it seems). "Disco Hit Single" and "Fascist" were the songs that stayed with me the longest. Remarks were made to the effect that the band had improved enormously.

Never having seen them before, I can only add to the above statement that they were fun to watch and a bit silly. Still, the subject matter was serious and I guess absurdity is the flipside. The Little Bears combine a sense of humor with a sense of perspective: both precious commodities these days. In time they may well make the move from seriously silly to viciously

jointed instrumentals, and the group said they'd like to continue in that direction. With a voice like Sue Anne's they ought to consider adding more vocals. It's moderately low but penetrating, and has the quality of demanding attention. "Can't Get Any Smaller" was the cohesive number, because of it.

They didn't move around much, but that may have been more a case of nerves than of inclination. Talking to Annie after the show I mentioned the way every song had had the same drumbeat and she admitted that her mind had gone blank at about the time the set started. "You mean every song has a different beat?" I asked. "Well," she said, "every other song, yes." The sound may not be polished, but it is distinctive and worth developing. You can see it develop right before your eyes, if you're interested: 8/29 at Wrex.

- Captive

6

RECORDS

PICK HIT LP

KILLING JOKE

What's this for...!

RELENTLESS RELENTLESS RELENT-
LESS RELENTLESS RELENTLESS
RELENTLESS RELENTLESS RELENT-
LESS RELENTLESS RELENTLESS
RELENTLESS RELENTLESS RELENT-
LESS RELENTLESS RELENTLESS
RELENTLESS RELENTLESS RELENT-
LESS RELENTLESS RELENTLESS
RELENTLESS RELENTLESS RELENT-
LESS RELENTLESS RELENTLESS
RELENTLESS RELENTLESS RELENT-
LESS RELENTLESS RELENTLESS
RELENTLESS RELENTLESS RELENT-
LESS RELENTLESS RELENTLESS
RELENTLESS RELENTLESS RELENT-
LESS RELENTLESS RELENTLESS
RELENTLESS RELENTLESS RELENT-
LESS RELENTLESS RELENTLESS
RELENTLESS RELENTLESS RELENT-
LESS RELENTLESS RELENTLESS
RELENTLESS (funk) RELENTLESS
(punk) RELENTLESS (broken)
RELENTLESS (slick) RELENTLESS
(ContraPUNTal) RELENTLESS
(buy) RELENTLESS (buy)
RELENTLESS (killing joke).

-Captive

FLESHTONES

All Around the World b/w
The World Has Changed
A & M

Alright! Now this is what I want
to hear after a long day over the
dishwasher. I apologize to all
of you who hate top 40 lyrics,
but I love words like: "Y'know
I love you baby. Well, well
well, y'know..." All Around the
World is a song for dancers.

The other side is not fast and
not slow enough. Technically it
is OK, but it doesn't quite make
it...y'know?

The Fleshtones have been around
for awhile. Ignorant am I, for
not having heard anything of
their's earlier. I may have no
sense, but I like this single.

-MM

MONOCHROME SET

Ten Don't for Honeymooners b/w
Juaita of Malacca

Ten Dont's for Honeymooners is a
well produced, well mixed and
rather boring song. Not that
it's a bad composition, but the
"yip-yip-ei's" remind me too much
of a bad Adam and the Ants
song.

Juaita of Malacca is better but
solely concerning the lyrics.
They are, as always, smooth and

pleasant to listen to, but the
words themselves are a bit much:
all about bad parts of town and
the taste of cat and the cane.

After hearing this single, I tend
to believe that the honeymoon is
over for the Monochrome Set.
Then again, perhaps it is only
the three year crisis.

-MM

JAMES CHANCE

Live In New York
ROIR Cassette

This is the guy who, say the
liner notes, completes what
Miles Davis started? Sounds
more like a white ripoff of
James Brown, and I don't like
the real Brown. But then
again, white ripoffs of black
styles are the history of
American popular music for the
past century, and it wouldn't
be surprising if Chance and his
bands, the Contortions and the
Blacks, get crowned "the kings
of funk" sooner or later.

Not from this, though, and not
just because it's only being
sold on tape. While the
Contortions grind out those East
Village no-wave licks like
dissonant street noises set to
a 4/4 beat, Chance sounds cold,
as in vocals that calculatedly
yip and halt, as in noisy sax
solos that raise musical
questions which are never
answered. While James ain't much
(though he has the potential
to be a big hit macho strut
star), and there are technical
flaws in the recording, the
band is quite danceable and
guitarist Bern Nix is almost
as burning as Chance is
freezing.

-Clark Humphrey

BLACK FLAG

Six Pack b/w I've Heard It
Before and American Waste

This three song EP by Black Flag
on S.S.T. Records is by far my
favorite from the band to date.
Black Flag seems to be one of the
few bands who manage to stay
hardcore, record after record,
without wimping out to commercialism.

Dez, their latest singer, really
stands out as well as Greg on
guitar. Six Pack is a totally
ridiculous song about everyone's
favorite subject - beer. Excellent leads on this particular
cut. My favorite on the EP is
definately "I've Heard It Before
not only because it's so true,
but because it's a great song
by a great band.

If you haven't got your Six Pack
yet, get a cold one from
Corporate Records.

B.F., a band which has a habit
of going through rapid personnel
changes, is now going through
another. Drummer, Robo will no
longer be with the band, a
tough spot to fill but we'll
see. Also, Dez is now playing
some back-up guitar. Well,
we'll just have to see in early
September when they come to
Danceland. Don't miss them or
their EP.

-Steve Fart

DAVID JOHANSEN

Here Comes the Night
Blue Sky Records

The night I saw the New York
Dolls on "Rock Concert",
Johansen strutting about the
stage in jail stripes, looking
so dangerous and inviting at once,
I knew this was the way rock
'n roll was supposed to be.
Their break-up was traumatic -
I thought the whole glitter/punk
scene common to NYC in 1973 had
gone down the tubes.

In a way, I was right. New York
rock will never be so fresh and
vibrant again. The Dolls were
a one-of-a-kind band. No one
has captured their sound since.
But the Dolls' break-up was
necessary for David Johansen's
musical transition.

"Here Comes the Night" is Johansen's third solo album to date.
The first, titled simply "David
Johansen", was uncoordinated and
raw, as if he really didn't know
what he wanted to do, and showed
him less than moderate success.
His second, "In Style", was a
soulful, full-of-hurt-and-pain
record. Good music to cry to.
I love it. "Here Comes the Night"
is a good balance between the
two previous efforts, and has
him back on the road to emotional
recovery. It's a very sensitive
album, but fun too!

Almost all of the songs are
excellent examples of D.J.'s
original approach to music, with
only two "filler" cuts - "Bohem-
ian Love Pad" and "My Obsession"
and two out of eleven ain't bad.

The best song on the record is
"Havin' So Much Fun". The rhythm
is sneaky and the message is
clear: "Ain't never going back
with you baby, well, I don't know
what I'd do, and I've been havin'
so much fun without you." A
very inspirational tune - listen
to it after you've just been
dumped.

Other mentionable cuts are:
-Party Tonight - The big city
alchoholics nightmare, complete
with a drunk-dance beat and
a great guitar solo by Blondie
Chaplin.
-Marquesa De Sade - An "I'll
show that rich bitch what she's
missing" song. Latin rhythms are
wonderful by Ulysses Dalvega and
D.J.'s vocals are fantastic, as
well as piano by Bobby Blain.
-Here Comes the Night - The title
cut offers real Doll's-ish vocal
posing by Johansen, and a Mott
the Hoople chorus. This song is
the most reminiscent of the
Doll's early power. Also, a
real party song.
-Heart of Gold - This is the most
hurting song on the album, and
my second favorite. Johansen's
voice is passionate but tender
as he sings: "You think I'm
all hard, but I've got a heart
of gold, and I need protection
from the cold." The piano is
sentimental and Elliott Murphy's
harmonica adds a hobo/country
feeling. Nice.

As you have probably gathered by
now, I like this record. It's
full of different styles and
beats - quite a fluctuation and
never boring. It covers subjects
from falling in love with a prostitute to nightclubbing to getting a lecture on sex education.
All in all, a exceptionally
human effort by D.J. Buy it -
it's good to know you're not
alone in the "rough and tumble"
world of today.

-Kathy Moschel

PICK HIT 45

EURYTHMICS

Never Gonna Cry Again b/w
Le Sinistre

Never... is a melancoly song.
It is impossible to tell exactly
what happened but still you
recognize the feeling and it is
there. The bass and drums are
strong, adding to the dancability
of the song and building upon
the helplessness of (yes)
another broken love song. Ann
Lennox sings about not crying,
not dying and going to the water:
"I just can't relate to you, I
just can't find a place to be
near you." The instrumentals
are nearly fast, and coupled
with the "sad" vocals, throw you
off 'til you remember that:
"I've shed more tears for you
than the ocean."

The flip side is slower. LS is
eerie with the opening piano and
percussion following you down
a dark street on an already dark
and thoughful night. Dark humor
is sinister. This song is
almost an instrumental with
vocal effects. A repetitive
song, again with strong feelings:
"Coming to me in my darkest
hour, messages...telling me
about your part."

The wonderful thing about this
EP is the intensity of both
songs. The Eurythmics are
repetitive but not boring." There
is something here that weighs
upon me, yet relieves a bit of
the pain leaving still, the sting.

The Eurythmics are Ann Lennox and
Dave Stewart, with help from
Jackie Liebreit (drums), Holger
Czukay (french horn), and the
visitations by Les Vampirettes.
Available at Corporate Records.

-MM

SYVAIN SYVAIN

Syl Sylvain and the Teardrops
RCA

This is pop. Ohh-la-la's,
bluesy sax, rockabilly piano,
tight horn section, and canned
crowd noises provide all the fun
clutter you could desire. Why
isn't it going gold? This sur-
passes by far the B-52's greatest
hits disc, and all it's tunes are
new. Try not to danse to "No
Dancing," I dare ya. Play
"Teardrops" and "Lorell" and enjoy
an exquisite aural sugar rush.
No wonder Paul's disbanding Wings
and Joe Jackson's fled to doing
Lounge Lizard covers. As sincere
a pure-pop record as you're likely
to get. The singer sure knows
his bops and doo-wops. Oh yeah,
better say he was the New York
Doll's guitarist.

-Clark Humphrey

RECORDS

SOLGER

This singles has been out a while, but somehow didn't get reviewed until now. Pretty surprising, that one. Especially since this 5 song EP just about sums it up as far as hardcore goes. The production is zero, and the pressing sounds like it was geared toward play on one of those see-and-say phonographs (you know, the ones with a nail instead of a needle.) Add a great sleeve (the cover photo's classic); don't add a label, leave it blank. It all adds up to one of the truest-to-life real hardcore records you'll ever find. Get it, there's probably not many of them floating around. Oh, yeah, American Youth and Raping Dead Nuns are great.

       -D.W.

SKINHEAD CLASSICS VOL. II

Own up time--I'm actually old enough to have bought and danced to these the first time around. Forget all yer 1980 ska bands, this is the real thing-- still unbeatable despite the muddy quality. (To think I thought all that distortion was part of the sound). "54-46 Was My Number" by Toots & the Maytalls is probably the best produced--but who cares, this record is indispensable!

SOFT CELL

Tainted Love/Where Did Our Love Go

Come dancing!! Just two young men (gasp) complete Soft Cell. A few months back, they gave us the truly memorable Memorabilia. Now, they've left the painfully bashful for producer Mike Thone (one-time tangled up with Wire). And that means on this showing, somewhat less obvious studio trickery. "Tainted Love" does a real seduction job. There you are, moving along to the wonderful synthetic beat when mmmm! they've gone and done and unbearably good segue into The Supremes' "Where did our love go". Mark Almond's voice is amazing. A fab hit!

       -Norman Bately

CHUNKS

NAR P.O. Box 21
San Pedro, CA 90733

If one had bought the "Cracks in the sidewalk" (Comp.E.P.) I would imagine you thought it was a piece of shit. Right? Sure, there was one hot Black Flag song, but the rest made you want to play frisbee. Well, there's good news: Chunks has dual purpose. Side one is great, but side two is a dinner plate serving up the same shit on a shingle that CITSW served on both sides. One exception on Side 2 is Vox Pop. A year ago, they also put out a single on the Bad Trip label: Cab Driver b/w Just Like Your Mom, real good, unfortunately unavailable. Vox Pop also features Pat Smear on guitar. Side 1 of Chunks consists of all good material: the Descendants, Chiefs, Minute Men, Black Flag, Stains. For $3.99, it's well worth it, and includes sleeve art by Ray Pettibone.

       -Catalyst

MAUREEN TUCKER

Around and Around/Will You Love Me Tomorrow
Trash

The sleeve lists her as "The Velvet Underground's Maureen Tucker," and this won't win a solo identity. Rather average versions of Chuck Berry and Goffin-King standards. Straightforward lounge vocals by one who had been one of rock's few non-singing women musicians, who now debuts as one of rock's few one-woman-bands. Recommended mainly to Velvet collectors, who will have heard about it anyway by now.

       -Clark Humphrey

SMASHCORDS

Rough Trade

This is one of the most aggravating records I've ever heard in my life...and not for the smug arty reasons they probably intended to set my nerves on edge with.

These guys are supposed to be from Federal Way or some other place around here. Maybe that was part of the joke too, although the Rocket have assured all of us that it is, in fact, God's truth. Rough Trade picked these guys up, and as far as I can tell what that amounts to is little more than a slap in the face to every hardworking band around these here parts. Real cute titles like "Brand New Rambler" and "Park my Car at the Rhumba Party"

are hardly any match to the pathetic sounds on this disc; some guys practicing in their bedroom, I'm told. What really pisses me off is that RT have always gone for the obscure, but never have they stooped so low as to make a joke out of the whole thing. I know they're trying to fill some kind of quota, but why do it with art school shit like this?   O.W.

101ers

Elgin Avenue Breakdown

What was Joe Strummer doing before the Clash became a reality? He was the lead singer and rhythm guitar player for the 101ers, a group the played for London pub crowds in 1975 and 1976. Their sets were a mixture of rockabilly covers and their own stuff, and they only released on record while they were a group.

On the A-side of that single was "Keys to Your Heart", a love statement by Strummer who "used to be a teen-age drug taker" but had now found the "keys to your heart". It had a great beat too, and shot up to number eight on the British charts. That happened around the same time Strummer befriended two young art students--Mick Jones and Paul Simonon. The 101ers broke up, and the rest is history.

Since the Clash became such hot shit, Andalucia records (I've never heard of them before) thought some money could be made by releasing "Elgin Avenue Breakdown", a collection of rare recordings by 101ers. I really love it, even though the sound quality on about a third of the cuts is real shitty.

Mr. Alcohol is bringing up your chin/Now violence leads to hospitals, informing next of kin", sound like something Dylan would have tried in 1965.

But no matter what you think it sounds like, "Elgin Avenue Breakdown" shows that Strummer had a lot of things going through his head during the days before punk. And there is a lot of raw energy and talent on this LP. It's definitely worth having, even if you aren't a Clash-head.

       -David Danelski

EASTERN FRONT II

Ed. Note: Erica, our famed
wandering reporter is in Korea.
Don't ask. So, as a desperate
creative alternative, here's
our first venture into that great
old form of non-verbal communication, the photo essay.

Satz of THE LEWD

T.S.O.L.

ALL PHOTOS BRIA CONRADUS

SIC PLEASURE

SIC PLEASURE

SIC PLEASURE

SIC PLEASURE

Olga of THE LEWD

Alex of T.S.O.L.

WARZONE

Trashing it

Hello Jello!

FLIPPER

FLIPPER

FLIPPER

9

LOCAL BIZ

SO WHAT IF THEY HAD A BOYCOTT AND NOBODY CAME?   by jeff greenwood

Last week, Seattle saw what was probably the single most important gesture on the part of the music community in years. Bands, promoters, and to a certain extent audience actually sat down to a dialogue concerning just exactly where each of them stood. Ostensibly (and quite incorrectly), their motive was whether or not to stand in force, boycotting all Steve Pritchard productions. This boycott would have affected shows at Danceland, the Showbox, and WREX. Initially, the question at hand was how promoters and bands were to come to terms with contracts, payment, and booking policies. It soon became clear these were all things that easily could be agreed on, and threat of boycott was laid to rest. The whole episode could have been easily avoided; so easily, that it seems almost absurd that the issue had been left unchecked, to rear its ugly head. Only in Seattle, I guess. What is most interesting is that for all its well intentioned pomposity, no one came out winner OR loser. No great deals were struck, no compromises met, and certainly no clear explanation of how the grand scheme of things will be worked out in the future. So what the hell was all the turmoil about, anyway?

TO PUT IT QUITE SIMPLY THE MONEY JUST ISN'T THERE...

As anyone well-versed in the Seattle club scene already knows. Jr. Cadillac, for the most part, make money for a night's work that would have a Spectator or a Blackout drooling if not foaming at the mouth. The problem isn't so much a matter of more respect for one band over the other, as much as the type of clientele that dictate a particular club's booking policy. Invariably, Jr. and the boys will consistently draw a better wage because of a better turnout at the door. It's a sad truth that most of Seattle's club-goers are not particularly interested in experimentation. The best rule of thumb seems to be "If you've seen 'em before, go again..if you haven't, don't go in unless the place is packed". Luckily for those a little more adventuresome, there are still one or two options; a few places one might see a new original band willing to take chances. Likewise, the clubs that offer those opportunities also take a lot of chances. Witness the Gorilla Room, closed at the moment due to legal problems with the liquor board, or WREX, who somehow manage to keep heads just above water, financially, as well as artistically. One would be hard-pressed to prove that anyone involved with booking or promoting new music in Seattle are in it for the money. If they were, they should have had their heads examined long ago, because to put it quite simply the money just isn't there. The same applies to the bands. If a reasonably talented musician wanted to make some dough in Seattle, the last place to attempt it would be in an original band. There are far too many

successful cover bands working in the Northwest for anyone to doubt the monetary gains of working in one of these outfits.

The rest of the country, believe it or not, is not all that far ahead of us, either. It may come as a shock to us when we consider that touring bands like the Stranglers, Joan Jett, or the Psychedelic Furs (all of whom have come through town in recent months) make no more than Hi-Fi or the Cowboys could in a night at Astor Park. And if that's not bad enough, imagine what Black Flag, DOA, or similar hardcore bands make. Nada... with a capital nothing.

Let it be agreed, at least for the moment, that no one is getting rich overthe exploitation of young new music talent in Seattle. The point made last week was simply that since there is so little money to be made, why not throw in a little respect, and recognition for the efforts Seattle bands have mustered in keeping a volitile scene alive. It was this simple point made collectively by a core of working musicians last week that prompted meetings, discussions, and the threat of boycott. It not only heated up an already tense community, but got at least a few folks worked up enough to talk openly with other musicians for the first time in their careers.

"We are asking for respect, organization, information, and a professional attitude from the promoters and the bands," said Sue Ann Harkey, one of the prime motivators in last week's episode. "What we asked for was extremely fair and deserving and within reason. We have to take into account the minimal audience we work with."

What was in fact asked for were contracts setting down guidelines as to the nature of payment bands were to recieve. This one overriding issue has been the source of a lot of aggravation in the new music community for months. Ever since places like WREX and the Gorilla Room have booked bands

WE ARE ASKING FOR RESPECT ORGANIZATION, INFORMATION AND PROFESSIONAL ATTITUDE

Gorilla Room have booked bands on a regular basis, the question of how much, and when has never been set down in writing. In the case of the Gorilla Room, it has generally been understood that an extensive guest list, poor attendance and lack of promotion could assure nothing more than a few bucks for a night's work. Brian Rennings, a promoter for the G. Room, has very seldom promised any amount to a band, and has thus far avoided any major disputes over payment. Many bnads last week expressed their willingness to put up with those conditions, simply because they felt that they had never been mislead over these wages. Apparently, not so in the case of those who had worked with Steve Pritchard.

In several cases, the bands felt that they had been told they would receive a percentage of the door, or a set amount, and that at the end of the evening ended up with

something considerably less. Factsbear this out in, a number of cases (some of them not involving Pritchard). One such case was a flat fee $50 offered Rapid-i as openers for the Punts at WREX. They still have not gotten paid. Part of the problem in their payment seems to revolve around a very nebulous agreement/disagreement between owner Michael Clay, Pritchard, Bev Williams (also of WREX), and former booker Wes Bradley, as to who actually should pay the band. It doesn't appear that the situation is going to resolve itself, and so for all intents and purposes Rapid-i made somebody else $50 richer.

Another more blatant case of misrepresentation was made last month when the Fix, from Michigan, played WREX. They and their Seattle booking agent, Pravda Productions were told the band would make $100, versus a percentage of the total made at the door, which ever was greater. At the end of the night they were given $53 and left to their own devices as to how to return home with less than enough money to cover their gasoline expenses (let alone food). The stories seemed almost endless, even though Pritchard has been involved in booking in Seattle for a reasonably short period of time. RPA, Spectators, Student Nurse, Audio Letter... each one of them had something to say about how they were handled. The most important thing to remember, however is

...IT IS VERY IMPORTANT THAT GREAT CARE IS PUT INTO PROMOTION.

that it is not a problem that only Steve Pritchard or WREX have had with booking bands. Mike Vraney, while at WREX for a brief perios last year also came up short at the end of the evening...prompting him to get out of the business for a while. Rescue Rock of the 80's ended their short career in promoting when the very same problem arose after a Showbox concert featuring RPA, Sundance, The Untouchables, and the Prefabs last spring.

One of the major reasons for the lack of money when it comes time to get paid, the bands agreed, was a serious lack of effective advertising. Steve Pritchard, when confronted with this admitted that this was probably true. His shows, especially the club dates in recent weeks have gone by barely noticed because of a lack of newspaper support. Pritchard mantains that it is the fault of editors leaving his shows out of their calenders, but it is fairly doubtful that so many could have been overlooked so consistently. Both bands and promoter agreed that alot of the butden rested in flyposting the city, and that both the band and club should be responsible for that. But the truth is, while most bands have postered, however meagerly, there have been few "official" club flyers (something WREX has been noted for paying greater attention to in the past.)

Dennis White, who represented some of the bands concerned explained: "When a local act opens for a touring act, especially when their pay is based in good faith rather than a contract, it is very important that great care is put into promotion. Alot of times there is only enough money to pay the headliner, when there could have been enough to go around if

only more people knew about the show."
The third major issue was the trickiest. Pay for the soundman. At this point sound is provided at WREX on a nightly basis at a charge ranging from $40 to $50 per evening. Many of the bands could provide a system of their own. Admittedly this is a task but not an impossible one. Harkey expressed anxiety over the fact that while

the soundman is secure in his payment, not so the band. The duties of the sound technician are to provide adequate equipment and knowledge and insure the smooth operation of the show. It is a vital part in any band's performance, and it appeared that most people concerned agreed that $50 was only outrageous when the bands make so much less.

During the negotiations it was suggested that the Club, not the promoter should bear at least half the cost of sound.

WREX owner Michael Clay has since agreed to help bear this burden. In the case of the Showbox, which demands a much larger system, sound is included in the rental agreement, and provided by Morgan Sound of Seattle. The case of Danceland is not so clear at this point, however; during the period that promoter Mark Brewster booked the club, a system was retained and used for each show. Now the room is without a regular system and one seems to be gotten in various manners, but seemingly this has not been a major issue.

The ironic twist is that no matter what gains, if any, were

made during last week's discussions, alot of the same attitudes still continue to prevail. Because the bands involved were not forced to take the action they had threatened, it is unclear if they will attempt to set up any sort of organized method of dealing collectively. The Gorilla Room will be reopened sometime in the future, and will probably be unable to offer any more than a showcase for new and working acts. That's more than likely the way most would have it anyway. As for Danceland, and the Showbox, the are of course available for shows to anyone with the financial wearwithall, and a good bill.

...ALOT OF THE SAME ATTITUDES STILL CONTINUE TO PREVAIL.

No doubt other club owner, promoters and bookers will look on all of this with the same lack of circumspect as usual. The PI is probably a little embarrassed for covering what they probably hoped was going to be some kind of scoop. Some people's eggs will no doubt have been offended, and others sensibilities heightened. So what if they had a boycott and nobody came? Well, according to Hardy:
"By establishing our own values and demanding their worth it will force promoters to work within that standart, and attract a creative promotional system." That in it'self should be enough. Good luck.

10

VANCOUVER  REPORT

CORINNE   MAH

Back again with an update on the downfall of Vancouver's club scene.

The past week's trusted grapevine has brought nothing but horrific news of more club closures.

Rohan's in Kitsilano (the only licensed live music club in that area) has just been sold for demolition. The manager says they'll stay open as long as they can, but it looks like it'll be gone by the end of September. Rohan's has been around for years as a bar, then as an all day bar with music, then as a night-time cabaret. In the past while their booking policy has phased out a lot of the granola and has become open to a much wider range of bands: from folk, rock, soul, R & B, to new rock, pop, and punk. Young, new local bands are also given a chance as opening acts. Alas, the price of progress.

Things have hit the skids down in Gastown as well. When the urban cowboy craze died, "Cowboy's" became Route 66, a rock club. Word has it that within days it will close due to lack of business. It's not yet clear if Route 66 has been sold and will re-open under new management or if the space will be used for something else.

Just down the street, Bronco's has not fared well from slack turnouts either. Bronco's used to be Dimple's Disco, a two level affair, then it became a country rock room with bands upstairs and a mechanical bull downstairs. This summer the club went rock, with lesser known (i.e. cheaper) bands downstairs and a showcase room upstairs.

Unfortunately, no one has been turning out to see the expensive touring acts (Chris Hall, Capitol Records Artist, The Spencer Davis Group, and Seattle's HIFI) and the club has been sold. The small downstairs room will remain open "for as long as we can hang in there", booking bands at only $1,200 per six day week. I've heard that the new owners are going to gut the interior and turn the place into a beer hall.

In Gastown, The Savoy continues to do well; they have a regular clientele, and they don't change with the trends. Gary Taylor's Rock Room is not exactly thriving, but Gary and staff have stick-to-it-ness, and hopefully will scrape through this bad patch.

Apparently, things aren't any better across Canada. Toronto, the "music-hub" is supposedly faring worse than Vancouver, with a stagnating scene. Grossman's, The Edge, and The Horseshoe (the only places worth going to) all closed down last month. I wonder what's going on.

It's like a breath of fresh air to go to The Commodore (although without air conditioning in boils in the heat). Capacity crowds continue to attend the shows. Most of these concerts are booked by Perryscope Concert Productions, who also handle video broadcasts of the big fights.

The line-up for the next little while is quite amazing: The Cure (from England) Aug. 26th, Icehouse (from Australia) Aug. 27th, Muddy Waters Aug. 28th, Peter Tosh (two shows) Aug.

29th, The Tubes Sept. 2nd, The Roches Sept. 6th. For confirmation of further dates and prices, Perryscope's number is 604-669-2125.

The more established bands in town are doing very well. Powder Blue's second LP "Thirsty Ears" is out now. Their first album "Uncut" did exceptionally well. I found Powder Blue's pop-blues much more fun and interesting when they were a struggling club band; they're sort of complacent now.

Doug and the Slugs are wrapping up their second album. "Cognac and Bologna" was a good first effort, but to fully appreciate the talent in the band, and Doug Bennett's bordering-on-obscene/cute humor, one has to see Doug and the Slugs live.

The new first album I can't wait to get my hands on is the Payola's "In A Place Like This". Oh yes—the Z.Z. Top crowd at the Coliseum booed the Payola's off the stage after 15 minutes - what can you say.

11

ACCESSORIES

COOL COVERINGS, $1 PAIR

MAINTENANCE ART WORKS MONGO

and or gallery

I was enticed into going to see this "performance piece" by a flyer which read to the effect that this woman turned garbage into art. Wouldn't that entice you? When I got there, I was handed a program of sorts which set up all kinds of premises which the artist asked you to accept before viewing the exhibit. It was about the stifled creativity of the common laborer, posing the problem of the co-existence of creative life and "maintenance work" (her term: work which maintains (only?) a reasonable standard of living). It also vaguely mentioned the "Woman in work factor", although this was never developed or even hinted at in the lecture (save for the fact that the "artist" herself was a woman).

Walking in, I saw photos mounted on the walls; no real planned display, simply placed where there was ample space. They were all photos of people at work. Okay. So what? Some were photos of Ukeles at "work" too. This is a joke; right?

The lecture began: she appeared in green standard work pants, an orange City of NY Sanitation Dept. t-shirt, and a green vest with orange glow-tape on the back to warn oncoming cars of something oncoming. Ukeles told us that she worked for the Sanitation Dept. of NY, had a baby, and became inspired. She was inspired by having to change so many diapers without the job ever being completed. She was inspired to examine the problem of mind-numbification in the ordinary worker. Okay. So she went out and shook the hands of all the garbage men

(or "sanitary art_s", as she prefers to call them), and talked with them about their jobs. For a year.

She found that they were blistered, calloused, muscle-aching, and generally not cosmetically attractive people. She also discovered that the public abused these workers by wrapping their garbage improperly and often assaulted them with such insults as "Get away from her you smelly garbage man!" Ms. Ukeles was obviously stirred--how could the public be so inconsiderate, so inhuman?! She saw the work of the garbagemen as artful, and set out to convince the masses of this theory.

She did not state any relevant facts such as salary, benefits, hours, etc.

Anyway, here is what she did to help these men: she asked workers to make one hour a day "maintenance art" rather than "maintenance work". (This could remain secret to the public, but ought to make the

worker feel better. Apparently, art in this case is a state of mind.

At the end of the year with the NYSD, she sent the men an 80 ft. long telex (which officials forced her to condense). She read a good 15 minutes of it, pouring out her heart with eloquent declarations such as, "We love love love you". Each sentence exceeded the last in ridiculousness.

For the end, I thought, she's going to cut off her left breast in reverence to these men. Either that, or she's going to say, "Well I've charged each of you $4 to hear about garbagemen for two hours. Good joke, hmm?" No. The whole thing was in earnest.

Oh yeah, there were also these plastic birds suspended from the ceiling and perched on the wall. I asked her if they were significant in that birds shit on garbagemen, too. Ukeles said the birds were symbolic of children who grow up and "leave the nest". The relevance of that flew out the window, for me. She further informed me that the bird whose heart had been pierced with a feather was "about death". That one I agreed with: I nearly died of boredom.

Many things were missing from this performance. The first that come to mind are verbal adeptness, visual interest, material substance, and PURPOSE. Mierle Laderman Ukeles was silly. But not four dollars' worth.

—Arlene Adler

KEYBOARDS FOR MILLIONS

Casio has these two wonderful new instruments, portable electronic keyboards. The $70 model contains a calculator, a preprogrammed German music box tune, a place for you to program your own tune, several rhythm tracks to choose from, and a one-and-a-half octave keyboard that can actually go up four octaves with different settings. The $150 model is a little bigger, can play chords (the smaller one can just do a note at a time), and has other features. Both have a light, cool sound and either work through built-in speakers or through your amp. The small one works either on AC current or batteries. You can take it places where you can't take an acoustic guitar. Pack one in your briefcase and play it while waiting for the bus.

—Clark Humphrey

corporate top 10

1.	Black Flag	6-Pack
2.	Soft Cell	Tainted Love
3.	Laurie Anderson	O Superman
4.	Dead Kennedys	Too Drunk to Fuck
5.	Tom Tom Club	Wordy Rappinghood
6.	Joy Division	Love Will Tear Us Apart
7.	Fartz	"9 Smash Hits"
8.	Bow Wow Wow	Prince of Darkness
9.	Kate Bush	Sat in Your Lap
10.	David Bowie	Ching A Ling

LPS

1.	Au Pairs	Playing with a Different Sex
2.	Delta 5	See the Whirl
3.	T.S.O.L.	Dance with me
4.	Killing Joke	What's this for!
5.	Chunks	Compilation
6.	Joy Division	Unknown Pleasures
7.	Anti Pasti	
8.	Warsaw	(Joy Division bootleg)
9.	UB40	Present Arms
10.	Siouxie & the Banshees	JuJu

seattle dj top 20

THIS WEEK	LAST WEEK	TITLE	ARTIST
1	4	Ha Ha Ha	Flipper
2	6	Heaven Up There	Echo & the Bunnymen
3	12	Nightline	The Rats
4	2	Boom/Das Ah Riot	Bush Tetras
5	11	Shadow/Leaving	Delta Five
6	10	Demystification	Zounds
7	8	Pretty in Pink	Psychedelic Furs
8	15	To Hell With Poverty	Gang of Four
9	-	Never Gonna Cry	Eurythmics
10	1	Too Drunk To Fuck	Dead Kennedys
11	5	The Right to be Italian	Holly & the Italians
12	14	Can't Be Happy	Fastbacks
13	9	What We All Want	Gang of Four
14	7	Obvious	Au Pairs
15	17	Tanz Mit Mir	DAF
16	20	Signals Calls & Marches	Mission of Burma
17	19	Poppas got a brand new pigbag	Pigbag
18	-	Because this world stinks	Fartz
19	-	As Seen on TV	Student Nurse
20	3	Primary	The Cure

12

RAMONES

"we can't play unless we're real sick.."

NEIL HUBBARD

March 6, 1977, brought New York's Ramones to Seattle. This show had an important impact on the local music scene. It gave Seattle youngsters the first glimpse of the "punk" phenomenon that was taking the East Coast and England by storm.

The first time I heard the Ramones was on a cassette in the Telepaths practice studio. Tomata duPlenty of the Tupperwares (later the Screamers) had just returned from New York with a cassette of the Ramones live at CBGB's. The tape was badly distorted, but from what I could tell, the Ramones' set sounded like a subway train roaring between stations, pausing for a screech of feedback, a quick 1,2,3,4, and on to the next station.

After this, the first Ramones album was released. Still my favorite, it contains the classics "Blitzkreig Bop," "Now I Wanna Sniff Some Glue," "53rd & 3rd," among others. Only one song clocks in over two and a half minutes -- "I Don't Wanna Go Down To The Basement" at 2:35. I wore the record out with almost daily playings, so you may imagine how excited I was to hear that the Ramones were coming to town.

Except they were going to appear at the (yeuch) Aquarius Tavern. Billed on a Sunday night with some drippy bar band, the show was destined to be lost in oblivion. Most of the Ramones' real fans too, would miss the show, as they were under 21.

So, the enterprising college student that I was at the time, I got on the phone to Sire

Records to see just what was up on this Aquarius gig. Referred by Sire to the Ramones booking agent in Hollywood, it was learned they would be doing three days in the great Northwest: Friday in Bremerton (!), Saturday in Aberdeen (!!), and Sunday in Seattle (!!!).

"Hey" I tell the agent with all my subtle candor, "Anyone who happens to see the Ramones at the Aquarius won't give a damn anyway." So he says "If you can find a better place, I'll give you the show." This, folks, is how one gets into Big Time Booking.

Finding a place for the show was the hard part. The Moore Theatre wouldn't have it, the Seattle Center was booked; along with every other small hall in town. But the Olympic Hotel's Georgian Ballroom was available. My partner (whom I decline to give credit to for being a blatant rip-off) and I secured the room with a deposit, notified the agent, and had posters printed. For the opening act, we booked the Meyce, the only deserving unit in town.

Friday night, we ferried across the Sound to Bremerton for the Ramones' first ever appearance in the Northwest. Prepare for culture shock. The Club, Natasha's, was a large community center type beer hall run by two mongoloid type cretins. Members of the audience, mostly Navy types were allowed to bring in their own beer, cases and cases of it. The rules also allowed the manly dudes to be escorted by one chicky under 21, but not under 18! The opening act, Crown, slogged diligently through their covers -- Boston, Kansas, Queen, while the crowd diligently guzzled their cool ones. They were obviously not prepared for the Ramones, and did not appear to care either. By the time the set was halfway over, most of the crowd had split. But the Ramones were great.

The band then travelled to Aberdeen for a show at the Rocker Tavern. Some shrewd character taped that Aberdeen show and it was available as a bootleg "Ramones at Your Birthday Party" for a while. Advance ticket sales for the Olympic Hotel show had been phenomenal, considering the short publicity campaign.

By showtime, when the Ramones arrived at the staid Olympic Hotel, chaos was rampant. In the lobby, middle aged conventioneers glanced warily at the fans

lining up outside the Georgian Room. The hotel staff seemed composed enough, but appeared poised for emergency action. The band, eager to get to their luxuriously appointed dressing room--the hotel kitchen--burst into the room where two police officers were preparing for it all to begin. The Ramones Four pile up "Three Stooges" style, mutter apologies and back out sheepishly.

Jim Basnight's Meyce were warming the crowd up with their innocent, energetic pop music. The Meyce were well liked, being a bright, enthusiastic young group. They played their hit tunes "I Want You," "Live In The Sun," "She Got Fucked," "Keep On Walkin," among others. Little did anyone realize that it would be their last public performance. Less than one year after their debut at the TMT show, the Meyce called it quits.

The Ramones took to the stage and proceeded to show Seattle the shape of things to come. Hard, fast, loud, hummable pop tunes with Mad magazine lyrics. Four leather jackets pounding out the sound. Tuning Seattle's pinheads into the speed of life in New York City. Seattle had been injected with the punk bug.

Perhaps times now are not all that different. What follows are excerpts from an interview with Joey Ramone. It took place at a Ballard party following the show. Much of it reads like it could have been done last week.
NH: Would you ever consider changing the style of your music?
JR: Naaa.
NH: Why Not?
JR: Uhmm..well, we like what we're doing, ya know...we're doin' what we wanna do, ya know?
NH: How long do you think you can keep on doing what you're doing?
JR: Well, we can just keep on goin', ya know. We have a lot of stuff written for the next album. I mean, if we wanted a change, we could change, we're not limited to any certain style or anything like that. It's not like we can't do anything else. We can do anything we want to do. It's just that this is what we wanna do.
NH: But how long do you think the public will accept that?
JR: There are still a lot of people who haven't even heard of the Ramones. We're not stuck in any one certain situation or style, ya know.
NH: What's your definition of the word "punk"?
JR: Well, punk is just...uhmm... a punk is just someone who wants to have a good time, ya know.
NH: Do you think that rock & roll has always been "punk" except that it hasn't been called that?
JR: Naa. There's a difference. Everybody's being called a punk now, and it's really a lot of bullshit.
NH: Where do you get all your energy?
JR: We're all hyper. We drink a lot of coffee.
NH: No ya don't! I had dinner with you tonight. Any special foods?
JR: Jack In The Box.
NH: Yea. But what I don't understand is--that food isn't very nutritious...
JR: We can't play unless we're real sick. So we go to Jack In The Box.

Ed. Note: The Ramones will be returning to Seattle within the next few months.

13

CALENDAR

AS OF THIS ISSUE, WE ARE OFFERING FREE CALENDAR LISTINGS FOR CLUBS, BANDS, ETC. PLEASE CALL IN ANY INFORMATION YOU WANT INCLUDED IN THE NEXT ISSUE BY FRIDAY, AUGUST 28. 634-0303. THE NEXT ISSUE WILL COVER SEPTEMBER 2 TO SEPTEMBER 15.

Danceland USA: 8/22: Visible Targets, Student Nurse; Vacuums; 8/29 Omni Beat from San Francisco w/ Discors

DEZ'S 400: 8/19: Cathedral 8/20-22: Reputations; 8/23 8th Avenue Blues Band; 8/24-26: Matinee Idols. 8/27: Red Dress; 8/29: Eddie & The Atlantics; 8/30:Battle of the bands showcase

Popeye's (in Olympia): 8/25-29: Bruce Maier Band; 8/30 Ronnie Lee; 9/6 Student Nurse;

Audio Letter: U.C.T. Hall on Sept 9

Hall of Fame: 8/19-20 No Cheese Please, 8/21-22 Citizen Sane, 8/26-29 Strypes.

Jeff Lorber Fusion at the Showbox August 21

Peter Tosh at the Paramount, August 30.

WREX: 8/21: the Rats from Portland; 8/22: Visible Targets; 8/26 Student Nurse/ Rapid-i; 8/27-28 Das Bloc from San Francisco; 8/29 Three Swimmers

FOR FURTHER CALENDAR INFO:
Ad Lib	854-3059
Astor Park	625-1578
Baby-O's	624-6558
Dez's 400	283-5825
G-Note	783-8112
Gatsby's	455-0666
Goldies on 45th	632-3453
Hibble & Hyde's	623-1541
Rainbow	632-3360
Shire	937-4362
Tugs	623-2813/
	762-0353
WREX	625-9739

STOP PRESS

The Toxic Reasons show, scheduled at Freeway Hall August 18th was cancelled when F. Hall backed out of their agreement. Apparently, the hall doesn't want hardcore bands playing there anymore.

Norman Bately has a new show on KRAB, Thursdays 10-12, 107.7 FM

The Fag House is no more. The eviction process (which the landlord commenced with no good reason) was apparently real ugly.

Rapid-i is currently recording an EP, to be out in October.

Mike Refuzor can now report what it's like having a mohawk when you're in King County Jail...

Contrary to P-I reports, Steve Pritchard will be continue to book WREX after all.

Husker Du has recorded a live EP, to be available soon

Tacoma's Famous Potatoes have been touring Eastern Washington and Idaho: they plan to return for a Seattle gig in the near future.

Sally Johnson, who books Vancouver's Smilin' Buddha, wants someone else to take the job Greg Simmmons is now managing Joe Despair & the Future.

Rumor has it Stephen Rabow may be hitting the commercial air waves again soon...

B+ movie series at WREX is no more. If you're reading this Tuesday afternoon, Myra Breckinridge, the worst movie ever made, will be playing tonite. A party, free beer.

Pop Defect are recording a demo with Enemy drummer Pete Barnes producing.

****
GORILLA ROOM BENEFIT TICKETS ARE AVAILABLE AT ALL BASS OUTLETS
****

FUNNIES

14

Issue #5

This issue seems to be all about the perils of promoting local concerts. The boycott of certain local concert producers draws out a long rebuttal from Steve Pritchard. He writes that he can't possibly be the big promoter in town because he can hardly control his own life. He admits to paying bands in beer, and points out the inherent risk in booking unknown local bands. A festival called "Rock Against the Liquor Board" is covered. Ten bands play their hearts out for free but the promoters still lost money. The economics of the music industry are harangued.

The review of another local concert includes a delightful typo — rapour for rapport — and congratulates the bands for bypassing promoters and doing the show themselves. Yet another review begins by giving kudos to the venue and not the bands: "The Roma [Tavern] has a great location right on the bus line between Ballard and the University, just up from the liquor store."

The Toxic Reason concert was cancelled when the venue cancelled the rental. The band members nonetheless really enjoyed their four days in Seattle, and to make up for the cancelled concert, Bria Conradus reviewed a Toxic Reason concert she saw in San Francisco.

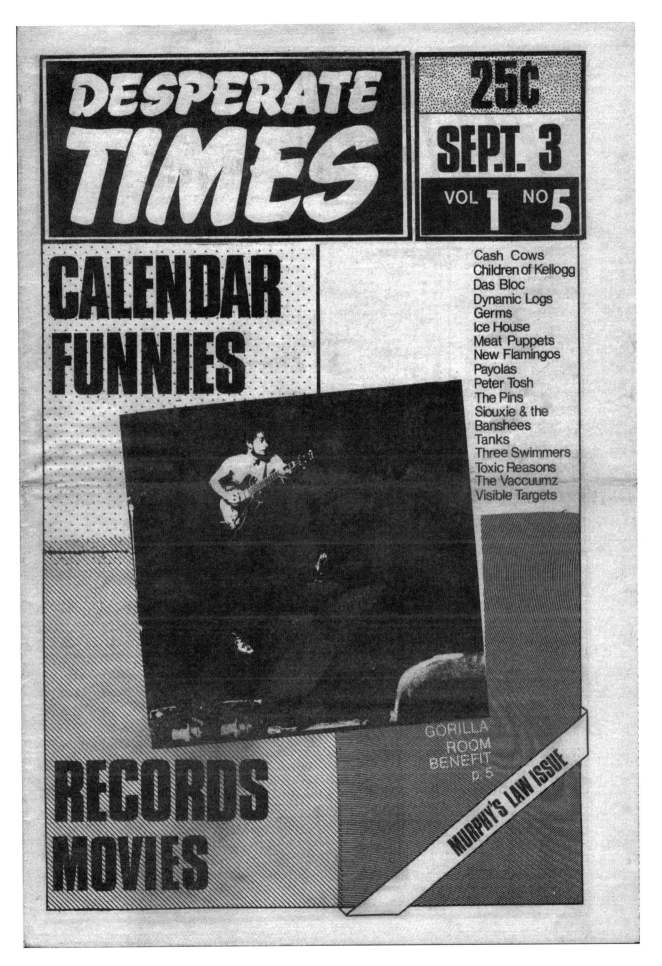

DESPERATE TIMES

25¢

SEPT. 3

VOL **1** NO **5**

CALENDAR FUNNIES

Cash Cows
Children of Kellogg
Das Bloc
Dynamic Logs
Germs
Ice House
Meat Puppets
New Flamingos
Payolas
Peter Tosh
The Pins
Siouxie & the Banshees
Tanks
Three Swimmers
Toxic Reasons
The Vaccuumz
Visible Targets

GORILLA
ROOM
BENEFIT
p. 5

MURPHY'S LAW ISSUE

RECORDS MOVIES

DESPERATE TIMES

Editor:
Daina Darzin

Associate Editor:
Captive

Art Director:
Billy Shaffer

Photography Director:
Skip Beattie

B.M. and D.B.
Maire Masco

Contributing Writers:
Berlin, Bria Conradus,
Peter Davis, Verna Doherty,
Clark Humphrey, Kathy
Moschel, Mark McLaughlin,
Wilum Pugmyr, Johnny Rubato,
Heidi Weispfenning

Contributing Photographers/
Artists: Bob Howanic,
Matthew Courtway Cam Garrett

Cover Photo Credit :
Skip Beattie

Special thanxes abound (We're
so fucking grateful round here)
1) To the manufacturers of
glass bottles, without which
life would be far more dull
2) To Murphy, whose law produces those moments which
let us see the dirty truth.
3) To Consolidated Printing,
for putting up with the un-
orthodox demeanor of our layout sheets 4) To Steve Pritchard, for giving us all sort
of swell controversy to write
about.
DESPERATE TIMES is published
more or less bi-monthly by
On The Edge Press, 4525 9th
Ave. N.E., Seattle, Washington, 98105. (206) 634-0303

OPINION

Hey, we gotta fill this space
somehow so here I am only
cause I'm the only fucking
body with enough speed in me
to be up at this death's-
door hour, when the sane and
middle class are copping z's.

This is, this here OPINION
space is spozed to deal with
the serious and pressing
issues of the music community
an' nothing serious & pressing
has happened lately, which I
for one find to be a fucking
relief. In fact, if one more
serious & pressing thing
happened, I was just gonna
puke. So, with no S&Ps to
deal with, I thought I'd
just put down some random
OPINIONs and quotes. These
were heard mostly in bars
at advanced stages of in-
ebriation, so take them with
that in mind.

Anyway, this is a contest
(I just decided that). Send
in your guesses as to who said
these things. The person
who gets the most right gets
a swell prize, like sex with
the local musician of your
choice. Hell, I know we're
all lazy, so I'm going to
make this into a nifty clip
& mail form (see below)
so get those guesses coming
in! Good luck, folks, and
remember that ultimately

MURPHY'S LAW ROOLS!

-Berlin

$1

IN THE MAIL

Thanks, but no guest list?

Greetings D.T.'ers,
I recently, quite by accident
came upon your magazine in a
record shop. I found your
magazine impressively good
for a local publication. I
regularly check out the
local band scene. In these
days of spiraling inflation
I still try to buy what
records I can afford.

My favorite local bands are
Section 8, The Visible
Targets, Portland's Untouchables, and at times, Three
Swimmers. I would like to
see your magazine review as
many independent, import and
off-the-wall records as
possible. It would also help
if you could specify what
particular type of music it
is such as hardcore punk,
dance-rock, reggae-rock,
electronic-pop, etc. So
people know what to check
out. Remember there is no
progressive radio.

Concerning your article
"local biz" in issue no. 4,
I think the owners and promoters of clubs and small
halls and also the band
members themselves should
make everyone pay for admis-
sion and eliminate the
guest-list. Surely members
of Seattle's "avant-garde"
and hardcore scene can afford
a few bucks. The band members deserve more funds.

Thanks, Tomas

P.S. The Room's show at WREX
was great. Especially their
political and social songs.
A very timely show indeed.
I can't wait for Halloween.

Nancy's watchin' you

To Whom It May Concern,

Please answer my cry for
help! I am a deranged
psychopath. I constantly
find myself hurtling into
so called punk clubs and
dancing my tuschy off! Help!
Help! Help! I know I must
be sick. Why do I enjoy
bands playing in clubs, the
noise (dare I say music? To
do so might offend Mozart!)
they produce, screaming
through my aural-orifice at
90,000,000 decibel (did I
spell that properly? Is
the Muzak turning me into
a gibbering, third grade,
illiterate? Will my hear-
ing be impaired? Will I
become impotent? Does "Cold
Water ALL" truly cuddle
milk?) OH GOSH! My mommy
was so disgusted the day I
dyed my hair chartreuse; if
she found out it went so well
with my green pubes mayhap
she would not frown so;
though I think she would
be upset at the paper clip
in my foreskin. She will go
into even greater depression
when I tell her my new lovers
name is Rover.

Somehow these clubs have
changed the weave of the
existence which is my life.
No longer do I feel a simple
joy in the playing of Go-Fish
or Crazy-Eights. Such simple
pleasures, The very reason
for life and breath before
I started smashing into clubs,
are now found only in the act
of spitting on people, or
playing a friendly game of
mumblety-peg with George, the
homosexual policeman who sells
me drugs.

I knew I was in a terrible
state of mental health when
I registered for the draft

a month ago, only because I
wanted the card to patch my
underwear. Then today I
had my nose tattooed; it
says "I love my asshole,
but I don't love you."

Help me someone, please?!
I must be stopped before
the clubs open again to-
night.

-Ronnie Reagan

Rebuttal #1

Dear Desperate Times:

In regards to "Nobody's"
letter in the last issue--
please inform your readers
that the gum of choice is
Hubba Bubba, not Bubble Yum.
(Bazooka will do in a pinch.)

Yours truly,

Rob Morgan

Comic Plea

An open letter from Billy
Shaffer to our readers:

This is the Art (?) Director.
Desperate Times has allowed
me this space to make a plea
for all you struggling artist
types out there to send in
your artwork. I am particularly interested in expanding
our "Funnies" section. So
all you closet cartoonists
get off your duffs. This is
your big chance! Imagine
seeing your work in a presti-
gious periodical like Desperate Times! Wow! Amuse your
friends! Impress your parents!

Do we pay anything, you ask?
Nope. At least, not yet. But
how can one compare monetary
rewards with the personal sat-

(CONTINUED ON NEXT PAGE)

Contest

1. Pipe down, bonerlip!

   _____

2. You've sucked so many
   dicks that if they co-
   vered you you'd look
   like a porcupine!

   _____

3. Heroin is not as good
   as sex but better than
   Led Zeppelin.

   _____

4. Can I have a cigarette?
   Can I have a joint? Can
   I have a beer? Can I
   crash here tonight?

   _____

5. I got crabs from the
   first woman I ever slept
   with, but I didn't mind,
   it was such a relief to
   get it over with.

   _____

6. Hi, I'm on the guest list,
   I'm one of the Heats.

   _____

7. The Vapors are without
   a doubt the most talented
   English band to come out
   of 1980.

   _____

8. I open soup cans with my
   ears.

   _____

Prize

If I win, I want to fuck:

☐ a. Steve Hoffman (Fartz)

☐ b. Annie Rose (& Thrillers)

☐ c. Mike Refuzor (DTZ)

☐ d. Ian Fisher (Cowboys)

☐ e. Lulu (Fastbacks)

☐ f. Todd Fuchs (X-15)

☐ g. Mr. Epp (& the Calculations)

☐ h. Upchuck (Fags)

☐ i. Suzanne Grant (Enemy)

☐ j. Other: _____

You

NAME _____

STREET _____

CITY _____

ZIP _____

isfaction you'll receive supporting Seattle's New Music
scene? Don't ask me. It's a
rhetorical question! Anyway,
send stuff in. We may not
print it, but we'll at least
look and give an honest opinion.

If you don't have any comic
strips, send drugs. We give
honest opinions of those,
too. Please include an SASE
if you want your art back.

Thanks,
Billy Shaffer

Rebuttal #2

An open letter to my critics:

I've never done a show at the
Arena or Paramount. In fact,
I've never produced a show
larger than the Showbox.
Yet, there is a common mis-
conception in Seattle that
I am Mr. Rock, a big succes-
ful promoter who controls
the scene. That is somewhat
laughable since I sometimes
feel that I barely control
my own life. Lately, I
have been the subject of
some negative and inaccurate
press in your magazine as
well as in the PI and the
Seattle Sun. This letter
is an attempt to clear the
air and unconfuse the issues.
I would like to try to explain who I am, what I do and
why I do it. First, a partial
list of my accomplishments
that I feel have been contri-
butions to the new music
scene.

January, at the Showbox, a
four-band punk show featuring the Subhumans. The
first punk show in Seattle
in months. We drew the
largest crowd ever, up to
that point, for a Seattle
hardcore show. It was an
excellent show, all four
bands were great. We broke
even. In April, I broke with
Showbox Attractions and went
independent. With Mike
Vraney, we produced the first
ever International Punk Explosion. Six bands for five
bucks from three different
countries. We added the
three local bands just because they asked. It was a
wild show, the kind no promoter in his right mind would
touch. The kids had a great
time and we made $150 each.
In May, with two friends, I
produced the Stranglers'
first Seattle appearance. I
felt it too was a good show.
I made $90. In June, I took
an act that nobody wanted and
everyone in the business told
me not to do it. It was the
great John Cale. The general
belief was that no one would
pay to see Cale. I charged
three bucks and sold over a
thousand tickets. It was to
this date my proudest show,
especially considering that
the Vapors had played there
the night before for $8 and
the Plasmatics were there
the night after at $10.50
advance. I felt Cale was the
best artist I had ever worked
with. The concert was a cultural coup. Things got busy
in July. Mike, Jim Lightfoot
and I did the Dead Kennedys.
We charged five bucks and
only had six days to promote
it. Jello was tremendous and
once again, the show was
successful. I made $150 and
got to see one of my favorite
bands. Also in July, I did
the Psychedelic Furs, one of
the most creative groups in
existence. Poor choice of
opening bands (my mistake),
but the Furs pulled it off
beautifully. I broke even
but would have made some
money if the guest list had
been controlled. Two nights
later, 9-9-9 at the Showbox.
Financially my most succes-
ful concert. I made $600.

All of these concerts had a
few things in common. First,
they were all shows that I
wanted to see and would've
bought a ticket for. Second,
they were not hard acts to
secure. No other promoters
were going after these acts
because they were all considered high financial risks.
Third, they were all done out
of one main, overriding moti-
vation: "If I don't bring
this show to town, then this
show won't come to town".
There was a serious cultural
vacuum and I wanted to try
to fill it.

I cannot even count the times,
through all this, that local
bands have called me and asked
to be put on a show. It almost always goes something
like this: "We want to play
that show, we don't care about
the money, we just want to be
on a good show". I usually
made verbal agreements with
local bands. If I made money,
they would make money, if I
lost money or broke even, I
wouldn't be able to pay them.
If I needed to give guarantees
to local bands to open for
national acts, I would choose
established bands with followings. Through this arrangement, however, I was to give
unknown or unestablished bands
a chance to play in a venue
where they would not normally
get that chance. They got
exposure and a chance to play
before big groups. Some bands
that have played for me under
these conditions includ the
Fartz, the Refuzors, RPA,
Idiot Culture, The Pudz, X-15,
Joe Despair and the Future, and
Autosax. The Fartz are an
exception because they always
say they don't want money
(just buy us beer if you make
some bread) but in all other
cases I've paid the bands
that played under those
conditions one the shows that
produce any profit.

Now I am suddenly being accused
of exploiting local bands.
Most of the accusations are
coming from bands I've never
directly booked (Audio Leter,
Rapid-i). I am not bothered
that the band members got
together and asked for more
orthodox booking policies.
They are looking out for
their interests. It's a
countercultural movement we're
dealing with, and that kind
of unity is needed in order to
survive. I met with represen-
tatives of some of the bands.
They felt that most of their
complaints could be dealt with
by having things in writing.
I agreed to have standard
contracts drawn up for all
future shows within seven days
and would deliver most everything the bands wanted within
my power. I have finished
the contracts and they are now
in use at WREX.

I feel that when I agree to
let an unknown band like the
Refuzors or DTZ play a show
that that's my way of supporting local bands who have something new and interesting to
offer. I am supporting
them, not exploiting them.
What other promoter in
Seattle has the guts or the
foresight to let the Fartz
or the Maggot Brainz play the
Showbox? Mike Vraney was
the only other one, but he's
not in Seattle any more. I
choose local bands because
I like the people in the
groups or because I like what
they're trying to do, not
because of some trade-off in
the business or because of
a favor owed. I try to get
good shows for the bands
that hunger for good shows
and don't sell out to get
them. I would like nothing
better than to pay these bands
good money for performing.
They give a lot and they

deserve it. I deserve a
decent income for what I do
and I am not getting it yet.
But I won't give up. I feel
that if I quit doing shows
that Seattle would get real
boring for new music fans.
Thank you to Desperate
Times for this space.

—Steve Pritchard

THIS IS IT!

FOR NOW

AFTER THIS ISSUE, THE STAFF OF DESPERATE
TIMES IS GOING TO TAKE A VACATION. WE'RE
TIRED AND BROKE. WE'RE GONNA GET SOME
SLEEP AND MAKE SOME MONEY. AND THEN
WE'RE GOING TO DO IT AGAIN. WE'RE STILL
LOOKING FOR ARTISTS, WRITERS, AND PEOPLE
TO SELL ADS AND DO OTHER BUSINESS STUFF.
NEW BLOOD AND NEW ENERGY (LABOR OF LOVE
FREAKS, THIS IS YOUR BIG CHANCE). TO
ALL OF YOU WHO'VE COME UP TO US AND
SAID YOU LIKE THIS RAG, KEEP YOUR EYES
PEELED. WE SHALL RETURN.......

2

MOVING VIOLA
PATTER POP FROM S.F.

DAS BLOC   WREX   AUGUST 28

Das Bloc is real obnoxious, but just cute and talented enough to pull it off. They're a shitkicker power pop band (if you can imagine that combination) with a tight, professional sound, in the same ballpark as the Romantics, more in attitude than musically. Their attitude is where the obnoxiousness comes in: Lead singer Owen Masterson pulls all that "HELLOOO, Seattle/

You gotta DANCE, you're not dancing, you gonna just stand out there and CLAP?" shit that is endearing only when Joan Jett does it. He also does I'm-a-rock-star poses copped from just about everyone, but mostly from Bruce Springsteen, Johnny Rotten, and Mick Jagger (if you can imagine that combination). The crowd bought it, though, particularly the women in

the front row. (Masterson looks like he gets laid a whole lot on the road). The second night, Das Bloc repeated both patter and costumes, but--OK, I'm a sucker for high- energy, badass rocking music, and Das Bloc has their shit down in that department. I'd love to see them again, just--hey, shut up and play. I'll dance, already, OK?

—D.D.

Rastamen, and a suprising number of babies and children, Now it seems to me that there's something wrong with that. Granted, it wasn't as loud as a lot of shows I've been to, but children's hearing is easily damaged, and whether you like the little critters or not, you've got to admit it wouldn't be fun to be deaf by 12. Anyway, back to the matter at hand. There was a rather strong smell of the evell marijuana (ganja to the reggae initiated) in the air. The first band that played w ere the Dynamic Logs, a local tavern favorite. They consist of 6 men and one woman, use diverse instruments like trombone, saxophone and flute, and have an upbeat, danceable bar band sound that relies heavily on horns and bass. It's not exactly my favorite style of music, obviously, (or I'd be writing for another local paper which shall go unnamed) but they're good at what they do. They played a short tight set and won the audience over pretty thoroughly.

During the break, I wandered around, discovered Fartz graffiti in the woman's bathroom, and listened to the reggae on the P.A. Would you believe an instrumental of the Bonanza theme mingled with the William Tell overture? Niether would I, but they played it.

Next up on the bill was the Rafe Gale Band, if I got their name right. They're more of a sould band, with emphasis on horns and percussion. There's 8 men all in white, and a woman (Shawna Ray--and I hope the spelling's right) who gets to deviate and wear a blue blouse. It took me a couple of songs to get used to her voice, which was rather high and piercing, but it eventually grows on you. They did one number called "Life On Life" where they asked for a little audience participation, with hands, voices, and such. It took a lot of work to get the crowd going, but the results were fairly satisfactory. It was another short set, but they went over well.

While I waited, I noticed signs of the renovation in progress. Carpets were ripped up and chandeliers were plastic wrapped. I wonder how they're going to get all the years of resins off of everything.

The crowd was quite friendly, sort of a party atmosphere, except that people seem to be much stingier with their drugs than in past years. Its just as well, I probably wouldn't have been coherent enough to write this. Anticipation was building rapidly. People cheered each roadie, change of lighting and pause in the music. Finally, after the audience had practically cheered themselves hoarse, Peter Tosh took the stage.

He started off with a fairly soft number to warm us up gently. His 7 man band was

(CONTINUED ON NEXT PAGE)

TIGHT ICE   ICEHOUSE and THE PINS

MOORE THEATER   AUGUST 26

What good a promotional campaign from a major record label can do. Icehouse, an Australian quartet formerly called Flowers (before they came to conquer America and get rich), is getting airplay on Seattle's "rock" radio station. Because of Chrysalis' promotional effort the Moore Theater was nearly filled for Icehouse's debut Seattle performance.

Icehouse does not play heavy metal (but one would think so if he/she judged their music by the crowd at their show). They play synthesizer and guitar based music in nearly the same vein as Ultravox. Lead vocalist/guitarist Iva Davies, looks and sings (when he wants to) a lot like David Bowie.

They didn't rely completely on their music to entertain the stoned and seated crowd (they should have played the Showbox). Icehouse had a fairly elaborate light show and a dry ice fog machine (which was used on "Icehouse"

and "Walls". Their set was rather tight and well rehersed. Some members of the audience even bothered to stand up and applaud the two songs which are apparently getting airplay ("We Can Get Together" and "Icehouse"). The crowd seemed to like Icehouse (they sure screamed and whistled a lot, like every time Seattle or sex was mentioned).

Oh yes, they did an excellent encore of John Lennon's "Cold Turkey" in which Iva Davies sounded exactly like the late Lennon. (Davies also sounds like Lou Reed on "Nothing To Do" which they unfortunately didn't do).

Seattle's own Pins opened the show! Neat. They played a full set of pointless power pop. The guitarist was cool though. He had one of the ugliest guitars I've ever seen. The crowd sure did like it, though, whenever the bassist said "fuck".

—Mark McLaughlin

TOSH REGGAE MON

PETER TOSH

PARAMOUNT   AUGUST 30

It was the last rock show at the Paramount. From now on they're booking goodies like the Osmonds. There was an air of one last fling in the crowd, and the security crew seemed calmer and looser than I've ever seen them before. They were letting people get away with all those picky little offenses like running and smoking (gasp). The audience was a lot whiter than I expected, with an assortment of hippie s, punks,

---

TIONS

THE SACRED AND THE PROFANE

ERIC SCHMIDT

excellent, and included one of the original Wailers, Dreamy Vision, on percussion. As well as being a fine percussionist, he should get the award for the longest dreadlocks of the night. Clear to his waist, they were. Note: I've always wondered how you wash dreadlocks. Anybody out there know? Tosh had a cap over his, which weren't revealed till much later.

His music seems to have a more pop-reggae feel, or maybe I should say accesible than a lot that I've heard. But don't get me wrong, this man may associate with the likes of the Rolling Stones but he's a true Rastaman. About halfway through the show he gave us a rap on Rastafari (the messiah), the whys and wherefores of reggae, including the statement that it was 85 billion years old (strange, that makes it pre-human at the least), Jah, and other important stuff. He also gave his approval of the audience, making us feel like the best little reggae fans this side of Kingston.

He danced, he smoked--and I don't mean cigarettes--and of course he sang. Classics like "Get Up Stand Up", songs about your heritage (if you're from the North Pole and black you're an African), songs with screaming guitar leads, about being a misfit, about pollution. And of course he did numbers about Rastafari and legalizing marijuana. The sound was clear, although bass-heavy enough to leave my ears a bit shell-shocked, and his voice came through so clearly that you could actually make out the words!

On the main floor, all the people except the fogies residing in the front rows, were up and dancing early on. In the balcony things looked pretty dead. It took "Get Up Stand Up" to get the boring brigade on their toes and they soon cosied back into their comfy little seats, content that they had done their duty by standing and even clapping (gasp) for one song. The band left the stage. We demanded an encore, and the M.C. came on to explain that this was no ordinary encore, this was Round 2!

The band returned to the stage and danced us through four more numbers, singing about Rastas and Babylon, and last, but of course not least, that pot-smokers anthem, "Legalize It". The M.C. came back and introduced the band members, but by this time my ears weren't funcioning too well, and I missed most of it. I retired to the lobby quickly to avoid more conversation with a rather over-friendly character (kept patting my ass), found no party, and slogged on home.

My complaints? I thought it was poor man's music from the Kingston ghetto. Other than that a great show, and a fitting finale for the Paramount.

Rock steady!

--Heidi Weispfenning

Eric Schmidt, a Seattle artist who has spent the last few years in New York, returned on August 23rd to perform excerpts from four verse plays to an audience that seemed equally divided between old friends and expectant first timers. It was an intriguing atmosphere; the lights dim and the floor littered with a variety of semi-precious simulacra. There were rhinestones, plastic cameos and pearls, and a handful of tiny St. Christophers beckoning from pie-shaped wedges of lucite.

The music started and a woman came out to introduce the pieces. Before leaving, she tugged hard at her necklace and more pearls went cascading to the floor.

Schmidt emerged, tall, thin, and oddly pretty, and sat down at a podium between lit candles. Gregorian chants boomed from the speakers as, draped in black, he began The Aunto Villageress: the 15th century. A woman imprisoned in the vatican is to be executed at dawn. Her monologue is a mixture of memories, prayers, and conversations with her only companion - a beetle, who's leg she has inadvertently crushed. In addition, she wonders aloud why the sentence has been passed (she's in love with a mythical giant, and suspects that this is the reason).

Incredible though it may sound, the piece worked. Schmidt's abrupt movements and intonations created enough dramatic tension to carry it off. When the tension broke it was deliberate: moving from tragic soliloquy to incongruous modern references (the beetle is at one point addressed as " O MY YW"), or babbling from word to word in a meaningless exploration of sound.

The Freezing No To All Questions Prison Of Bent Things didn't fare as well. The outfit was remarkable (yellow pants and frilled yellow sleeve garters). The props were remarkable (a circular wooden fence equipped with sharp blades to be revealed at appropriate moments, a strobe light, and a wonderful machine that spat out pearls when cranked). But the total effect, combined with the phrases used, was not remarkable. In fact, theatrically it was almost prosaic.

When Ten Things Get Dead I Give You Ten Thanks was a lover's diatribe directed at BLANK. Example: BLANK, who is ultimately charming and ultimately lucky, seems to want MY pity."

The character sometimes accused itself, sometimes accused those outside of it. In a man's suit covered by a filmy pink negligee, Schmidt maintained his self-sufficiency: "I do not agree with the happiness of ANYTHING."

"else," he added.

The Matador Of Spit Cobras began with a Spit Cobra (one Miss Fitch) clambering up to the second level. Once installed, she read a circular pattern of assertions

regarding her love for the Matador. The Spit Cobra wore a frothy white dress and nonchalantly threw out such statements as "Your love inspires me", "I love you more than you love me", "I am sincere in my dislike for you".

Meanwhile the Matador came out, his black sequined jacket reflecting slivers of light around the darkened room. The pattern looked

like a back drop shot of THE GALAXY. He spoke of his glory, and his beginnings ("Where's Eric?" "He's in church praying. He wants to be the Matador of Spit Cobras!"), and ended with a warm appeal to someone (a Spit Cobra?), in which he was totally convincing. "You have a nice face," he said, giving the last line a sense of both commencement and finality.

Schmidt writes well, moving from the urbane to the eso-

teric, the mundane to the mythical, with barely a twitch. His unusual sense of timing adds to the quality achieved. But, that night at least, his vocabulary of gesture and sound didn't quite come up to the level of the text. Despite this lack he had his moments, and they were definitely worth seeing.

-Captive

4

ROCKING AGAINST THE

So there's the clubs who are rolling in the income from their efficiently dispensed $2.50 mixed drinks, while wrestling with the existential question, , "How many times can you book the Heats?" There's the clubs that juggle artistic integrity with the desire for profit, while trying to stay two steps ahead of the liquor board, fire department, and tax man. An then there's the Gorilla Room, whose trials and tribulations with the aforementioned regulatory agencies must be the classic promoter's Murphy's-law-acid trip-nightmare. The Gorilla Room is real loose and takes outrageous artistic chances, comes up with some true bombs and some killer-set evenings that are better than anything else in town. Sad truth, creativity and shrewd business sense do not often reside in the same person. In their inimitable style, the G. Room put on a wonderful benefit show August 30. The bands sounded great. The crowd had a terrific time. The proceeds were supposed to cover the G. Room's extensive debts so that they could reopen. The show actually lost money. And then, after the club's hangers-out had gone through a day of eulogizing, the G. Room announced they were reopening after all This Friday. For a month (other liquor board penalties still await) and then the plan is to move to another location. Or something like that. You can never tell. This may be completely inaccurate by the time you read it.

For everybody who loves the joint, see you this weekend.

To those who have never been there: you only got a month, go. It's one of the few truly great bars in Seattle.

What follows is photos and notes about August 30, the Gorilla Room's almost-last hurrah.

Daina Darzin

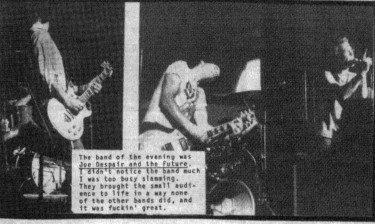

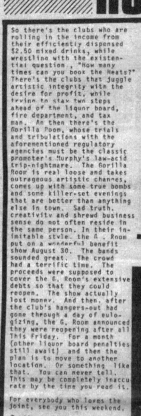

The band of the evening was Joe Despair and the Future. I didn't notice the band much I was too busy slamming. They brought the small audience to life in a way none of the other bands did, and it was fuckin' great.

The Deans opened the show with only a few people in the audience. I like this band when they rock, as they did in their first two numbers. Most of the other songs they did were slower, and I found their music and their enthusiasm if fun to watch.

The Executives are a pretty good band to listen to, but I loathe their image, and listened to them from the door, so I didn't have to look at them. They performed a couple numbers that really sounded tight and fast, among others that did not impress me too much.

Student Nurse is beginning to grow on me. A lot of their material still bores me, but much of what they played sounded exceptionally good, and had the audience moving. "Garbage" is one of my favorite tunes, and it alone makes their 4-song E.P. well worth having.

The Enemy did a really cool thing. Not long after their first number, the guitarists and singer left the stage, and we were treated to a powerful drum solo. Because it was so unexpected, it annoyed a lot of people, and I liked that very much. They performed "Bang Bang You're Dead" and "I Need An Enemy" with so much energy that the audience went wild. They've never been better, and I hope it won't be long before we are treated to another single.

The Fastbacks were the suprise of the evening for me. I don't like their single, and didn't expect to enjoy them. But their first number was an explosive fast, really great song that left me stunned. They have many good songs. But the ones they recorded seem, to me, their most boring and poppy tunes.

5

LIQUOR BOARD

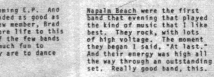

**ALL PHOTOGRAPHS
BY SKIP BEATTIE**

Rapid-i is already a very hot band. A lot of people told me they were there because of the good things they had heard of this group. The band did tunes that will be featured on their forthcoming E.P. And the funk sounded as good as always. A new member, Brad adds a lot more life to this band. One of the few bands that are as much fun to watch as they are to dance to.

Napalm Beach were the first band that evening that played the kind of music that I like best. They rock, with lots of high voltage. The moment they began I said, "At last." And their energy was high all the way through an outstanding set. Really good band, this.

DTZ/Maggot Brains Bonanza: the last act, fittingly enough. "Return with us now to the days of ancient Rome-- the warrior musicians (barely outfitted for one-to-one combat) do battle with a jaded audience armed with beercans and foul saliva..."

That's about what happened. No drum kit, just an overturned keg. The cymbals were trashcan lids-- also used to ward off flying beercans. It didn't take long to get a small riot going. Between one bass solo and a 60-second harmonica run, the only sound to be heard was small pieces of tin bouncing off of larger ones. They managed to capture the spirit of GR in one fell swoop and, actually, it was a lot of fun.

—Wilum Pugmyr

The Rats, from Portland, are a great band who do loads of good raock material. I like the way the bassist sways her bass to and fro to the beat of the songs. Their guitarist is superb, and his vocals are screamed with lots of feeling. Their drummer has a cool "snotty" attitude when he sings, a style that reminds me of Jlohnny Rotten. They have two albums out.

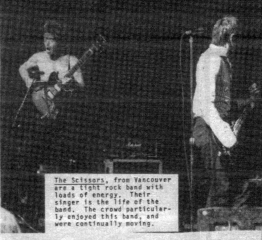

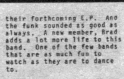

The Scissors, from Vancouver are a tight rock band with loads of energy. Their singer is the life of the band. The crowd particularly enjoyed this band, and were continually moving.

The Fastbacks

LAYOUT BY BOB HOWANIC

6

FASTBACKS
U MEN

U.T.C. HALL   AUGUST 26

U.C.T. Hall has the feel of an Elk's lodge, what with fake wood paneling, scenic pictures, a teeny trophy case, and a polyester fiber-fill plush rug. The accoustics are better than other places I've been to, but the stage is too small. I really liked the broken-down juke box in a forgotten corner of the room. It adds a "nice touch".

The Fastbacks have got the fastest hands I've ever seen, and the most in-control playing I've ever heard. Hot energy! These guys are so fast, you don't even see their hands when they play. Hot set! Four very talented people, two girls, two guys, make up this soon-to-be-written-on-leather-jackets group. The two girls, one on bass, one on guitar, share vocals. They harmonize beautifully and clearly. They're so in tune they don't need to scream the lyrics out. The guitarist in the pink shirt is <u>very cool</u>, but should stop trying to dance and play at the same time until he knows the rhythm better. I loved the unpredictable drumming, in fact the drummer looked like a pro and sounded like a pro.

The question is, folks, is it live, or is it Memorex? LIVE of course. No way could you get 20 bodies slamming for over ten minutes to a bunch of lipsyncing, simulated players!

"This is 1957!"

No, it's too powerful to be 1957. U-Men is the perfect indecision band. They warmed up with some 30 second songs and then went into the heavy stuff. The Sid-a-Jello-like singer screams like the best of 'em, when you can hear him over the loud drums and dominating bass. They're so good you kind of overlook that. I did not hear the guitar from where I stood, I really think the bass dictated the set. One thing guys, next time TURN UP THE VOLUME!

Basically, U-Men kept me guessing whether to love them or not. The material ran hot and lukewarm. Come on, it's very hard to come to a decision when there are these factors involved:

1) Who they played with.
2) How shitty the sound was.
3) Not hearing the guitar.
4) How'd they function in a packaged place.

Conclusion, folks:

Draw your own.

-Verna Doherty

STUDENT NURSE
VISIBLE TARGETS
VACCUUMZ

DANCELAND   AUGUST 23

This was what I call a funny concert. The music, for the most part, was enjoyable, and the various haps and mishaps of the show were rather amusing.

According to custom, the doors opened at 8:00 and the first band went on at 9:45. The Vacuumz play kind of poppy, PIL-y dance music. I liked them, although they'll be better when, given a little more time, they're more comfortable with their own style of music. The little kids dancing around were great, though.

During set changes, I went outside, where the cops were checking cars and being jerks. For a while it looke like a good (sic) case of harassment the way they were treating one guy.

After a beer run, I went back up the infamous Danceland stairs. Unfortunately, I had missed the first part of the Visible Targets set. Worse than that, the sound system was having problems. Even so, the VTs have played much better. I think they were dissappointed by the crowd (only around 30 people) and the P.A. Hopefully, they will do another (all-ages, please!) show with better luck.

<u>Student Nurse</u> walked on stage. Helayna flashed a smile, and you knew everything was going to be alright. The two new members, on bass and guitar, are wonderful additions giving the band more energy, more impetous in their music and seemingly more enthusism to the whole band's stage presense. A wonderful rapour with the audience was established when a home-made particle board bass (?) was brought out. It sounded great, better than any wash-tub I've ever heard, and the crowd loved it. Everyone, that I saw, was dancing and inbetween songs jeers and taunts were exchanged quickly before the next song. Most of their music in melodic, and all of it is innovative. The last song, after three encores, was a particularly beautiful instrumental, that the band claimed was improvised. If you've not heard <u>Student Nurse</u> yet, you really should. I have never heard them sound better, and if this is any indication of what's ahead, Seattle's in for a treat. <u>Student Nurse</u> is incredible!

One additional note: This concert was sponsered and promoted by the bands themselves. Congrats.

--MMM

7

DISORDERLY

NEW FLAMINGOS
HIBBLE & HYDE'S

Sure did like these guys a lot better before they told me they'd been together, in different incarnations, for years. Some things are charming at a band's second gig, and beyond-the-pale lame thereafter. One of them is Rock Moves. Turn Back To Audience, Turn Around Upon First Downbeat. Strum Guitar In Broad Emphatic Gesture. That stuff, you know? The New Flamingos' singer/lead guitarist does that, in kind of a frozen-grimacy way. There were basically two parts to the set: the first was amorphous new wave originals (Pretenders/Clash/Costello run through a blender together). All the songs were designed to be catchy, like

        THIS IS THE HOOK
        THIS IS THE HOOK
        THIS IS THE HOOK
        ....OH, YEAH

After 15 minutes of this, I was ready to leave. At this point, however, the NFs (perhaps inspired by a real funny, drunk black dude who

was dancing around solo on the floor) launched into a cover of James Brown's "I Feel Good (I Got You)", and finally seemed to be having fun with something. For that song, there were wonderful, high-energy and compelling. A few reggae-edged originals followed, which were better than their new wave material by a good

deal. R&B is what the New Flamingos obviously really love, and that's the direction their original material should be going. Fuck being trendy. This band is pretty good technically, particularly on instrumentals, where they don't blow it with Presenting a Stage Show. You want a stage show, hire the afore-mentioned drunk guy. He was great.

-Daina Darzin

RUBBER SHEETS
ROMA TAVERN 8/15

The Roma has a great location right on the busline between Ballard and the University, just up from a liquor store. It serves good diner food all day, reasonably-priced non-Coors beer, two pool tables and a cool juke box. During the height of disco fever, somebody put in a dance floor, a wall of mirrors, and a PA. With the action spread across three intimate rooms, you can do whatever you want.

It's a well-kept secret, this Roma Tav. Only 20 or so paying customers saw Rubber Sheets play there on the 15th. Not that I'd recommend this frat-punk band to many; the guy in the scrub suit, for instance, has got to go. They're like what the Kingsmen must have been when first starting out: cute fake cockiness, a set full of power-pop standards, no unifying "look". Rubber Sheets don't do "Louie Louie" but they do a great "Fever," in a cross between the Peggy Lee version and the Kingsmen-Cramps arrangement. One female singer is quite tall and has a quaint miniskirt; another was decidedly dressed down, in faded white jeans and matching sneakers. They've got a great organist who uses a great old lounge organ; were it my duty to make them stars, I'd build the sound around that organ, have them do more surf tunes and cut out the Devo and Bowie covers. You just can't sing back-up for "Suffragette City" in faded white jeans.

-Clark Humphrey

THREE SWIMMERS
CHILDREN OF KELLOGG
WREX JULY 30

Last time we told you where Audio Leter got their name; this story leads off with the origin of the name of this Audio Leter spinoff.

Children of Kellogg has nothing to do with kiddies getting addicted to the morning white sugar fix. The title's from a recent KCTS documentary about the Idaho mining town whose children are growing up mutated or deformed or just ill, while the city fathers insist that the industrial waste couldn't have done it and won't you just leave us alone please? After the band was named and the gig announced, word came that the mine would be shut down and the whole town put out of work. Your own private Idaho, indeed.

Couldn't hear what Sue Ann Harkey was singing about, but it sounded nice. One of two charter Leter members still in that group, and one of the leaders of the affairs reported in the last issue's "Local Biz" piece, Sue Ann has a yowl that belies her quiet appearance. She also plays a mean fret. Frankie Sundsten and Annie Mulcahey on bass and drums make an ensemble of glorious noise and sensual beats. The few tunes where they played it too cool were more than compensated by the ones where they gave it their all. Most everyone there liked them.

THe 200 or so weren't there, of course, for C of K. They were there for the possibly-last sight of Three Swimmers. The band that wanted from the start to be the Next Big Thing may be no more, largely because Mark Smith's connections paid off and he's off to England to hit the big time with Dave Allen, ex-Gang of Four, and Barry Andrews, ex-XTC and Fripp;s League of Gentlemen.

It was clear why so many lover the Swimmers. They are Seattle's tightest, slickest, most "professional" band. Smith has his English accent down pat, and all the boys have dreamy fashion-plate faces. A perfect combination for those Seattleites who wish they were rather in London, who really appreciate it when a local band sounds like it's not from here.

I know it's sacrilege in some circles to say I never loved them, but I had some uncomfortable feeling about their groove thang. Like, can you be a socialist and still believe in the star system? Why do they leave the impressions of more radical chic than radical? If they've got all these important things to say, why does it come out like a clique of Americans insulting Margaret Thatcher?

The did have their moments, like songs that ended with one last bar of guitar after the drums had stopped, like a strong rhythm section. But they're not God.

--Clark Humphrey

Photo: "Two Swimmers" by Cam Garret

8

PAYOLAS

In A Place Like This
IRS

You may have heard the closing tune, "China Boys", which was played occasionally on a certain dead broadcast station. On the LP, it's an anticlimax, 'cuz the tune before it, "Comfortable" is an all-time power pop great. It's got riffs and hooks borrowed from punk, ska, folk-novelty, MOR, and probably a few other places as well, along with a catchy lyric in the vein of "Pleasant Valley Sunday" and "Respectable Street". In 2:45, it's hard to ask for more.

The title tune provides a day in the life of a worker at a defense plant, a tale which 60,000 Boeing folks and their dependents know too well. There are several mediocre selections, and the token ballad has one of those syruppy string sections that's so bad it's fun. Might be Payola$ sort of snide attack on the token-ballad syndrome that has even heavy metal acts going sappy to get airplay.

—Clark Humphrey

CASH COWS

Virgin UK

"An album for the price of a single," says the cover. Here it's an import for the price of a domestic. You get the new Flying Lizards single, Beefheart, live PiL, XTC, Human League, Mike Oldfield, and the first vinyl by the Professionals, the new band led by Cook and Jones, the heart and spine of the Sex Pistols if not their soul. Theirs is the second weakest cut here, after Gillan.

You can actually get a Cash Cows for something close to "the price of a single" if you head up and buy the Canadian version, not imported here. That one doesn't have PiL, or Professionals

but does have a great piece of Magazine's Play LP, dynamic chanteuse Valerie Lagrange, and the serious side of Nash the Slash.

As good samplers should, both Cows show off the label's acts at their best, helping you choose your selections of regular-priced stuff. If only enough of these artists were released over here to warrant a state-side Cash Cows. Will there ever be a U.S. Nash, new Lizards, Professionals, Lagrange, or Human League?

—Clark Humphrey

THE A's

A Woman's Got The Power
Arista Records

They should have named this album "Aesop's Fables for Forlorn Lovers and Hopeless Men"; where on the A's first release, they couldn't stand girls, now they've hit puberty and can't live without them. Sometimes the theme works, other times, no.

The first time I listened to this record, I was disappointed. The next few times, it grew on me, but now as I disect it for this review, I'm disappointed again, mostly with the production - it's choppy and nothing seems to fit together. Maybe Rick Chertoff had an earache or something, because the A's first record (which he also produced) was great - I connected with it immediately, it was a strong, solid production.

Songwise, six of the ten songs click. "A Woman's Got The Power", the title cut, starts off Side 1 with a Motown feel. It has a mildly funky beat and breathy high-pitched background vocals coupled with flowing synthesizer. This is one of the fables - directed to the female listening audience, it gives tips on how to pick your man up once he's reached the scummy-depths- of-humanity syndrome.

"Electricity" follows. This is a slow song, with stirring vocals. Another lesson to be learned here girls, of how to keep sexual control over your man's feelings about himself and his life in general. Give him a quick pick-me-up...it's OK!

Next in line is "Heart Of America", which starts off with a marvelous beat and horns, but soon crashes into the dirt with sappy lyrics all about that 4th grade essay "What America Means To Me". Too bad, because this is the only song that really captures the A's old sound. For the patriotic only.

Ensuing is "How Do You Live", and they ask that age old question, "How do you find the strength to go on, how do you live with a broken heart?", the answer being, "I stay at home and cry, I lock myself away and hide." This song could have been a classic 10 - 15 years ago. It has a "roller skate palace" beat, at least thats the visual image that comes to mind.

About now, all the opening guitar licks are beginning to sound the same. The last song on Side 1 is "When The Rebel Comes Home". A medium good song, but nothing to write home about.

The first three songs on Side 2 are hardly worth mentioning - just some more stories, this time about Johnny, Jackie, and Bob. They are good to listen to when you really don't want to listen to anything. Then we get to the two prime cuts on the whole record.

"I Pretend She's You" is the forlorn lovers song with a solution - simply transfer all the qualities of your old mate on to your new one; just pretend the magic is there. This is a really wonderful song. And the production isn't half bad either. I love it.

The last song is "Insomnia". It has a frantic (!!!) beat and the vocals are squeaky, like Richard Bush is almost over the edge. This would make a great background track for that choreographed nightmare we all have of running, running, running, but we don't know what from. My heart starts to pound just listening to it.

After the A's first record, which was so astoundingly first rate, "A Woman's Got The Power" sounds so different that it's a shock. They sound like a whole new band. I'm not saying it's bad, but it is obscure commercialism at it's best (a sell out?). This from a "punk" band???? Ah, well, they said the same thing about the Clash... we'll see....

—Kathy Moschel

KID CREOLE & THE COCONUTS

Fresh Fruit in Foreign Places
Ze-Sire

Join Creole (Mr. Darnell to his friends, including you) as he goes the whole wide world, following W. Eric's advise, to find the woman of his dreams, one Mimi. Along the way, he simultaneously revives the rock opera and invents a calypso revival. It had to happen, after ska, that calypso, the first west indies-inspired pop and Mitch Miller's failed dream for a positive teen-dance alternative to rock 'n roll, would emerge, and where else but on Ze. It's the most light-hearted concept album yet and tons of fun for everyone. Find a record store that will play a whole side of it for you and you'll be hooked if you've got any fun in you at all.

—Clark Humphrey

PICK HIT LP

SIOUXIE & THE BANSHEES

JUJU

Time flies. The first couple of listens did nothing for me. I thought "it just sits there. These songs don't do anything." Normally I'm a snotty listener; if it doesn't imbed it's claws in me by two listenings - forget it. But one night, in a full moon cycle, I played "JuJu" very loudly and bounced off walls and crawled on the floor. Claws. Psychedelic drones. Scary lyrics. Siouxie relaxed, powerful, full of feeling. But sometimes it even sounds as if they're having fun - a new side to the Banshees' dark sound. All members share songwriting credits. No longer a studio-tour replacement shock troupe these people are a group. Less sparse and less arranged than "Kaleidescope" and the 1980 single "Israel" b/w "Red Over White", but more energy and more horror movies. "Shrunken heads under the bed", and a "little voodoo dolly". Music's answer to Edward Gorey? Siouxie's lyrics suggest unmentionable abominations without being explicit. Your imagination fills out the sketches and the music takes you there "nails are deep in your hair".

—Johnny Rubato

TANKS

Bongo Congo b/w March of the Slugs
Capitol Records
775 Union
San Francisco, CA 94133

Hey! Only positive adjectives here for Bongo Congo. The vocals wail, the beat is fast, the bass is strong. Even the lyrics are good: "There's always something coming out of the woodwork. There's always something and it looks like a new world." A gutsy band that's not telling you to fuck off. Over and you got a follow-up to X's Los Angeles. "It's not a path, it's just a... dusty road".

March of the Slugs is slower but will knock you up just the same.

This is a great band if their single indicates anything at all. Tanks are not a band to sleep to. They're a band to get off your ass with.

—MMM

NAKED SKINNIES

All My Life b/w This Is A Beautiful Night
Naked House Records
1585 N. High Street
Columbus, Ohio 43201

These three guys and gal have found it. I can't compare them to Joy Division because the first time I heard this single I thought they were Joy Division.

Particularly Beautiful Night. It's so close! Very amazing with Mark Eitzel on moaning vocals, and John Kricko on a bass line that definitely has recent roots. Nancy Kangas on organ fills the background nicely.

All My Life (for someone to talk to) is somehow endearing. Again Mark Eitzel is like Ian Curtis reincarnated.

I like this single, although I can't get excited over even this close an imper-

sonation. J.D.'s fan's
should hear this for thrills
and chills.

-MMM

TIKIS

Surfadelic b/w Junie
World Imitation Records

Remember "Wipeout?" Well,
you don't have to anymore.
It's been reproduced 80's
production style by the
Tikis. Lush, plasticized,
and absolutely stinking
of the 60's. I kind of
like it, but then I still
listen to the Ventures
every once in a while.

"June" is also surfing
music, but a slightly
different style. Plus,
unlike the A-side, it
has vocals. Which are
awful. And the vocals
pretty mych center
around the lyrics. Also
awful. Imagine a surf-
style love song--remember
all those carefully
worked out harmonies?
Well, you can forget
them too.

The only exceptional
thing about this
record is the Free
Tiki you can send away
for. But you can find
a reasonable facsimile
in the nearest gumball
machine. Come to
think of it, with a
pocketful of pennies
you can probably find
the record in there
too.

-Captive

MEAT PUPPETS

5 song 45
World Imitation Records

It's loud. It's fast.
It's...HARDCORE. Except
for a strange litte
instrumental called "Out
in the Gardener" which
features a stuttering
rhythm line a la Beefheart.
"In a Car" and "Foreign Lawns"
are short, hard, and smeared
with screaming vocals in an
'8 packs of cigarettes later'
rasp. Actually, there are
two singers, but they're
brothers and sound the same.
Each song is recognizably
different (yeah, they can
even play their instruments)
and by the third hearing all
you want to do is see them
live--so the excitement
doesn't have to stop when
you get up to flip over the
record.

-Captive

HERTZ

Hertz Records
Demo Cassette

Last minute addition: DT has
just received a killer cassette from the Hertz. Distributed exclusively through mail
order (send a dollar and a 47
minute blank tape to: Hertz
Records, P. O. Box 93412 Boston Mass, 0213B, and they'll
make you a copy.) This EP
contains a stunning all drum
solo version of "Winchester
Cathedral"-- Fey Doneaway in
top form.

Although none of the 28 songs

really match up to their highly touted single, "The Match
Game Theme Song", there is a
fairly bizarre (live?) cover
of "What's New Pussycat?" with
what seems to be a horse neigh-
ing in the background as She
Bernstein shrieks "Whoaa-o-o!
This band is almost as strange
as Smegma, and a lot more danceable if you can move that
fast. They claim they're a
fuck band but don't believe it
unless you're in the habit of
mixing speed with your spanish
fly.

Included is a promo photo of
the band. They have some rather
unusual tastes in clothing. It
Hertz, guitarist, is dressed
in plaster bandages and tubu-
lar gauze, held together by
oversized bandaids.

Although litigation concerning
the use of Gene Rayburn's favorite song has been dropped,
new problems have arisen from
a certain car rental agency
whose name is quite similar to
that of the group. "We were
here first. Who cares?" quip-
ped the enigmatic Ms. Bernstein. Lawyer fees have reportedly held up production of
their first album, and judging
from their highly touted demo
the real losers in the battle
are us listeners.

--Jeff Greenwood

COMPILATION

We Do 'Em Our Way
Various Artists
MFP Records

You've heard all the originals
and most of the cover versions
have had a birthday or two,
but this is a party record
worth owning. If you like
party records. It's just like
a thumbful of 45's on a friday
night with school a weekend
away. It wears on you, like
most compilation albums- something about having to hear the
songs in THAT order over and
over again.

There are, however, a few cuts
that you might have been meaning to to pick up, and $5.99
is about what the singles
would cost anyway. Think of
the additional stuff as bonus
tracks. The hot ones are:

The Sex Pistols (of course)
doing "Stepping Stone", and
sounding like they really mean
it. They managed to turn one
of the wimpiest hits in history into an anti-love anthem
to the rebound set. The average is one sneer per every
fourth beat, and it's not a
short song.

The Slits with "Heard it
Through the Grapevine". Throb
bing reggae with hot-and-cold
running vocals. This one I
will never tire of hearing.

The Stranglers doing "Walk on
By as though they'd written
the damn thing. The bridge is
a bit long, but then they always are with this band, and
the bass/keyboard sound works
perfectly with a hint of the
old-R & B feel.
Those Helicopters have a decent "World Without Love"
(sounds a lot like Ian Drury
but not as substantial), U.K.
Subs are listenable with
"She's Not There" (though it
sounds too much like the original), and Hollywood Brats
manage to sound almost like
Patti Smith in "Then He Kissed
Me" (same problem).

The Devo cover should have
been "Secret Agent Man" (it's
"Satisfaction"), and the Flying Lizards'"Money" is something you'll be tired of in
no tire if you aren't already.

- Captive

PICK HIT EP

GERMS   (SAVE US EVER HEUPE)

GERMS

What We Do Is Secret -
In Memory Of Darby Crash
1958 - 1980
Slash Records

Here we go again, but this
time there's more than one
would expect. There are
four songs on this that
should have been on (G)
album. That's OK though
because that's what makes
this E.P. so great. "Circle
One", "Caught In My Eye",
"No God", and "My Tunnel"
are all exceptional. Any-
body that told me the Germs
were always lousy live can
stick it! There are two
cuts recorded live from the
extinct Starwood, December

3rd to be exact. Which
should deflate a few people's
conceptions of the Germs.
I'm not talking out of my
ass! About the time the
live cuts were done which
incidentally was the Germs
last show, it was more or
less a reunion since they
had previously broke up.
Darby was going through a
pretty heavy self realization
trip and was basically trying
to break free of his old
image. This shines through
clearly on the beginning of
the live stuff. It's really
too bad too,because only a
little more than ten days
after the Starwood gig he
died of an intentional
overdose. Musically the
material is excellent.

This E.P. is recommended to
people not previously aware
of the Germs and definately
to those addicted already!

"Everything works in circles!
It's like something you've
done eight years ago but all
of a sudden it feels exactly
like you're at the same place
doing the same thing. It
may not be that same thing
but the feelings there!
Well, that's circles. Everything works on circles."

"It's your circle, you can
do what you want with it..."
              -Darby Crash (No mag
              interview, 1979)

              -Peter Davis

PRETENDERS

There is not really much I
want to say about this album.
If you liked the last
Pretenders you'll probably
like this one, unless you're
tired of the sound. (You

know, uncomplicated beat with
treble-y guitar and Chrissie
Hyndes sultry, sour voice
making threats and complaining
in a pretty way). My
favorite song on this album
would have to be 'Waste Not
Want Not'. It has a ska
inspired beat and is probably
the gutsiest on the album.

-D.C.

10

BACKGROUND....
TOXIC REASONS

by: BRIA CONRADUS

Ohio Punks Hit & Miss Seattle

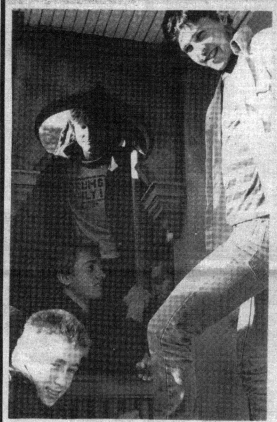

Maybe you saw the posters; Toxic Reasons from San Fransicico, at the Freeway Hall, Tues. August 18. But there was no show. A day before Toxic Reasons were scheduled to play, Pravda Productions recieved a letter from the managers of the Freeway Hall stating there would be no show. (ie. no more punk at the Freeway Hall). Toxic Reasons, in Vancouver, received only a few hours notice of the cancellation but came to Seattle anyway. They spent four days watching T.V. and eating at Skipper's Fish & Chips. What did we miss? A fucking great band!

Actually from Dayton Onio, Toxic Reasons have been cruisisng the west for about six weeks. Their first Pacific side gig was in Vancouver with DoA and the Dead Kennedys at the Com modore. It was a good show with 2000 people, but afterwards they ended up loosing their drummer ("a wimp") to road fatigue (and five stitches). They then picked up J.J. Kill ex-drummer for No Exit, and headed south for San Fran. The Band is: Ed Pittman-vocals, Bruce Stuckey-lead guitar, Rob (a Brit)-rhythm guitar, Greg Stout-bass, and J.J.Kill -drums.

It was in San Fransicico that I saw Toxic Reasons play. They

played with the Dead Kennedys on a friday night at the Fab Mab. I was hanging out by the pin ball machines when the music hit me like a strong wind. I had to check it out.

The crowd was hot and sweaty but it was worth it. Ed Pittman comes at you like a freight train. He's a very powerful singer with a strong voice. J.J. Kill had only been playing with the band for a few days but you wouldn't have noticed. Lots of energy and rhythm packed into J.J. who is an extremely talented drummer for his age, 16. The high point of the band, at least for me, is the lead guitar player. Bruce Stuckey is real cool. He has great control over his instrument and played with such feverish emotion that he ended up bleeding all over his pick ups at the end of the set. After th show Bruce handed his guitar to a squid (in the Navy) standing next to me. The guy tried to give it back but Bruce just walked away, glad to be rid of the piece of shit.

The next night Toxic Reasons played with Flipper. This time I tried to pay attention to what they were playing. Most of Toxic Reasons' set is fast paced but they can also play some real nice slow and melodic music. In comparison, Toxic Reasons is as dynamic as the Dead Kennedys and their

songs reflect the quality of early Clash stuff. They had the whole club dancing. One song that stuck in my mind is 'Ghost Town', a song about Dayton. It has real eerie reggae inspired sections broken by fast paced walls of sound.

Toxic Reasons lyrics are not your avdrage swill. They've got that 'something-is-definitely-wrong-here-and-we're-going-say-something-about-it' tone. They take their political ideas seriously (as seriously as possible) and aren't afraid of talking about it. While in San Fransciso, Toxic Reasons was interviewed by Ruth on the Harmful Emmisions show, radio K.U.S.F. They played a few songs and the interview continued with the band drinking, swearing, and discussing their ideas on politics..."Adolph Reagan". The chief engineer of KUSF was so moved, he got out of bed, drove to the station and turned the show off. The radio listeners were treated to five minutes of silence and an apology for technical difficulties.

The guys in Toxic Reasons

are agaist the violence that stains punk and all agree "No Nazi Shit". They believe that it's the "weekend punks", the jocks, that come to clubs to kill punks. Punks end up bloody and blamed for such social decay. They also believe punks should look out for each other and unite against the people in society who oppress with the power of their money.

As for the new music scene, they find New Wave to be a real "cop out". Big bands are alienated and have forgotten "what it's like to be local." Toxic Reasons found the Seattle scene "awful boring"and think it's being "shit on." But it's nothing new. All over the country clubs are being shut down and local bands are getting squeezed. There is little/no interest in local acts and the record labels are especially unsupportive.

Toxic Reasons haven't really had to deal with too many record company hassles even though they think they've

been screwed by BOMP in L.A. Still, their single with War Hero b/w Somebody Help Me has sold-out 1000 copies. There won't be new copies of this single until the band can get the master from the ex-drummer who stole it when he left the band. Before they leave the west coast they'll be working on a new single with East Bay Ray. It will be a three song E.P. and should be available in about six weeks

Toxic Reasons will be taking off to the east soon on a

"sleep on the floor tour". They're planning on going to Phoenix, Tucson, through Texas, and into the south. The band said they're used to playing the south and will be glad to be on home turf, but they won't take "no shit from rednecks". After they tour the east and spend some time in Dayton they plan on coming west again in about four months. Seattle will get a third chance, (T.R. was also booked at the Gorilla Room), to see Toxic Reasons.

-Bria C.

11

ACCESSORIES

MAN IN YOUR VANITY, $1.50

MOVIES

Breaking Glass

Director: Brian Gibson
Screenplay: Brian Gibson
Cast: Phil Daniels, Hazel O'Conner
Music: Hazel O'Conner

BREAKING GLASS, a dynamically entertaining and energetic film, just completed a very limited run at the Neptune Theater in the University District.

If you wern't one of the lucky few to catch this movie, either at the Neptune or this year's film festival, then keep your eyes open. BREAKING GLASS is the best movie about what is going on in music, and the business of it, to date.

Hazel O'Conner, an extremely talented lady, not only scored and performed all the tunes in this film; but turned in a helluva performance as the star of it as well. Her personality and music constantly reach out and snatch you around the neck like a vice grip.

For example: there is a sequence in the film where she is in a concert hall filled with 10,000 obnoxious punks (where would we be without the stereotype? Thank you Hollywood). Suddenly there is a power outage. O'Conner ignores it and without benefit of mikes, or other electronic paraphernalia, siezes upon the instant to hiss out the song, "Who Needs It?" (opening lyrics: living in the shadow of a mushroom tower, who needs it?).

The audience thinks this is great and gets into it. Here is this unknown singer blasting a song at one very pissed off crowd, and the topper on this is they can only see her from the light of two flashlights being held by her manager, Phil Daniels, who some may remember from QUADROPHENIA.

Though it must be admitted that Brian Gibson, the writer of the film, has indulged himself in a trite bit of cheap theatrics, the sequence is so well carried off by O'Connor you tend not to notice.

The story (yes, believe it or not there is even a pretty good one; which makes it not only an exception as a film about new music, but as a movie too), deals with an idealistic singer's rise to fame after she latches onto a very bright manager who believes in her, and who she eventually dumps on because she has sold out and her subsequent neuroses and guilt complexes make her afraid of what he stands for as regards her past and beliefs. It should be

mentioned that Phil Daniels turns in a remarkably good performance as the luckless manager who gets shit upon several times before he wises up and bails out.

The music makes original and wonderful use of the sax and the lyrics are of exceptional merit. I'd seen the film three times and picked up the soundtrack a month before I ever noticed the words to such songs as "Blackman": "...I am the darkness, you are the light... I am the alcoholic pissed in the park. I am the girl who sold her body to the dog, I am the truth. Love it..."

The short run at the Neptune is a disappointment from the standpoint of not enough people having the opportunity to see the film. On the other hand, if you've ever subjected your ears to the excuse for a sound system in that place, it may be just as well. Perhaps next time around the theater which books it will have a decent sound system; as was the case this year when the film played at the Seattle International Film Festival.

As a last bit of advise on BREAKING GLASS, if you are one of those people who equate movies with drugs as others with popcorn, take a hint: you don't need any. This movie is so hot it will burn your eyes out. However, if you must indulge, I suggest no more than three joints. Anything more is over-doing it.

—T.C. Rice

REGGAE
SAT. 11-7
3407 FREMONT
45 & LP
weekly from JAmaica

MURPHY'S LAW:
(one of the great philosophical truths of our time)
EVERYTHING THAT CAN GO WRONG, WILL.

RADIO

KRAB

RADIO IS NOT DEAD! KRAB features New Music, Reggae, Heavy Dub, or Punk five times a week on 107.7 FM.

Life Elsewhere
Thursday 10pm-12am

Your Unpopular Hit Parade
Friday 10pm-12am

Third World Music
Saturday 12:30pm-2pm

Swell Maps
or Acrylic Waves
Saturday 12am-3am

Bleed With Me
or Start At The Start
Sunday 10pm-12am

ROSCO LOUIE GALLERY

The Rosco Louie Gallery opened in 1978 bent on raising hell on the art front. As Seattle's only modern art gallery, we are charged with the responsibility to showcase the most exciting and innovative talents in the fields of visual arts, performance art, poetry, new music, film, video, fashion, and revolution. We don't rely on fascist politicians for funding, so we can get away with just about anything.

Our fall schedule contains the best artists to be found anywhere. We hope you appreciate it and if you don't, well, fuck you.

INCITES '81

5
Rios Memi
11/27-12/12

6
ROSCO LOUIE'S GREATEST HITS
12/13-12/24

7
PETER SANTINO
12/31-1/19

1
BILL WHIPPLE
9/3-9/22

3
NIRMAL KAUR
10/15-11/7

2
BETH ELLIOTT
9/24-10/13

4
CORK MARCHESCHI
11/5-11/25

87 S. WASHINGTON ST. SEATTLE, WA. 206 682-5228
HOURS: MON.—SAT. 11:00-6:00 (NOV. & DEC. SUNDAY NOON—5:00)

12

C A L E N D A R

ASTOR PARK
625-1578
5th and Lenora

BABY-O's
624-6558
122 Cherry

DANCELAND, U.S.A.
624-4732
1510½ First Ave.

GATSBY'S
455-0666
12700 Bel-Red Road
Bellevue

GOLDEN CROWN
622-5304
1616 Fourth Ave.

GORILLA ROOM
345-9393
610 Second Ave.

HALL OF FAME
633-5500
4518 University Way

HIBBLE & HYDES
623-1541
608 First Ave.

RAINBOW
632-3360
722 N.E. 45th

WREX
625-WREX
2018 First Ave.

THE SHOWBOX
621-8864
1421 First Ave.

U.T.C. Hall
632-3705
Fifth and Aloha

POPEYE's
2410 W. Harrison
Olympia

THE SHOWBOX

9/23 The Go-Go's
9/25 Leon Redbone
10/2 Siouxis and the
      Banshees

U.T.C HALL

9/2 Ai-Ai...
9/9 Audio Leter

ASTOR PARK

9/15-19 The Cowboys

BABY-O'S

9/2-5 The Untouchables

GATSBY'S

9/16-17 The Heats

WREX
9/3   Shatterbox
9/4-5   The Frazz
9/9   Skinny Ties
9/10-12 The Enemy
9/17   Flipper
9/18   The Pudz
9/19   Red Dress
POPEYE'S
9/6   Student Nurse

CORPORATE TOP 10

albums

1. Au Pairs   Playing with a
                      Different Sex
2. Delta 5
3. Cabaret Voltaire Red Mecca
4. Warsaw   Joy Div. bootleg
5. Siouxie & the
    Banshees   JuJu
6. TSOL   Dance with me
7. New Age Steppers
8. Bill Nelson   Quit Dreaming and
                      get on the Beam
9. Motorhead   No Sleep till
                      Hammersmith
10. Killing Joke   Whats this for

singles

1. Dead Kennedys   Too Drunk to Fuck
2. Soft Cell   Tainted Love
3. Joy Division   Love Will Tear Us Apart
4. Delta 5   Shadow
5. Echo & the
    Bunnymen   A Promise
6. Bauhaus   Passion of Lovers
7. Bowie   Chig a Ling Song
8. Black Flag   Six Pack
9. Siouxie & the
    Banshees   Arabian Nights
10. Eurythmics   Never Gonna Cry Again

Pick hit of the week: Meat Puppets

02786

GEN. ADM.
AUG 30, 1981

PARAMOUNT PRESENTS

PETER TOSH

30

SEATTLE PARAMOUNT THEATRE — SEATTLE WA

PETER TOSH

30

GEN. ADM.
AUG 30, 1981

02781

S	M	T	W	T	F	S
		1			4	5
				9		11
		14				
20						25
			30			

s   e   p

13

STOP PRESS

FUNNIES

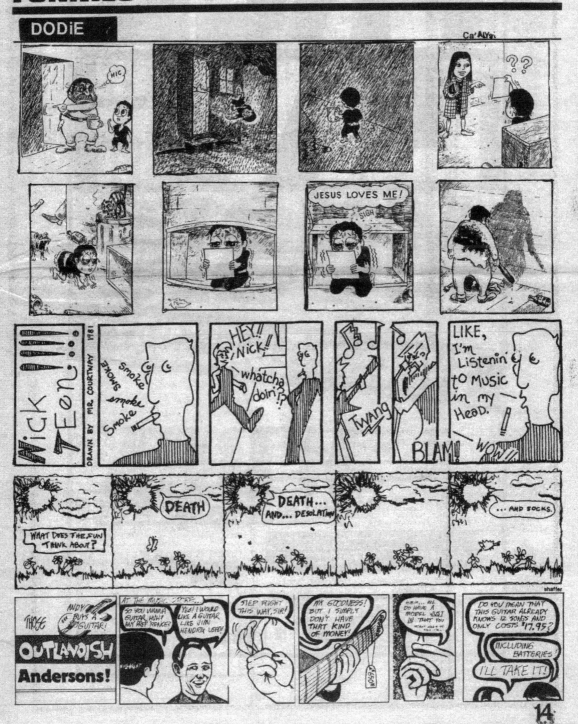

Issue #6

After a month-long hiatus and an increase in cover price, Desperate Times returns. The look and feel of the newspaper is different; the layout is sloppy, and there are no photo credits. Local bands Sleeping Movement and the Gargoyles are on the cover, along with the statement "Brave New World Apathy."

The annual Bumbershoot music festival is slammed for including an unpopular local cover band on the bill: "Who did these guys have to fuck to get this gig?" Even so, the Frazz, a local cover band, gets a great review in this issue. Local band Solger reveals in an interview that they have nine or ten original songs, but also do Germs and Black Flag covers. There is a silly discussion trying to define hardcore versus punk versus teeny-bopper.

The Vancouver Report is replaced by a section called Illegal Aliens. Useful information in this new section includes this tip for seeing bands in Vancouver: bring your own booze.

Neil Hubbard continues his important narrative of Northwest punk with the history of the Showbox Theater. The 1981 DEVO concert at the Showbox was a life-changing event for many Seattle musicians. The last word in the last issue of Desperate Times may appear to be filler; rather, it reads more like a bad omen. It reports that commercial promotion company Concerts West is taking over the Showbox and planning to book straight rock. RIP.

DESPERATE TIMES

NEW PRICE 50¢

VOLUME 1 NO.6   OCT. 7 1981

The Allies
Channel Three
The Cure
The Dicks
D.O.A.
Enemy
The Frazz
Gargoyles
Go Go's
Gun Club
Ian Dury
Leon Redbone
Pronoia
Specials
Stains
Suburban Lawns
U-Men
The Villians

Sleeping Movement

The Gargoyles

BRAVE NEW WORLD APATHY

DESPERATE TIMES

Editor:
Daina Darzin

Milk & Cookies:
Dennis White

B.M. & B.D.:
Maire Masco

Director of Photography:
Skip Beattie

Records Editor:
Clark Humphrey

Movie Editor:
T.C. Rice

Contributing Writers:
Berlin, Captive, Catalyst,
Criss Crass, Joe Despair, Buz
Dirmedosaquez, Gillian,
Scott Hartwich, Tad Reedy,
Johnny Rubato, This Reviewer,
Heidi Weispfenning

Graphics & Layout:
Catalyst Jr., Mark
Michaelson, Mold, Bob Newman,
Billy Shaffer

Ad Manager:
Xan Johnson

Bookkeeper:
Heidi Weispfenning

Typing:
Carole Pearsall

Distribution:
Paul Klassona

Special thanks to Square
Studio for the use of their
space

DESPERATE TIMES is published
more or less bi-monthly by On
The Edge Press, 4525 9th N.E.
Seattle, Washington 98105
(206) 632-4049

IN THIS ISSUE

OPINION

Ok, we're back, hopefully a bit less crazed and better organized. We still need writers, artists, photographers, ad salespeople PARTICULARLY IN VANCOUVER B.C. AND PORTLAND. Please give us a call (note new phone number.) Also, if anyone has sent us any stuff that's gotten returned, please let us know, ok? The post office is fucking up.

Because of all the wierd changes going on with Seattle venues, this opinion is about what's happening at that last bastion of hope, DCT Ball. This is the only game in town, ok? The Gorilla Room will not reopen (barring miracles), the Showbox is going to be nice, clean straight rock, Eagles will be nice, clean new wave, nobody has been able to make Danceland work, Freeway Hall don't want no punks, no more.

The punchline is, why did the doors open two hours late at the Social Deviates/Gargoyles show? The police distinctly do not like less-than-respectable-looking kids loitering on corners drinking beer and smoking pot (which is about the only thing you can do while waiting for the doors to open. This complaint is in no way about the audience at this show, who were being really patient and reasonable about the whole thing). The police do do things like call up landlords and bitch about who they're renting to, landlords do get nervous and refuse to rent their hall out to punk gigs, so, independent promoter types, let's not fuck up this one, ok? Seattle without a hardcore club is fucking Death Valley.

—Daina Darzin

A NOTE:

you probably noticed that DT now costs 50¢. Why, you ask? Because we NEED THE CASH, really bad. Nobody expects to make any money off this rag, but it would be nice to break even once in a while, and, you know, these is inflationary times we's living in. Such is life.

2

THE GO-GO'S
FLESHTONES
EAGLES AUDITORIUM

If you want to read about the show, go to paragraph 3. I'm gonna digress for a while.

Those people who are older than they look will remember the old hippie-psychedella days Eagles Auditorium. For the rest of you, you know what the Showbox looked like before they tried to make it respectable, like during the Punk Explosion? Eagles was like that, concrete hallways and cold, low lights, acid-tripping kids slumped against the wall. So the New Eagles has spotless red carpeting and a graffiti prevention squad monitoring the bathrooms, and goddamit, I wish this city could have one lousy hall that the owners were willing to keep loose and dirty. Also, for some reason, the stage for the Go-Gos/Fleshtones show was on a small riser in front of the main stage (which is much higher up), making visibility next to zero. Something was also causing a a heavy reverb and separation in the sound. Eagles is a weird, cool hall architecturally, and it's got all that history, I'm sorry they didn't do something more imaginative with it.

There is also a bit of sniveling that I just have to get out of my system; security is security, but the John Bauer Co. runs a heavy door. It took me 45 minutes to get into this show, even though I cleared a press pass a week before the show. The high points of this experience were 1) the two large blond jocks on the door who would not let me leave my purse as collateral and go inside to look for someone from the Bauer office who could tell them I was, in fact, supposed to be on the guest list. 2) the security guard who, when I started to bitch about having to wait outside for a long time, pushed me and told me "honey, ya wanna see the show, ya pay your $7.50 like everybody else". Not nice, guys. Ok, I feel better now.

The punchline is, when I finally got let in, the Fleshtones' set was starting and I was so pissed off that it took me about 15 minutes to realize how much I liked them. The Fleshtones have an r&b flavored, heavy-on-the-harmonica sound (the stuff that makes J. Geils Band oldies such a trashy pleasure) with an overlay of rockabilly. They have a lot of energy, and I could have listened to them much longer than their brief, opening-band set.

Very bright lights went on during the break.

I liked the Go-Gos' bubble-gum silliness better at the end of their set better than at the beginning, however, this kind of cute 60s bop-til-ya-drop stuff needs a little sleaze and sarcasm to make it work today, and the Go-Gos stayed irritatingly happy-ditsy throughout.

The most interesting song they did was "Automatic", featuring a coolly discordant melody and lyrics about vending machines. The other decent material happened at the end, mainly a rocking number that sounded like a Chuck Berry cover even though it was probably an original, and their hit "We Got the Beat", which has a neat Tarzan-movie jungle-drum rythym line, and got the rather sedate new wavette crowd to do something vaguely resembling the pogo in its original, slamless form. The crowd loved the Go-Gos; they did a number of encores.

If you like performers who come off 'I'm-just-a-cute-little-girl-and-isn't-this-all-FUN', you, too, will probably love the Go-Gos. Yawwwwwwwwwwwwwwwn.

—Daina Darzin

LEON REDBONE
SHOWBOX

FROM MAGAZINE TO LEON REDBONE
ANOTHER EPITAPH

It doesn't seem like that long ago that the Showbox did its first show. Magazine at the Talmud Torah. New music in a Jewish bingo parlor...I remember wandering around dazedly, wondering what we were doing in a hall this big, with chairs and tables, and so much wall space just begging for graffiti.

Now here I was, covering what looks to be the end of the Showbox as we know it. Once again it's changing hands, but now everyone wants it. With Paramount gone, Seattle needs a smaller hall for all those wonderful mainstream acts that aren't yet up to filling the Arena. So guess what group of music fans gets it up the ass again.

The Leon Redbone show was rather a fitting finale; nostalgia, it's true, but with a definite touch of the bizarre. I got there twenty minutes after the time stated on the poster, hoping that the doors would be open so I wouldn't have to get any wetter than necessary. Surprise! Not only were the doors open, but the first act was already playing. As a double shock to my nervous system, there were neat rows of chairs all over the floor. I actually had to sit down for the entire show. Horrors!

The first act was a local character called Baby Gramps. He's of indeterminate age, (all I could see were beard and hat) plays acoustic guitar, and sings in an incredibly scratchy voice. He's a pretty funny guy, doing songs like "Your Feet's Too Big" by Fats Waller, and the Walt Disney song, "Nothing At All":
    "To be a bat's a bum thing
    A silly and a dumb thing
    But at least a bat is

something
And you're not a thing at all."
which should strike a familiar note with all you "Illuminatus!" fans out there. He also did a sort of "elephantrilogy" one of which was "Through the Hole in the Elephant's Bottom". You'll have to go see him yourself to find out what it's about 'cause I won't tell. The last song in the set was "The Teddy Bear's Picnic" which had some lyrics I didn't remember from my childhood about them frolicking in rubber novelty shop underwear. Hmmm. For his encore, he did an excellent impression of Bob Dylan.

The intermission seemed awfully long, considering the minimal set-up they had to do. The audience started getting irritated, hooting, stomping, and generally carrying on. I felt like I was at the Coliseum waiting to see The Who or something. Anyway, Mr. Redbone finally chose to honor us with his presence. He's traded in his straw panama for a black felt number, and his sideburns have grown out to meet his moustache, giving him that turn-of-the-century mutton-chop look. I couldn't decide whether the atmosphere was that of a Harlem club in the 1920s, or an old bordello somewhere in the Deep South. He did "The Sheik of Araby," which is the song that got me interested in him a few years ago, and followed with a tape of some Hungarian soprano singing, while he made a shadow puppet of her mouth. Then he paused, took a Polaroid of the audience, and continued with another song. I couldn't tell you what it was, he really mumbles those lyrics like an old bluesman.

Another amusement was his imitation of a whale, done with a syringe full of water and an airhorn. His set consisted of fourteen songs, including "Champagne Charlie," "Your Cheatin' Heart," "Shine On, Harvest Moon," "Diddy-Wah-Diddy," and other such elderly classics. After the first few

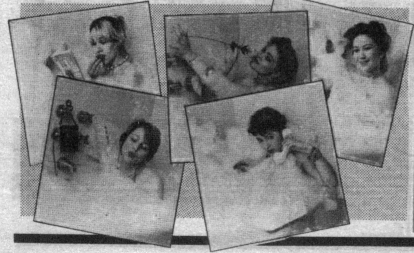

3

VIOLATIONS

numbers, he brought on his backup musicians, a clarinet player who doubles on sax, and a tuba player. All the musicianship was excellent, and his fingerwork on the guitar was pretty incredible. He was called back for an encore, of course, played two songs and left, the house lights making it clear that he wouldn't return again.

The hall cleared immediately, which also seemed strange for the Showbox, and I stood outside for a minute or two to see what sort of people had been present. It was an older crowd, which I'd expected, but many of them had obviously never heard anything about the Showbox, as they were dressed very nicely. Can you imagine someone in their "going to the symphony" clothes encountering the horror of the bathrooms in that place? The thought amused me so much I splurged, went to a bar, and treated myself to a few beers. G'night John-Boy.

--Heidi Weispfenning

BUMBER SHOTS & THE ALLIES

What I wanna know is: who did these guys fuck to get this gig? One of the hot local band showcases, playing between Chuck Berry and the Tubes, to a near sold-out Coliseum audience? Because the Allies--formerly Bighorn--SUCK. Dressed in cute little matching black jumpsuits, they did bland amorphous rock that would have sounded lame at Hibble's on a slow Wednesday.

So that this review will contain something besides slag, what follows is some suggestions as to what bands would be much better for a show like this, for future reference:

-X-15   -The Pudz
-Napalm Beach   -The Fraza
-The Rats   -The Cowboys
-Red Dress   -The Enemy

(This is assuming the Bumbershoot people want to go with somebody reasonably mass-appeal. I think RPA would sound real cool in the Coliseum, myself . . . .).

--Berlin

THE TUBES

And then there's The Tubes. Too early to label punk, but too late to pin as glitter, these guys have been cranking out their unique brand of techno-shock-rock for almost 10 years, dragging around enough props and costumes to stock a high school drama department. Still, they were never in the right place at the right time to secure massive $ucce$$.

The first two times The Tubes played Seattle, the show resembled an overblown rock-n-roll-travelling-circus and insane asylum, incorporating the band (9 musicians at the time) 20 or 30 dancers and about 15 tons of shit; 30 or so televisions, three movie screens, smoke machines, giant rubber cigarettes, etc. etc.

Well, times have changed. The costume changes are still there, but the 20 choreographed dancers have been watered down to two Tubes cheerleaders, and the props were kept to a bare minimum. The stage was done up in blue, with two blue "tube" lighting columns and a smaller "tube" in which Fee Waybill changed from secret agent coat to scuba diver to crazed murderer back to Fee.

The set consisted primarily of tunes from the new "Completion Backward Principle" LP, a few choice Tubes "hits," and a couple of unreleased gems including "Hey, Sports Fans," a great number in which Jock-in-the-box Fee Waybill hits whiffle balls into the crowd while guitarists Roger Steen and Sputnik Spooner play ping pong. Heavy stuff.

Highlights included a great rendition of "Attack of the 50-Foot Woman," and Fee Waybill as Jacques Cousteau singing "Su Su Sushi" to a girl with a Japanese wig and octopus arms. "Suck a tentacle," indeed!

Even though the show was very entertaining and obviously well thought-out, it was still a bit of a disappointment to anyone who knows what these guys are really capable of. Not that the fault lies solely with The Tubes themselves. As musicians, this seven-piece unit was as on top of it as ever. Waybill, Spooner and Steen, along with fellow band members Prarie Prince on drums, Rick Anderson on bass, Vince Welnick on keyboards and Mike Cotten on synthesizers, all turned in top-notch performances. (Even though Spooner looked a little like he was gonna die.)

Part of the problem was the fact that you had to deal with the Coliseum. But the biggest hassles were all those jerks who had no idea what The Tubes were all about and were just there cuz, hey! it's Bumbershoot! Thus,

forcing us to deal with lots of KZOK-rock-rock-rockers, along with just about every other type of person imaginable. And some Tubes fans, too. Of course, in a way this was good, as it enabled The Tubes to shock and offend lots of unsuspecting family types, and after all, isn't that what this is all about?

All in all it was a fairly hilarious and worthwhile endeavor, what with the motorized drumset and keyboards that would actually drive around the stage, the "Citizen Kane" type sales pitch speech by Fee, Quay Lewd (Yes!, Quay Lewd!), singing "Tubes World Tour," etc., etc. and so on. But one couldn't help thinking about the "old days" ... what this band used to be ... and hopefully (providing Capitol puts up more money for the next tour) what this band will be again. Until then, "let's make some noise!"

--Bux Dirmedosaquez

4

DRUNK AND

SLEEPING MOVEMENT PRONOIA
WREX OCT. 1

Sleeping Movement is a new, dynamic, heavily populated band that features Upchuck as lead singer and high priest of the festivities. Pony Maurice added backup vocals in-between wan mysterious looks and high energy dancing, Dahfny Raphael and Gordon Deucette played guitar, Mike Davidson on bass, Ben Ireland on drums, Barb Ireland on keyboards and vocals, and Lee Lumsden on percussion. That's a lot of people. Happily, it is also a lot of talent, as was demonstrated that night.

With so many styles to choose from, at least one song out of the short set had a particular appeal no matter what. Slow, fast, muted, shrieking, punkoid, technoid, straight rock-n-roll. Even a ballad! Upchuck, dressed like a candy cane in spots, was in excellent form and his voice sounded better than ever. (I could've sworn I head "Jacuzzi Floozie" in there somewhere, but it must have been an aural halucination—spurred perhaps by a stage whisper of "Old clones never die...")

A record should be out in January (the band is considering an LP), and when asked about video the response was, "we're working on it." That medium comes to mind since, though the songs are memorable, the look is a bit more polished than the material. They might open for Siouxsie, so prepare yourselves. Sleeping Movement's first show was as good as The Fag's last. For anyone who hasn't gotten the message, SEE THIS BAND.

Pronoia shares two members with SM, but their sound is more consistent and less theatrical. Vocals and instruments were traded, but the basic line-up is Frater Raphael on electronic keyboards, G. Deucette on guitar, M. Davidson on drums and Tor Midtskos on bass. The word "Pronoia" is a Gnostic term meaning "first thought." At least, so claims the band. It actually seems to be an anglicized revision of

Ennoia—but you don't care about that, do you? You want to hear about music, not aeons.

Pronoia was very tight, and the emphasis was on drums and bass. I found myself thinking of early Magazine and Killing Joke, although neither is really apt. It's the idea of accessible music built on an obscure base. They do it very well, but by the last song of the first set (of two) it began to sound too familiar. The sound was very controlled and alternated spareness with lush variations. Barb Ireland's guest vocals on the first song made a nice contrast. As far as first impressions go, this is a band that you could see again and again without getting tired of them: the songs are distinct enough to sound better every hearing (as opposed to bands that knock you out the first time only to bore you to tears thereafter). I will take this chance to remind my confused readers that familiar does not mean repetitious or boring. The sound isn't brand new but it's good enough to attract a real following.

—Captive

SOCIAL DEVIATES GARGOYLES
U.C.T. OCT. 3

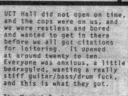

UCT Hall did not open on time, and the cops were on us, and we were restless and bored and wanted to get in there before we all got citations for loitering. It opened at around twenty to ten. Everyone was anxious, a little bedraggled, wanting a really stiff guitar/bass/drum fuck, and this is what they got.

The Maggot Brains cause a peculiar allergic reaction in some people, to others (themselves included) they

are God, and to the rest they are a riveting hardcore band that manifests in a person's mind a feeling of chaotic confusion. They were particularly satisfactory last night. "Now more than ever"... A maggot endeavor!

The Social Deviates packed that nefarious crushing weapon that got the folks jumping about, causing a tendency for bashing and trashing. The set was impeccable and paltry. The good stuff!!!

CHILDREN OF KELLOGG U-MEN
U.C.T. OCT. 2

UCT Hall is getting a lot of attention these days as the "new place" in town to show local bands, especially those performing non-commercial music, and those with musicians too young to play WREX. UCT is an all-ages hall and one prompter. Greg Simmons, is attempting to make it into an all-ages club with shows on a regular basis. The addition of a good sound system and lights added immeasurably to the atmosphere of the hall and the quality of the show.

The U-Men started promptly at 10:00. This was their third gig and even with some problem strings and some obnoxious hecklers, it is obvious that these three guys and one gal are great. The U-Men have developed a sound of their own with discordant cord smashes fitting into the original bass and vocal parts. While the drums could have been louder for this shown, vocalist John Bigly's performance took up

the slack. With eyes rolling, his voice was sometimes subdued and sometimes searing. The U-Men play many original songs, however, their version of The Cramps song "Can't Find My Mind" was particularly good. Definitely a band to watch.

Children of Kellog were next. There has been a lot of talk about this band, but nothing came close to the real thing. The bass and drums seem to support everything front woman Sue Anne Harkey does. I'm not exactly sure what she does—but whatever, it's incredible. "Experimental" is a term that might be used, as Harkey used various pieces of metal to attack her guitar or bass. But it is a cohesive style that's hers and not an experiment. "Illusion Is Real" was one of my favorites, along with another song I didn't catch the title) where Harkey plucked and strummed a violin and made droning/moaning sounds with her voice. This song was repeated as their last encore to everyone's cheers. Now I know where all the talk comes from.

—MM

DISORDERLY

THE FRAZZ
WREX SEPT 4

THE FRAZZ
Wrex

The best way to see the Frazz would be in the company of an extremely cute but dumb date who you intend to try to seduce later in the back seat of your car, wearing a prophylactic. Your date should have teased hair and insist you tell her you love her. Which you should do, even though you just want to get in her pants. If this sounds obnoxious and sexist, it is, but so were the early sixties, and that's the point of the Frazz.

60's cover bands are generally not my favorite type of entertainment, but the Fratz are great. Unlike most groups, who crank out mouldy oldies with the attitude of hey, let's return to the good ol' days when life was FUN, the Frazz peg the period for what it really was—crass, mindless, greedily commercial. Their stage show is just on the edge of Tubes-style nasty parody: their lead singer wore a brocade dinner jacket. They did "Wipeout" and "Woolly Bully". They had fringed, bare-midriffed go-go dancers with Valium eyes named Suzy and Barbie. They hawked their single during the set ("special offer, only $2.00, we'll autograph it for you, anything you want") and then Suzy and Barbie circulated among the crowd with copies. The whole thing was real funny, and terrific. (The record didn't grab me much, though. Without Suzie & Barbie's blank stares, the Frazz are just another good-ol-days 60's cover band.)

–Daina Darzin

Strong playing by The Gargoyles kept the atomic mass in a demented state of jostling and bustling while they pounded out attitude for twenty minutes or so. Then on came their brothers, The Living Gargs.

Excellent! They played for about eight minutes and then the singer got pissed at a guy who was spitting his beverage at him. He dove off the stage and onto the guy, fists flying, and tackled him on the floor while the rest of the group, plus the audience pushed and shoved each other. Somewhere in the middle at the beginning of the end, a girl was hit hard and sent reeling and bleeding to the ground. Quickly, security flocked to her and rushed her to a back room.

As we departed I looked back at the destroyed hall and tried to figure out a reason for the detrimental things that keep repeating themselves, and I couldn't find any that make sense. I wonder if this shit is justifiable...or if it ever was. Yes, creepy violence scares me.

--This Reviewer

THE ENEMY
WREX SEPT 10

THE ENEMY: With Friends Like These

In physics it's called the Third Law of Thermodynamics. In Seattle, it's called The Enemy. Conversion, constant change and a certain logic have kept The Enemy in the foreground of the local scene. They're hated, they're endured, and they're endeared. They play what they want and how they want to play it.

To take four individuals, with all their miserable problems, whacko personal lives and differing points of view, and combine and develop them into an artistic unit that has as its' goal producing original music is no easy task for any-one. The Enemy has one up on every Seattle punk band, they've had six years as such a unit and the relationship they've attained comes through in every performance.

I've only been seeing the band for a year and a half, but even in that space of time I've seen them twist their music dramatically, gaining a broader base of popularity than they've ever known. Sure, it's easy to pass them off with a sneer, "fuckers wimped out," or pin the label "new wave disco" on the back of their coats when they're not looking, but it's more than that. It's growth and change. And I can't sneer at that.

Yeah, there have been nights I've been pissed at them, shows that made me leery of mentioning I was there, times they played more rotten covers than KJR, but they've kept me coming back. There's always one song, one hot move that piques my interest. Laser Eyes. Rumblings. I forget. Creature Feature. Undermined. Just to hear one of these tunes is worth a night at the Golden Crown, drinking expensive beer and sharing the dance floor carefully with semi-literate Alaskans wearing AC/DC baseball caps.

Their recent performances have been sketchy. They've had to play too long, too many covers and to audiences that only come downtown on Fridays to wear strange sunglasses, funny ties and call themselves "New Wavers." That's unfortunate, because The Enemy needs to concentrate on playing only their material and just for a set or two a night. That's when I've seen the amazing occur. That night at WREX, with Suzyon Arab costume singing Want Me, with a slight change, to "you only want my 981." The Gorilla Room Fiasco, with Barnes' drum solo/joke followed by four fast tight tunes. Anytime they do Flipper Baby.

Go watch The Enemy. Not once or twice and then ignore them like all your friends, but several times over several weeks. And don't listen to the covers. Go out and buy some aspirin wrapped in tinfoil from some guy on the corner and pretend to get high. Then come back inside and listen to their songs. Be impressed.

By the way, George, the check you guys gave me bounced ...

--by Joe Despair

c.1981 Hungry Voice/Joe Despair

6

ILLEGAL ALIENS

THE VILLAINS
COMMODORE BALLROOM, VANCOUVER, B.C.
SEPTEMBER 19

I'd never even heard of the Villains before arriving in Vancouver last time. What I expected was a trendy, lame, skinhead ska band; what I got was an hour's worth of the most intense dance music around. They're a fun band to watch as well, with an added 6th member serving as one of the main focal points. He was the only black in the band (the rest being white English skin-heads).

What makes The Villains unique is that they use steel drums, which gives their music a bouncy, melodic feel. No other major ska band that I know of use steel drums. The Villains have their own sound and they should be proud of it. I guess they moved from England and have made their home base in Vancouver.

They'd just gotten back from a major Canadian tour and played to a middle-of-the-road looking, sold-out crowd. Everybody liked the band and most were dancing to their infectious, uptempo beat. All in all, a good time was definitely had by everyone.

Oh, yeah. The opening band is hardly worth mentioning but I will anyway because they were so bad. They're called Sweet Dick and they played uninspired reggae cover tunes. The worst thing about 'em was that they all wore these long white robes with hoods. Talk about a gimpy looking band; these guys were embarassing!

I also want to mention that The Villains have a 4-song 12" E.P. out that's well worth obtaining. It's on Skinhead Records and should be available soon as a Canadian import. It's called "Life of Crime," which is one of the tunes; the other three are, Urban Skins, Ska Music, and an old Sam the Sham and the Pharoahs tune called Wolly Bully.

When The Villains come to Seattle make sure you get to see 'em 'cause they're hot! Until then...keep on skankin'.

--Criss Crass

D.O.A.
SMILIN' BUDDHA
SEPTEMBER 26

For those left inconsolate by the closing of the Gorilla Room, the Smilin' Buddha in Vancouver is the best substi-tute to be found in these parts, and is well worth the three hour trek. The Buddha staff can be a bit hostile--Igor, the bouncer, is over 300 pounds and YOU NO GO BACK HERE BANDS ONLY and he means it, the guy at the door is very insistent about seeing ID--but they're kind of funny, as is the spaced-out little old man who tends bar. Good news: the Buddha serves hard liquor. Bad news: it's $2.00 a shot, they stop serving at 1:00, and do not give you a break on the American/Canadian money exchange. So it's better to sneak in your own, also bring your own drugs, Vancouver was not plentiful in that depart-ment (believe me, we looked).

The Buddha was hopping for DOA's last show prior to their departure for a tour of England. (They're booked at the Lyceum, Grayhound, Rock City, and hope to pick up some other gigs while over there. After that comes a Canadian tour.) This was obviously their home turf-- DOA were having a much better time than at their recent Danceland USA show. They played a long, loose, high-energy set, incorporating most of the material from Hardcore '81. The place was noisy, heavy on the slamming and black leather jackets. All in all, it was the best time I'd had all month. The Buddha's schedule for the next couple of weeks is included in the calendar in back. Grab someone with a car and hit the road.

-Daina Darzin

7

MOVIES

GALLIPOLI

Director: Peter Weir
Cast: Mark Lee
Mel Gibson
Music: Jean Michel Jarre--
OXYGENE

For those of you unversed in British (or any other) history: Gallipoli is located in Turkey near what was Constantinople and is now Istanbul. It is also the location of one of the greatest defeats of the Allied powers in WWI, all thanks to the planning of Winston Churchill and the mismanagement of the British generals during the invasion.

This debacle did not do much for the career of Mr. Churchill nor for those of the thousands of Australians, New Zealanders and Britons who lost their lives there. Not suprisingly, the invasion of Gallipoli resembles our own involvement in Vietnam. Director Weir has used this to create the most provocative antiwar statement ever filmed.

The story is of a very special, and, I might add, platonic relationship between two young

sprinters. Mel Gibson, who recently appeared in Mad Max, plays the part of a realist who is coerced into joining the service because, well, there isn't much else he can do. Mark Lee, his counterpart and friend in the film, is the idealistic young seeker of adventure. For Gibson's character, superbly played as is Lee's, there is no sense in fighting another man's war. Lee, on the other hand, goes to his death at the end of the film, willing to die with the brotherhood of a soldier as his only comfort; finding glory even in the eradication of what had promised to be a gratifying life.

Normally it would be in extremely bad taste to reveal the ending of a film, however, in the case of Gallipoli, there is little or no question from the beginning as to how the film will end. The movie is about the sadness and the joy of meeting one's destiny. There have been complaints about how the film finishes, but really there is no other way, or place, it could. To carry the story further would be useless.

Weir has created a powerfully moving film. Those of you familiar with his work, Picnic at Hanging Rock, The Last Wave, will find that he has surpassed himself with this latest effort. No film in the past ten years has been so incredibly devastating to the senses. Viewing of this movie and contemplation of everything it implies requires a minimum two-day recuperation period.

—T.C. Rice

AC/DC let there be rock

The new AC/DC movie, "Let There Be Rock" has something for everybody. For all you diehard, heavy metal, AC/DC freak rockers, the appeal is obvious. The concert scenes and the sound system display the band favorably, and the personal, of somewhat inept interview footage should make AC/DC fans drool with the chance to "meet" their heroes. For those of you who enjoy a good laugh, one look at the movie crowd is enough to send any knwolegeable concert-video goer into hysterics. Monday night's group seemed more intent on looking cool and being stoned than having a good time getting into the music. The general atmosphere was one of submissive apathy, with an occasional drunken roar when AC/DC logos were flashed or the band members were initially shown. Needless to say, not a head was bobbing. Finally, for those of you who can't spare 12 dollars to see AC/DC in person, this movie is a welcome relief, costing only five dollars.

The sound system was adequate, but a bit distorted. The volume level was perfect; quieter than a live concert, but more intense than the sound of a typical movie at your local theater. Although seven speakers lined the sides and back wall of the hall, the lack of speakers above the screen made it seem unbalanced for anyone sitting at the front. The film quality was good, with a constant stream of excellent concert footage. The cameraman appeared in a few shots, which detracted from the feel of the entire concert scene.

The format approach taken by the film producers works unusually well. The first several sequences deal with the band and roadies' preparations for a live gig in London. As the film unfolds, the concert footage is punctuated by interviews with band members, all of whom appear somewhat sloshed. This provides several welcome breaks from the pounding music. The interviewer seemed a bit lacking in original question material, making it difficult to get a real feel for band member's personalities.

Prior to Bon Scott's death, he and Angus Young were obviously the entire live appeal of AC/DC. Angus duckwalks across the stage countless times in the manner of a Chuck Berry high on uppers. His lead guitar isn't the world's most original; what is incredible is the manner in which he combines his stage antics with his musical performance. Bon, for the most part, controls the rest of the show. His straightforward slightly macho delivery is very believable, and he seems to be enjoying himself. The rest of the band simply standing or seated, waded through such AC/DC classics as "Whole Lotta Rosie," "Rocker," and "Bad Boy Boogie." (12 or 13 tunes were shown in the entire movie.)

If you have any interest whatsoever in AC/DC, don't miss "Let There Be Rock," otherwise, the price is a bit too steep to risk the experience.

P.S. Bye, Bon!

—Scott Hartwich

John Waters & Divine

In the history of the cinema there have been certain films which have been noted as high points in the change and development of the craft: in 1903 there was The Great Train Robbery, in 1915 D.W. Griffith's Birth of A Nation, 1927 saw Al Jolson sing in The Jazz Singer, Orson Welles came out with Citizen Kane in 1941, and in 1981 Peter Weir will convince every kid under the age of 18 not to register for the draft.

John Waters was born in Baltimore, Maryland, and spent most of his time at the flicks, lapping up the sleaziest ones eagerly (Scum of The Earth, Faster Pussycat Kill Kill, etc.). After leaving the NYU film school following a marijuana bust, Waters began peddling his films as midnight shows along the West Coast. Waters had made five films by this time (early 70s) but it was not until Pink Flamingos (72) wa released that his name became legend. The film attracted an immediate following, and the ritual of the midnight film was born.

All of Waters' films are set in Baltimore, "the sleaziest city on earth" and nearly all have featured the 300-lb star Divine, playing his roles in drag, but insisting "I'm an actor, not a transvestite. A transvestite is a man that lives in drag or gets off sexually in drag. And I don't do either of those. I'd ruin all my costumes, number one-- it costs too much money to clean, and that never really comes out." Divine's presence in the films invariably makes them center around him, as the main source of energy-- this somewhat weakens the depth of the other characters and the storyline. As a result, Waters' last film, Desperate Living (77-there

is a soon-to-be-released-in-the-west film called Polyester) was a bit more cohesive, was more a complete story than a diary of one person, but at the same time, lost the sense of outrageousness that Divine brings.

Pink Flamingos-"the sickest movie ever made, and one of the funniest," concerns Divine, the filthiest person alive, who becomes involved with a couple called the Marbles who set out to "out filthy" Divine. Their claim to fame is kidnapping young girls, impregnating them, and selling the babies to Lesbian -couples. But is that enough to beat a person who eats dog shit off the street....?

Female Trouble-follows the escapades of Dawn Davenport (Divine) who starts out as a high school J.D. mashing her mother under the Xmas tree, and ends up in the electric chair. Along the way she delivers her own baby (and ends up throttling her later), becomes a model, bride and mass murderer.

Desperate Living-the story of Peggy Gravel and her 400-lb black maid on the run after killing Peggy's husband. They end up in Mortville, a never-never land run by evil Queen Carlotta and her black leather male goons. Peggy joins the Queen, her maid dies, but the women of Mortville revolt and all live happily ever after.

Yes, 'outrageous' is a word often used to describe Waters' films-the cavortings of his mob do their best to trample down every barrier of convention, in every area conceivable, going so over-the-top you'll either be disgusted or "get sick all over yourself with laughter,"

8

INTERVIEW

with: **SOLGER.**

by: Catalyst

9

INTRO

Solger formed in June of 1980

Paul-guitar, Kyle-vocals, Doug-bass, Tor-drums.

Inspired by The Germs and Black Flag, the desire to expend pent-up energy was excuse enough to start their own band. Solger was a short-lived outfit, only performing a small handfull of shows. If not for their E.P. they would be lost in total obscurity, save only for those in Seattle who saw them. Ironically enough, their E.P. is doing well in San Francisco Too bad tho, it's now been a year since their break-up. Hopefully, bands in Seattle will get more attention because of bands like Solger. Who knows, maybe the whole music industry will wake up. Wishful thinking, huh?

Cat: How many songs did you have in your repertoire?

Doug: About nine or ten.

Cat: Was that the extent of your show, or did you throw in some covers?

Doug: Yeah, we did covers.

Cat: Like, such as ...?

Kyle: What We Do Is Secret; Germ's song. We did a Damned cover; Stab Your Back, but we changed it to Suck Your Cock or Suck My Cock.

Cat: More black humor. What impressed you about the Germs or Black Flag?

Doug: My opinion is that bands like Black Flag, Germs are punk bands. They are hardcore, not teeny-bopper bands. A lot of bands come on and they think they're going to be hardcore, but they're teeny-bopper music. It's like 1-2-3-4-5-6... you know. Let's have lots of fun.

Kyle: Black Flag has lots of energy. That was their big thing.

Cat: What's your real definition of hardcore, then?

Kyle: Noncompromising. Black Flag didn't compromise I know when they first came here all these guys who arenow into hardcore-I won't mention any names-

they didn't like Black Flag at The Bahamas because Black Flag weren't compromising. They said you had to compromise and Black Flag didn't. You know, they didn't. Hardcore put out. They didn't like it, but now it's like, Black Flag or something. They wear the headbands and everything.

Doug: Loud, fast power that's annoying but in the right perspective. A lot of music is annoying and you don't want to hear it cause it's a bunch of shit. You can take the band seriously. They don't get up there and dance around and shit.

Kyle: It's a real adrenaline rush.

Doug: It's not repetitious.

Cat: You guys had a pretty good following?

Doug: No. Too many trendy people in Seattle. We felt better doing shows out of town. I don't know--I didn't give a shit.

Cat: Do you think it was basically the amount of ignorance?

Doug: I don't know. I though Solger was a good band. I watched bands in Seattle for years and years, and I thought the band Solger had energy and were taken more seriously than any other bands.

Kyle: When we were playing there weren't the people there are now. There are a lot more people in the scene now.

Doug: Like the trendies, they wouldn't admit they liked it.

Cat: Would you guys say you basically made a start of things around here, and then everybody jumped on the bandwagon?

Kyle: The way I look at it, even though I don't want to put this in there--

Cat: You don't, huh?

Kyle: Oh, I don't care. All these other bands are U-District stupid, wanna-be-poppy, hopefully-make-it-like-the-Undertones--

Doug: Buddy, buddy--

Kyle: Yeah. I think our attitude was more of a-- you know, like I was really into the L.A. scene, and that was more of what I wanted. There weren't the bands like that around. Just go out and attack. Before that it was all Psycho-pop and Zipdad kind of music.

Cat: Were you trying to attract a certain crowd or were you out doing it for yourself?

Doug: That's the way we got our kicks. I didn't have nothing to do and I wanted to play in a band and we got together. None of us even really knew each other.

Kyle: It was also a chance to be somebody. You know, before you're just sitting around and watching these stupid bands and you wanna be someone and you can do it and you can do it better than them.

Cat: It's just the fact that anybody can do it if they try hard enough?

Kyle: Well, not everyone can do it, cause not everyone wants to do it. But if you want to do it, you can do it.

Cat: How did you guys meet?

Kyle: OK, first of all I met Paul. I saw his ad in the paper. He wanted to start a new wave-punk band basically. I wanted to get in a band cause I saw Black Flag at The Bahamas. I got a kick out of that and thought this was what I wanted to do. So I called him up, and I asked him if he'd heard of The Germs and all that, and he had. So, we got together at a store, and I got practice space at the Showbox. Then we put up a poster on the wall and I guess Doug saw that. Tor came in by asking if he could practice. At first we said no and then we took him.

Doug: Tor is a good drummer. I just wanted to say that. I thought he added a nice touch.

Kyle: He didn't have the power we could have used. Those are the breaks--he was an artist.

Cat: Would you say he added a pop influence--the artistic touch?

Doug: He was rather an artist within himself. In that sense he added a nice touch to the band cause he didn't play a typical beat. You can hear it on the record--boom!

Cat: Did you accomplish anything?

Doug: Yeah. I learned a lot about playing on stage. I think everyone should be in a band that does a lot of politics and stuff, but it's like, you know, flogging a dead horse. You gotta make your point, maybe, but you can't do it all your life.

Kyle: If you've said it once, what's the point of playing 400 shows if it's going to be the same thing? You've done it.

Cat: So basically it was personal accomplishments that you suceeded in?

Kyle: Everyone but Paul. Paul wants to become more famous.

Doug: That's why the band broke up--this is my opinion. Paul may give the typical rock star story that he got bored, but the real reqson was he met Upchuck

Cat: Was there a special idea behind the E.P.?

Doug: Just that we existed.

Kyle: Well, we made a tape, I don't know why we made a tape, but we made this tape. Then Doug said he'd put up the money to make a record.

Doug: We didn't follow the typical band rule. We didn't go to the studio. We just had Phileppo Scrouge do four-track recording. We did guitars in the Showbox dressing room, vocals at the Gas Chamber in the washer and dryer room, and we had it recorded at the Lawrence Gospel Recording Studio. No one can say we made any profit off of it. No one kissed our ass--we kissed no one's ass.

His Foreplay Was Murder

yes, FARTZ!!!

What the F**k?

BULL SHIT!

ASTOR PARK: 10/6-10 Allies and Impacts 10/27-8 Shyanne 10/31 Johnny and the Distractions

ASTOR PARK 625-1578
5th & Lenora, Seattle

BABY-O:10/31 No Cheese Please

BABY-O's 624-6558
122 Cherry, Seattle

DANCELAND 624-4732
1501 1/2 First, Seattle

EAGLES AUDITORIUM:
10/9 Siouxie and the Banshees 10/28 Student Nurse, Prefabs, Vacuumz, 10/31 Rastafarians

EAGLES AUDITORIUM
7th and Union, Seattle

EUPHORIA (503) 235-4300
320 S.E. 2nd, Portland

EUPHORIA: 10/12 Insex, the Rats 10/28 Marty Balin

GATSBY'S 455-0666
12700 Bel-Red Rd, Bellevue

GATSBY'S: 10/8-10 Kidd Afrika10/13-17 No Cheese Please 10/19-20 Strypes 10/21-24 Sequel

GOLDEN CROWN 455-0666
1616 4th Avenue, Seattle

GOLDEN CROWN: 10/13 Annie Rose & the Thrillers

GORILLA ROOM 345-9393
610 2nd Ave. Seattle (not open currently)

HALL OF FAME: 10/31: Beats

ha ha ha ha

HALL OF FAME 633-5500
4518 Univ. Wy., Seattle

RAINBOW: 10/12-13; Eddie & the Atlantics 10/14-17 Dynamic Logs 10/21-24 Clantons

HIBBLE & HYDES 623-1541
608 First Ave., Seattle

SHOWBOX 621-8064
1421 First, Seattle

SMILIN BUDDHA: 10/9-10 Subhumans, Gentlemen of Horror, VXN, Replacements 10/12-14 No Prisoners 10/15-17 Chronic Condition w/ Special guest 10/19-21 Replacements

SMILIN' BUDDHA 604-669-3136
109 E. Hastings, Vancouver

UTC HALL: 10/8 Student Nurse Little Bears from Bangkok, Mr. Epp & the Calculations

UTC HALL 632-3705
Fifth & Aloha, Seattle

MANIAC WHO KILLED, AND DEVOURED.

WREX 625-WREX
2018 First Av., Seattle

WREX: 10/7-11 Napalm Beach 10-/14 Rolling Stones party 10/15 New Flamingos 10/16-17 Enemy 10/21 Engram record release party 10/23,24 Romeo Void with Student Nurse, Sex Therapy 10/27 Echo & the Bunnymen with The Enemy 10/28 Fastbacks 11/6 Really Red (country punk from Texas!?) 10/30 Blackouts, Student Nurse 10/31 Halloween party 11/4 the Romantics

Battle With Army Continues

BORN. FIGHT BACK Calendar

DRINK

10

RECORDS

foetus underglass

Spite Your Face b/w O.K.F.M.
Self Immolation Records

YOU'VE GOT FOETUS ON YOUR BREATH
Wash It All Off b/w 333'
Self Immolation Records

I suspect that these two groups are actually one and the same: call it intuition. "Wash It All Off" is a spiffy electronic number with pseudo-disco bass and a singer who sounds mostly like himself but, for clarity's sake, could easily pass at times for Richard Hell or James Chance. The lyrics are hysterial ("Super-califragilistic Sad Masochistic!") and the backup vocals are the Residents meet Alvin and the Chipmunks. "333" is a little like Smegma, a little like Metal Machine Music, and quite melodic. Somehow. It features chanting and shrieking in faraway voices.

"Spite Your Face" has more amino B-ring silliness and a chorus of "See my voice I'm not complaining/Hear my teeth no cavities!" Hey, it grows on you. "O.K.F.M." DOES sound like Phillip Glass, albeit bargain-basement version. The sound coagulates into ominous techno sounds on top of a heartbeat bass, and someone begins to wail, "OK, freeze mother!" Visions of baby blue helmets...

If you want to hear something that truly sounds like NOTHING ELSE, buy these records. I don't know how new they are, but they're hard to find. If you want to order them yourself, contact 35 Bracken Road, London N2, England. A few are available at Corporate or Tower. The sleeve notes such forthcoming releases as a solo single by Phillip-Ex Fug, and a triple LP-Foetus On The Beach. Don't ask. These discs are Highly Recommended.

--Captive

psychedelic furs

Pretty In Pink b/w Mack the Knife

"Pretty in Pink" is the "pick hit" of the Fur's second album. Quite popular at WREX, I hear. It's one of their more melodic tunes, very hummable and danceable. Sticks in your head. I like their second album's style better for boppin' down the street, but the first one's best for sitting around being cozy on cold nights.

"Mack the Knife" -remember this? Bertolt Brecht by way of Bobby Darin? He may have croaked but the Pyschedlic Furs carry on his music, changed to suit them. You'd never realize what it was if you didn't notice the lyrics. It's been revamped to the Fur's style completely. Butler really snarls out the lyrics, and it sounds a lot nastier this way.

Heidi Weispfenning

iggy pop

Party"

Arista president Clive Davis must have decided Iggy needs to make hit singles. So what do they do? Bring in former Monkees' producer and songwriter Tommy Boyce to produce four songs (strings, horns, and echo) and let some other guy from the same school produce the rest. No hits here, although "Eggs on Plate" has Iggy in good form and features the memorable line, "who left Murph the Surf on my ceiling." On most of the songs Iggy's personality is submerged in the clutter. With the exception of the occasionally inspired guitar of Ivan Kraal the musicians sound bored. It's rock and roll, but it doesn't rock. A definite disappointment after Iggy's fine Arista releases, "New Values" and "Soldier." The carefully touched-up photo on the cover should have tipped me off.

--J. Rubato

the stains

John Wayne
Was A Nazi b/w Born to Die

Typical harcore deep from the heart of Texas. "John Wayne" I must say is a real clever song and is all truth. Especially the chorus-
"He was a Nazi...not anymore
He was a Nazi--life evened the score."

This is real fun stuff, I mean, who really wanted to grow up like John Wayne anyhow? "Born to Die" is your usual angry punk outlook song. Don't misunderstand me, this is real good and worth having. But there has been an onslaught of hardcore lately and it does get dull here and there.

--Catalyst

the dicks

Hate Police

Texas punk? This is the Stain's sister band. I like "Hate Police," it's good original material with halfway good lyrics. Not real fast thrash punk, but it does have its' own punch! The flip side is a bunch of shit, I think. Well, I didn't like it too much. But then again, I didn't give it a second chance. See what you think first.

--Catalyst

channel three

This is fast, loud, hardcore music for either the connoisseur or novice. Another great band from Southern California with some incredible work by guitarist Kimm Gardener. "I'm Not a Gun" is fast but stupid. "Manzaner" is faster and definitely the best cut from this E.P. Highly recommended.

Posh Boy Records/P.O. Box 38861/
Los Angeles, CA/90038   --MM

the frazz

Little Bit of Soul/Venus
Du-Tel

You wouldn't know from the cheap photocopying of the Rob Morgan sleeve how clean the record sounds. It's possibly better-sounding than the originals, at least better than the moth-eaten copies of the originals that you're likely to find around town. Marty Frasu and his Northwest Go-Go Squad left any sense of tacky camp outside the studio door. Sincere, straightforward covers are the items on the menu and they're served up hot. Only a political conspiracy or a lack of interest in the surf organ can keep this from being a hit. Precisely the sort of accessible, joyous pop that the Reganoids' Muzak monopoly does not want heard. So hear it.

--CH

billy idol

Mony Mony b/w Baby Talk
Chrysalis, US

This is the first solo effort from the singer of the now defunct Generation X, and what an effort it is! The A side is a cover of an old Tommy James and the Shondells classic that manages to bring life to the silly bubblegum hit, complete with soul sister back-up vocals.

Billy's voice is in perfect form on the fun packed tunes and Baby Talk definitely rocks the hardest of the two. It starts off with a single guitar riff and from there goes into a flawless hard pop rock n' roll masterpiece. I wish I knew who played what and who his new band is...guess we'll just have to wait and see. I've heard that Billy's in England recording an album and then going back to New York to embark on conquering the States. In any event, this sneak preview without a picture sleeve should satisfy various rock entusiasts since it has universal rock hit appeal.

Here's wishing Billy Idol the best of luck with his new solo career and I highly recommend picking up this hard to find 45.

--Criss Cross

the vains

The Vain's post-mortem release must be considered the definitive harcore relase to date in the Seattle area. Guitarist Criss Cross, bassist Nico Teen and drummer Andy Freeze combine their respective talents to create an original trip of raw punk anthems with heavy metal overtones. The innovative, if crass, guitar work comes across successfully, managing to make all of those overly familiar punk chords exciting for a change. The solo guitar portions stand out due to their originality: Crass refuses to rip off typical leads, preferring to experiment; the lack of polished precision he displays actually adds to the overall brutish feel of the music.

Lest the listener expect perfection, he or she should be prepared for some rather raspy vocals on "School Jerks" and "The Loser," both sung by Criss Cross. Nico Teen's vocals on "The Fake" turn out more smoothly, helping to make it the slickest of the three numbers.

The production is of average quality, but excellent considering only eight tracks were utilized. What it manages to accomplish involves the way in which it keeps the sound quality or style in "sync" with the music; in other words, the rough-edged production matches perfectly the rawness of the music.

The Vains weren't lacking in humor, as indicated by the sleeve's front cover artistry. Portions of an annual page as well as printed lyrics with hidden meanings make up the rear cover.

Credit is definitely due Randall Fehr for the layout and Chris Millan of Vanguard Press for the print job.

The no-bullshit approach to hard rock demonstrated by these wee lads (18, 17 and 16 at recording time) makes the Vains 45 a worthwhile venture in music--well worth owning, trashing and buying all over again.

Scott Hartwich

zru vogue

Nakweda Dream/Kyoomye-lo-nimbes
Adolescent

It's slow, pulsating, ethereal, comforting and disturbing at the same time. The crooner lets out a scream just where you don't expect it. They're quietly confused about the world, but sure enough about themselves to claim to be "infinitely tall."

For a change of pace, the flip gives us some more African rhythms, complete with marimbas, (when's Dumi going to make a record?) jazz horns, and studio (instead of "found") vocals. Much too short.

--ch

hi-fi

Demonstration Record
First American

The first rock record in years, besides reissues, to have come from an organization controlled by Mr. Jerry Dennon, a producer entrepeneur who might have been God at one time for his work with the Kingsmen, Sonics, Raiders, Bards, Goodtimes, et al. Not worth the wait. The sound of hippie blues clones trying too hard to prove that they're up to date. A far better Hi-Fi demonstration record is to be found under the title Stereo Spectacular at your local Radio Shack.

--CH

frank johnson's favorites

Ralph

Take the liner notes with a pound of salt, then hear all the outtakes and rarities on this new Ralph sampler. The label's longtime schizophrenia between electronic vaudeville (Residents, Renaldo and the Loaf) and avant guitar heroes (Fred Frith) really stands out, but if you love one side of that duality you'll at least be able to sit through the other side. One listen to the Residents' Beatles cover will make the newly-convered burn all copies of "Stars on 45 XVII" in existence.

--CH

gary numan

"Dance"

"Dance" is not a get-up-and-move-your-butt disco record, nor is it a robotic pogo record, it's Gary Numan's way of saying "I'm tired of the same old thing."

Numan's latest effort is a mix of the same old synthesizer stuff with glittery soul rhythms and new, more human ideas for a change. It has lyrics with references to boys, elegant bitches, paid-for love, sex, loneliness, and boring New Romantics.

At 9:01 "Slowcar to China" is an example of good material spread too thin. To appreciate this, you have to be in a quiet, unstirring mood. Even then, it doesn't make a big impression.

"Night Talk" is quite a bit better, and it is a city rhythmic sex song:
    "Take things slow you can
        crack
    Like your face I don't
        understand
    How you smile and pretend
        it's fund
    Do you laugh when the rats
        come round to play"

"A Subway Called You" must be Gary Numan's answer to The Fur's song "Into You Like a Train." It's the song most likely to be released if there was still a "rock of the eighties" on the air. It's wonderful.

"Cry the Clock Said" is a slow, sad song about changed feelings "Maybe as a game you lost. Well someone I know lost the whole damn world."

Side two starts off faster with "She's Got Claws" and then goes right into another .trong one called "Crash." It's a flawless song. During "Boys Like Me" there's an accented voice whispering and laughing sexily in the background. Nice touch. "Stories" is a pretty little soft song about loneliness and new-found love. "My Brother's Time" has a piano riff that's vaguely familiar, a rich, jazzy sax, and nice lyrics. If you're impatient though, it sounds slightly bland. "You Are, You Are" reminds me a little bit of "We Are Glass." It's a very upbeat tune in the right place. The last one, called "Moral" you've probably heard before, except then it was called "Metal."

This is a lopsided album, yet well done because he leaves on a strong note, saving the best for last. I like that balance.

--This Reviewer

suburban lawns

IRS.

The Rezillos did a better flying saucer song, though the Lawns' one has a nice line about "smoking, drinking, stale burritos." Here's another line from the LP: "Couldn't wait/depend on fate/ the perfect mate/computer date/ I filled out a form/ and she filled out a form/ our date was merged/and love was born." If that amuses you, so will the Lawns. If not, then be warned that their legendary single "Gidget Goes to Hell" is still banned and doesn't appear here.

--CH

the cure

... Happily Ever After
A&M

And they all lived happily ever after, except elitist Lou who bought The Cure's Seventeen Seconds and Faith as imports for a total of $25.98 plus tax when he could have waited to get both records in one package for $8.66 or less, depending on the store.

It's been a depressing month for me, and there's little better to aid depressed states than The Cure. Hard to describe the sounds, but the first disc is sort of like a man who had earlier been screaming in panic, then calmed down, got a sober look at the scene around him, then screamed again, only this time quieter and stronger. The other disc sounds sort of like search through the heart to find a way back to sanity. Quite morose, quite good. Includes "Primary," a not-too-old single played at rock disco joints by DJs who thought it was just like U2. But it ends soon enough and the record goes back to its serious business. A double album that leaves you wanting more.

--ch

s.p.k.

Information Overload Unit

The information overload unit is you and the question posed is how much can you take before something snaps and there you are convulsing on the floor, spittle running off the side of your mouth.

First some information: SPK are a group from Australia or New Zealand rumored to consist of a mental patient and his nurse grooving together under a heavy Baader-Meinhoff influence. They have one single out on Industrial, "Slogan/Factory."

A handly little booklet called Dokument One that comes with the album provides a list of song titles plus photo-collages of children with birth defects, porno ads, and a tied-up mouse interspersed with cut-up paragraphs about psycho-neurotic soldiers and paralysis drugs. You've probably seen this type of decadent literature

many times before, but you cannot deny its startling effect.

Each song is carefully crafted to bring you a variety of sensations, "schizophrenia, manic depressive psychosis, mental retardation and paranoia." I might add slow nausea, physical disorientation and a heartfelt contentedness with the world around you.

Some might call this a downbeat album, but parts of it make me feel really good, like all those static rushes and airhammer feedback attacks that get your blood pumping in the morning. Not to mention some keen electronic syncopation. They've even got a sense of humor. Check out these lines from "Kaltbruchig Acideath":
    "Yeah. That was from
    the time with the bottle.
    Later on I went to the
    doctor and he told me I
    was pregnant. Cus I
    didn't want any baby I
    injected some acid into
    my stomach. Blood and
    fetus came out about a
    minute after. Actually,
    it was twins."

Wow. Is the human race damned, or what?

They speed up, they slow down, they throw up, they're a lot of fun. They're SPK who stand for, at different times, Surgical Penis Klinik, System Planning Korporation, Selective Pornography Kontrol, and Socialist Patients Kollektiv. But here is what they really stand for:
    "Not only is the historical
    complexity of ambient
    information increasing,
    but so is the ability to
    receive and interpret
    incoming signals. What
    appears today to be either
    a noise-wall or a non-
    interpretable foreign sig-
    nal, will in five years be
    considered simplistic/
    familiar."
                SPK RESEARCH

--T. Reedy

the gun club

Ruby Records

A 4-piece outfit from east L.A., sort of a combo of R&B, Ry Cooder and The Cramps thrown together. But these guys have got their own feel totally. This album is very pleasurable and I enjoy listening to it a lot. They seem to be kind of gloomy with a heavy upbeat/upswing. They really are very tight and will definitiely gain lots of recognition. If you like good rock, this is a definite must. Watch out, Cramps:

--Catalyst

urgh!

A&M

Aural elaborations on the "no such thing as new wave" argument of an early DI editorial. C'mon, just try to explain why any two of these 27 bands should be on the same record. Some four dozen bands were

filmed at specially-arranged sites to make the movie that this is a preview of, so you can imagine what kind of bootlegs we're in store for if we're lucky and someone in the project is greedy enough. They've done as good a job as anyone can of sequencing this so the wide variations of style and attitude don't interfera as badly as they could have. The one to play for your mother or anyone who doesn't understand your music, even though few of the acts are at their best, probably due to the presence of the film crews, who, I'm told, worked in frontstage pits with fans fenced out.

--CH

tom verlaine

Dreamtime
Warner Brothers

Once there was Television, now there is T.V., a Manhattan-rock original, with an album of guitar-heavy ballads that take a few hearings to get to you. It's a contender that could have been a champ, if the mix hadn't made it so Petty. I'd like to blame the producer but none is listed. Try to forget how bland it sounds and in a while Verlaine's voice will come through, a voice that deserves better than to be barely audible in the back of the record.

--CH

the specials

Ghost Town
Chrysalis

Strains of sirens approaching. Listen...wierd Arabic Bossa Nova. Listen closer...
    "This town is nothing but
    a ghost town/all the
    clubs are been' closed
    down".
Familiar.

    "This place is coming
    like a ghost town/bands
    won't play no more/too
    much fighing on the
    dance floor".
Yeah, too familiar.
They wrote it about their hometown, Coventry. It travels well.

D.W.

ian dury

Spasticus Autisticus
Stiff
This is definitely the most irritatingly infections thing since Dury's Hit Me days. It's sort of an out of the closet anthem dedicated to the deaf, dumb, blind and otherwise malformed members of our society. Sly Shakespeare and Robbie Dunbar join Ian and ex-Blockhead geanius Chaz Jenkel, turning out a highly danceable, extremely positive single. It chugs, churns, and all the stuff neo-disco is supposed to do, then suddenly it bursts into a jazzy bridge that chugs, churns, and all the other stuff jazzy bridges are supposed to do. Don't buy it if you don't like to dance. If you do, throw down those crutches and see again.
-D.W.

ACCESSORIES

GORILLA ROOM NEWS

Ok, here's the latest update; the landlord, health department and the liquor board have apparently decided that the Gorilla Room won't reopen. Here's how it works: the health department will not give the room an ok (although renovations have been made and everything meets standards) until they have written permission from the landlord stating that he approves the G. Room management's use of the property. Which he won't, because he wants them evicted. The liquor board has stated that should the

Gorilla Room overcome that obstacle and reopen, they intend to come and visit every single night the place is open.

David Brown, the G. Room's new manager, is really pissed off about this and says the G. Room is going to reopen, somewhere, if it's the last thing he does, just to show 'em. He's looking in the International District, where people are probably a little more tolerant of noise and craziness. Good luck, folks, keep the faith, all that shit.

— Daina Darzin

POK A DOT

M-F   11 to 6
SAT   12 to 5

782 6812
521 NW 43rd

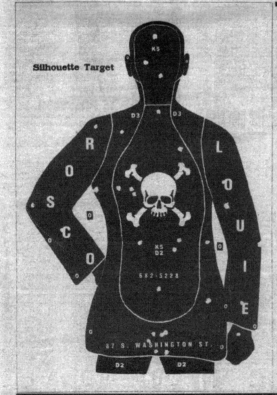

Silhouette Target

BRAVE NEW WORLD MUZAK

It's not an act of rebellion to sing about death and war now that the new fiscal year has begun and with it the implementation of greed and destruction as not just official policies but official virtues. It's not cute to wear a swastika today, it's just dumb at best and unconscionable at worst. After Atlanta, songs like the Victim's "100% White Girl" just sound pathetic.

The Specials hardly ever gig in the UK these days, because of shows that were crashed by Nazi youth groups dressed as skinheads drowning out the music with "Seig Heil." A story in Billboard last month traced one of the English riots to the burning of a building in an Indian section of one city by a skinhead gang. Pop music is being subverted to promote evil here, too: a modern American evil of self-centered apathy, reflected in

the endless airing of bland-chic dirges about sailing and being happily married. Brave New World muzak that encourages mindlessness.

What is the underground doing to resist mindlessness? Promoting an alternative mindlessness is no answer. Even light entertainment is political in the attitudes it inspires. Boogie-til-you-puke rock, metal and punk versions alike, just helps folks kill themselves so the right wing doesn't have to bother with killing them.

Romance music could be about loving and caring, but the records billed as "new romantic" are just white disco— Reganculture for the young and rich, while C. Cross is Reganculture for the middle-aged and rich.

--Clark Humphrey

STOP PRESS

Maybe radio really is dead. Apparently some of the old blood at KRAB are going all out in an effort to cut out the soul and new wave shows, the argument being that they're too commercial. Which leads us to the question of why these plastic commodities are not being financed by commercial stations. If you want to have airwaves left to listen to, send a letter of protest to

 KRAB RADIO
 2212 South Jackson
 Seattle, WA 98144

Tell them what shows you listen to and why. Alternative radio should live up to its name.

The Vacuumz' Kim Nomad was not permitted to play WREX last week because of lack of ID.

The Golden Crown is slowly opening up to new music thanks to R.H.A. and friends.

X cancelled at WREX for Halloween to play Corvalis ????? but are rebooked for November 13 at the Showbox and 14 at WREX.

Bassist Phil Otto has left Rapid-i to keep up with other commitments. Hopefully, their EP will still be released.

Ex-Showbox lease holder Muffin is reportedly flying to New York to tidy up some things with FBI.

Social Deviate Peter Davis is trying to put together a taped compilation of local bands. In the meantime, Engram Records is still waiting for delivery of the Seattle Syndrome.

Upchuck's latest endeavor is making a video-disk of his new band Sleeping Movement, primarily for sale in Japan.

Several local bands are planning a pre-Halloween costume party at Eagles on October 28. Featured bands will be Student Nurse, PreFabs, VAcuumz, and more

X-15 are changing their set and style with 16 new songs, 2 guitars, drums, no bass

Mike Refuzor is serious about the Gargoyles, but is looking for a drummer, who must be able to play loud and not be afraid to break his drum skins.

Perryscope Productions from up North are thinking of bringing Simple Minds to Seattle. As of press time, they still don't have an opening at for the Siouxie & the Banshees show.

Concerts West has taken over the Showbox, and are planning staight rock with a beer/wine license. Remodeling starts in January.

FUNNIES

NEXT ISSUE: WHAT'S HAPPENING ON HALLOWEEN, SIOUXIE & THE BANSHEES, ROLLING STONES, SUBHUMANS, OTHER SHIT...

THE SUMMER OF 1981 | 135

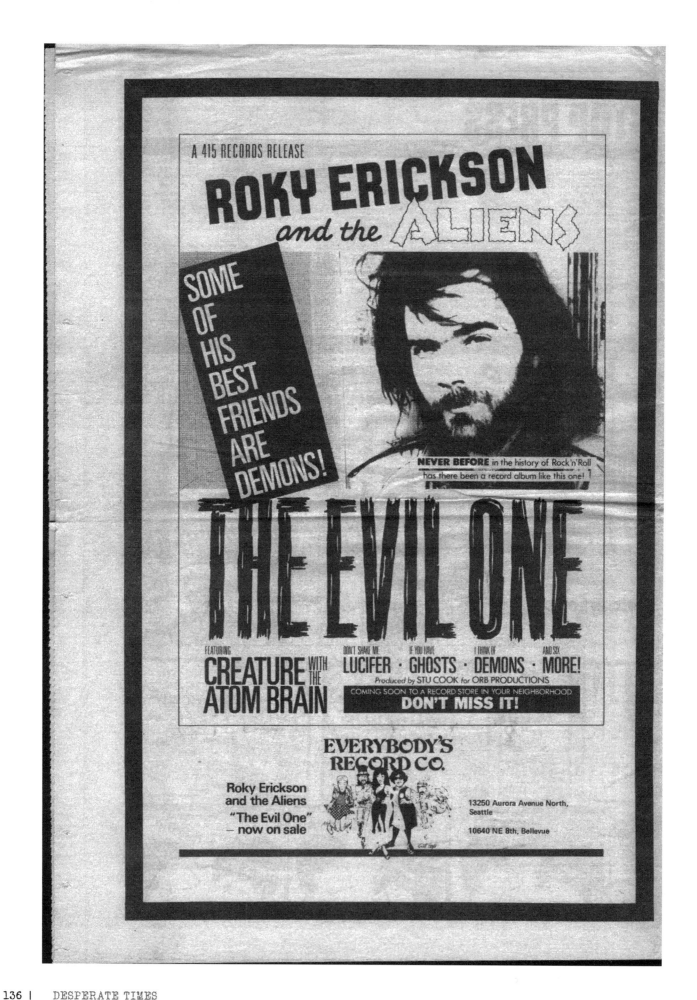

WHAT ELSE WAS GOING ON?

Every year is special in some way or another. Years are easily defined when we are students: school starts and ends the year, and is further broken up by terms and coursework. We also emotionally connect and remember individual years by the weddings, births, divorces, and deaths that occurred. Generations find identity in years marked by important events like world wars, walking on the moon, or terrorist attacks. Otherwise, the passing of years is hardly noticed; for most of us, it's just enough to get through the month. Technology has done us no favors by condensing our experience of time into instant communication and 24/7[30] news coverage. This is one reason why "Today in History" stories are popular, as well as a convenient filler. For a short moment we get to reconnect with the ongoing timeline of the world around us.

There is clearly a "time capsule" quality about this book because *Desperate Times* was such a short episode in a very busy year. *Desperate Times* captured a moment in time that can be placed on the time scale of a year, a decade, and even a century. So here are a few of the remarkable events that occurred in 1981 and why *Desperate Times* was not the only important thing that happened that year.

DO YOU REMEMBER?

It might be argued that the biggest event in 1981 was the royal wedding of Prince Charles to Lady Diana Spencer. The ceremony was televised and about 750 million people around the world watched. Most of these people watched it the same way I did, on a black-and-white television with an aerial antennae.

1981 was also a year noted for assassination attempts. Ronald Reagan was shot by John Hinckley, Jr. on March 30. Reagan's famous quip to his wife Nancy, "Honey, I forgot to duck," was sampled into a hit song by New York City band Three Teens Kill Four. The event's legacy was further nailed when an early skate-punk group took the name JFA, or "Jodie Foster's Army," as a nod to Mr. Hinckley's efforts (Hinckley had said he tried to kill the president because he wanted to

---

[30] 24/7, shorthand for 24 hours a day, seven days a week, fifty-two weeks a years, etc. The 365 days of the annual year are completely contiguous and non-interrupted. Hours and days and years don't matter when you are always "on."

impress actress Jodie Foster). Reagan survived, and supported private gun ownership for the rest of his life.

There was also an assassination attempt on Pope John Paul II on May 13. The Pope later met with his potential killer and forgave him. This papal audience was not requested, and is possibly the most notorious papal absolution in modern Catholic history. The Pope also recorded several pop albums that never made the music charts, but were a great tax dodge for someone. A month later, on June 13, a teenager took some pot-shots at Queen Elizabeth II while she rode her horse during a parade in honor of her birthday, the Trooping the Colour ceremony, in London. England has strong laws controlling guns and ammunition, and the unhappy youth only had blanks to shoot, so the Queen was never in any real danger. The newspapers commented on how well the Queen kept control of her horse.

Not all assassination attempts fail. Tragically, the Egyptian president Anwar Sadat was assassinated on October 6, 1981. Sadat had led the 1973 Yom Kippur War against Israel. But later he worked for Middle East stability, including the secret 1978 Camp David Accords facilitated by president Jimmy Carter. (Sadat and Israeli Prime Minister Menachem Begin were awarded the Nobel Peace Prize for the peace agreement in 1978.) The murdered Sadat was succeeded by Hosni Mubarak, who ruled Egypt from 1981 until ousted by a popular revolt in 2010, a critical moment in the Arab Spring of 2010-2012.

In 1980, the population of the United States was 227 million, with 7.1% unemployment. By 2010, the US population was 308 million, with 9.6% unemployment.[31] In 1981, the minimum wage was $3.35, which is what most of us were earning (if we had a job) as dishwashers or clerical workers. By 2009, the average minimum wage was $7.25. In May 1980, the price of gas peaked at $1.41 ($3.07 per gallon in 2010 dollars). In May 2012, the national average for a gallon of gas was $3.73. In Seattle the price was over $4.00.[32]

IBM released the first computer designed for small offices and homes, the IBM PC-1550, on August 12, 1981. This was significant because personal computers had been popular with hobbyists since the release of the Altair 8800 in 1975, but the IBM-PC was the turning point

---

[31] These figures were gathered from the US Census Bureau and US Dept. of Labor, as reported in August 2012.

[32] Numbers as reported by the American Automobile Association (AAA) in July 2012. See http://fuelgaugereport.aaa.com/.

when computers became a standard fixture of every office and eventually of most homes. But the release of hardware meant nothing without the release of software, and the addition of important software programs like WordStar and VisiCalc (and, most importantly, games) gave computers a useful purpose for every household. The impact of computers for personal use is still being determined. But even back then people recognized the historical sea change, and Time magazine named "The Computer" as Machine of the Year in 1982.

MTV began broadcasting in 1981. Video killed the radio star, and digital killed everything else.

HISTORICAL TIMELINE FOR 1981

JANUARY

1.03 John Lennon and Yoko Ono's album *Double Fantasy* is the top selling album. The former Beatle was assassinated on December 8, 1980.

1.04 *The Official Preppy Handbook* tops *The New York Times* trade paperback best seller list, and remains on the list for 65 weeks.

1.05 Berkeley police arrest eight demonstrators protesting Selective Service System registration. Conscription ended in 1973 after the Vietnam War, and an all-volunteer military was established. Registering for conscription, or the draft, at the age of 18 was reinstituted in 1980. It is still the law for all males between the ages of 18 and 25 to register with Selective Service; however, the law has not been enforced since 1986.

1.15 The first nuclear bomb test of the year is held at the Nevada Test Site. There will be 17 nuclear bomb tests in 1981 in the United States.

1.20 Ronald Reagan is sworn in as president of the US. Also on this day, Iran releases the 52 American hostages they had held for more than 14 months, in exchange for the return of $7.9 billion in frozen assets.

MARCH

3.01 Irish Republican Army member Bobby Sands begins a hunger strike at the Maze Prison in Northern Ireland. He dies 65 days later, at the age of 27, from self-imposed starvation. British Prime Minister Margaret Thatcher refuses to give ground, and nine more people die in the 1981 Irish Hunger Strike.

3.03 William S. Burroughs, Jr. (b.1947), writer, dies.

3.05 President Reagan asks Congress to end federal legal aid to the poor. The next day President Reagan announces plans to cut 37,000 federal jobs.

3.30 President Reagan is wounded in an assassination attempt by John W. Hinckley Jr.

APRIL

4.10 The Brixton riots begin in London. Over the next two days, more than 300 people are injured and 150 buildings damaged. The riots are blamed on economic and social policies implemented by Prime Minister Margaret Thatcher.

4.12 *Columbia*, the first US space shuttle, is launched from Cape Canaveral, Florida. The Space Shuttle program ends on July 21, 2011, after a total of 135 launches and only two failures (Columbia breaks apart during re-entry on December 16, 2003 after 27 successful missions, and the Challenger explodes during takeoff on January 28, 1986).

MAY

5.11 Bob Marley (b.1945), Jamaican reggae artist, dies in Miami.

5.13 John Paul II survives an assassination attempt.

Date unknown Tim Paterson, the creator of the Quick and Dirty Operating System, leaves Seattle Computer Products to work for Microsoft. Paterson is best known as the original author of the DOS operating system.

JUNE

6.01 Cable News Network, commonly known as CNN, celebrates its first year of broadcasting news 24 hours a day, 7 days a week.

6.05 The US Federal Centers for Disease Control publish the first report of a mysterious outbreak of a sometimes-fatal pneumonia among gay men. The disease was named Acquired Immunodeficiency Syndrome (AIDS) in 1982.

6.12 The movie *Raiders Of The Lost Ark* premieres.

6.22 Mark David Chapman (b.1955) pleads guilty to killing John Lennon on December 8, 1980. He was sentenced 20 years to life in prison.

6.25 The US Supreme Court decides that male-only draft registration was constitutional.

JULY

7.03 The Toxteth riots begin in Liverpool, England. Rioting continues for several days and spreads across the country, eventually including large disturbances in Birmingham, Leeds, and London. The riots are blamed on police intolerance under the Thatcher regime, poverty, and racial issues.

7.07 President Reagan nominates Arizona Judge Sandra Day O'Connor to the US Supreme Court. O'Connor was sworn in as the first female justice on the US Supreme Court on September 25.

7.08 First issue of *Desperate Times* published.

7.09 Nintendo releases the video arcade game Donkey Kong.

7.17 In Kansas City, Missouri, 114 people are killed when a pair of walkways above the lobby of the Hyatt Regency Hotel collapse. Also on this day, Israel bombs Beirut, killing approximately 300 civilians.

7.22 Second issue of *Desperate Times* published.

7.29 Britain's Prince Charles marries Lady Diana Spencer at St. Paul's Cathedral in London.

AUGUST

8.01 The US rock music video channel MTV, founded by Bob Pittman, makes its debut. The first music video shown is "Video Killed the Radio Star" by the British band the Buggles.

8.03 US air traffic controllers (PATCO) go on strike, despite a warning from President Reagan. Two days later Reagan fires 11,500 air traffic controllers.

8.05 Third issue of *Desperate Times* published.

8.12 IBM introduces the IBM 5150, better known as the PC, along with PC-DOS version 1.0. The personal computer ran at 4.77 MHz with 16 kilobytes of memory and sold for $1,565.

8.13 President Reagan signs the Economic Recovery Tax Act of 1981, popularly called the Kemp-Roth tax cuts. In addition to changes in the tax code, the bill authorizes tax-deferred Individual Retirement Accounts (IRAs) for individuals. Also signed into law is the Adolescent Family Life Act (AFLA paid for abstinence-only sex education programs in public schools).

8.19 Fourth issue of *Desperate Times* published.

8.28 James E. Hansen publishes an article in Science magazine entitled "Climate Impact of Increasing Atmospheric Carbon Dioxide." Hansen later popularizes the term "global warming." The United Nations begins monitoring the ozone after British scientists find a hole in the earth's atmosphere over the South Pole.

SEPTEMBER

9.03 Fifth issue of *Desperate Times* published.

9.19 Half a million people attend Simon & Garfunkel's concert in Central Park.

OCTOBER

10.6 Nobel Peace Prize winner and Egyptian President Anwar Sadat is assassinated by an Islamic fundamentalist. Vice President Hosni Mubarak assumes the office the following day. Mubarak rules Egypt until the Egyptian Revolution in February 2011.

10.07 Sixth and last issue of *Desperate Times* published.

10.8 A planted bomb is successfully defused at the University of Utah. It was the fifth of 16 bombs later attributed to the Unabomber, Theodore Kaczynski.

NOVEMBER

11.29 Actress Natalie Wood (b.1938) drowns off Santa Catalina, California.

DECEMBER

12.12 Martial law is imposed in Poland to crack down on the Solidarity labor movement. The arrest of labor leader Lech Walesa galvanizes the popular movement and brings international attention to the labor struggles in Poland.

12.28 The first American test-tube baby, Elizabeth Jordan Carr, is born by cesarean section in Norfolk, Virginia.

A FEW WORDS ABOUT RADIO

The role of radio in disseminating information and entertainment has been largely displaced by the internet and streaming media, making it nearly impossible to imagine how important live radio was during the 20th century. In the 1980s, college and community radio stations were crucial in promoting alternative music. Believe it or not, people actually listened to specific radio shows at specific times — you can see the ads for some of these shows in *Desperate Times*.[33]

There is not sufficient space, nor is it appropriate, to discuss here the debacle of the consolidation of radio, television, and newspapers that replaced local programming with homogenized, corporate content. I will say only that in my lifetime radio stations aired programming that was unique to the station's local broadcast area, which was often quite small.

For example, before 1982, the station wattage of University of Washington station KCMU covered only the campus and a few city blocks beyond it. The signal was so weak that radio reception was affected by the weather. In 2000, KCMU became the first radio station in the world to stream high-quality audio on the internet, 24 hours a day, seven days a week. In 2001, KCMU was renamed KEXP and began broadcast, satellite, and internet streaming through a partnership between the University of Washington and the Experience Music Project museum. Today it is one of the most widely listened to radio stations in the world.[34]

College radio was hugely influential in the spread of alternative music across the country during the 1970s and 1980s. These stations were often the only places where independently produced music received airplay. In addition, there were also stations run at high schools, as well as pirate radio stations that operated without FCC licenses.

The only commercial radio station in the Seattle area that played alternative radio was KZAM-AM, known as the "Rock of the '80s." When KZAM was sold, a grassroots effort was launched to protest the threatened change in music format. Petitions were circulated and a protest concert[35] was organized, but to no avail. (When the University of Washington threatened to close down KCMU, there was a similar response from loyal listeners.)

---

[33] *Desperate Times*, No. 1 pg. 15, No. 2 pg. 13, No. 5 pg. 2, 12, No. 6 pg. 12

[34] KEXP, 2010 Annual Report to the Contributors, http://kexp.org/about/2010AnnualReport-lite.pdf.

[35] See Wilum Pugmire's description of the "Save the Wave" concert on page 1.

The story of Seattle's KRAB radio station is particularly interesting. Lorenzo Milam had a vision for a unique type of media he called "community radio," which would be run and supported by local communities. In 1962, Milam was granted an FCC license and launched KRAB radio in Seattle. Run primarily by volunteers, the station aired pretty much anything. But this model of community radio turned out to be virtually impossible to sustain economically. In 1985, the station license was sold to a commercial radio conglomerate.[36] The frequency is now run as KNDD by Entercom Communications Corporation.

---

[36] See notice about KRAB in the Stop Press section, *Desperate Times* No. 6, pg.12.

RECOMMENDED READING

This is a list of books relevant to the time period of *Desperate Times*.

Ash, Timothy Garton. *The Polish Revolution: Solidarity*. Yale University Press, 2002.

Azerrad, Michael. *Our Band Could Be Your Life: Scenes from the American Indie Underground 1981-1991*. Back Bay Books, 2002.

Baker, Danny. *Sniffin' Glue & Other Rock-n-Roll Habits: The Catalogue of Chaos, 1976-1977*. Illustrated ed. Sanctuary Publishing, 2000.

Beresford, David. *Ten Men Dead: The Story of the 1981 Irish Hunger Strike*. Atlantic Monthly Press, 1997.

Berger, George. *Story of "Crass"*. 2nd ed. Omnibus Press, 2008.

Bone, Ian, ed. *Class War: A Decade of Disorder*. Verso, 1991.

Chantry, Art. *Instant Litter: Concert Posters from Seattle Punk Culture*. Real Comet Press, 1985.

Duncombe, Stephen. *Notes from Underground: Zines and the Politics of Alternative Culture*. Verso, 1997.

Eisenstein, Elizabeth L. *The Printing Press as an Agent of Change*. Cambridge University Press, 1980.

Gaar, Gillian G. *She's a Rebel: The History of Women in Rock & Roll*. 2nd ed. Seal Press, 2002.

Hayward, Steven F. *The Age of Reagan: The Conservative Counterrevolution: 1980-1989*. Reprint. Three Rivers Press, 2010.

Humphrey, Clark. Loser : *The Real Seattle Music Story*. 2nd ed. MISCmedia, 1999.

Kelley, Mike; Jim Shaw and Niagara. *Destroy All Monsters Magazine* 1976-1979. Primary Information, 2011.

Pohl, Frederik. *In the Problem Pit*. Bantam Books, 1976.

Postman, Neil. *Amusing Ourselves to Death: Public Discourse in the Age of Show Business*. Revised ed. Penguin Books, 2005.

Prato, Greg. *Grunge Is Dead: The Oral History of Seattle Rock Music.* ECW Press, 2009.

Sabin, Roger and Teal Triggs, eds. *Below Critical Radar: Fanzines and Alternative Comics From 1976 to Now.* illustrated ed. Codex Books, 2002.

Tow, Stephen. *The Strangest Tribe: How a Group of Seattle Rock Bands Invented Grunge.* Sasquatch Books, 2011.

Triggs, Teal. *Fanzines.* Chronicle Books, 2010.

Vale, V., ed. *Search & Destroy 1-6: The Complete Reprint.* V/Search, 1996.

Vale, V., ed. *Search & Destroy 7-11: The Complete Reprint.* Re/Search Publications, 1997.

Vee, Tesco and Dave Stimson, authors; Steve Miller, ed. *Touch and Go: The Complete Hardcore Punk Zine '79-'83.* Bazillion Points, 2010.

Waltz, Mitzi. *Alternative and Activist Media.* Edinburgh University Press, 2006.

Wertham, Fredric. *The World of Fanzines: A Special Form of Communication.* Southern Illinois University Press, 1973.

Yarm, Mark. *Everybody Loves Our Town: An Oral History of Grunge.* Crown Archetype, 2011.

ADVERTISER LIST

This is an inclusive list of all the advertisers who supported *Desperate Times*. For this they will get absolution.

Acrylic Waves (KRAB)

B Plus Films

Cellophane Square

Crème Soda

Deaf Cat Records

Everybody's Record Co.

KCMU

Little Bears From Bangkok

Popeye's

Corporate Records

Danceland

Dreamland

Flypostering

Kitchy Koo

"Photography"

Pravda Productions

Reflex Records

Reggae

Rock Against the Liquor Board

Rosco Louie Gallery

Seattle Bands Magazine

Showbox (Steve Pritchard Concerts)

Showbox (Space Muffin Productions)

Skyking

Split Enz

Square Studio

Student Nurse

The Dub Store

The Gorilla Room

The Spectators/Idiot Culture

WREX

VENUE LIST

This is not meant to be an inclusive list of all the venues that were active during the summer of 1981. It is only a list of the venues mentioned by name in *Desperate Times*; therefore all the venues listed below existed during or before 1981. The venues are listed by city.

SEATTLE
And/Or Gallery
Aquarius Tavern
Astor Park
Baby O's
Bumbershoot Festival
Seattle Center Coliseum
Danceland (aka Danceland, USA)
Eagles Auditorium
Freeway Hall
Gorilla Room
Hibble & Hydes
Moore Theatre
Olympic Hotel's Georgian Ballroom
Paramount Theatre
Roma Tavern
Rosco Louie Gallery
Showbox
Stomping Ground
Talmud Torah (later the Showbox)
U.T.C. Hall
Virginia Inn
Washington Hall
WREX

PORTLAND
Clockwork Joe's
Euphoria
Urban Noize

VANCOUVER, B.C.
Basic Street Blues
Commodore Ballroom
Devonshire Hotel
Gary Taylor's Rockroom
John Barley's
Misty's Disco
Rohan's
Route 66
Smilin' Buddha
Spinning Wheel
The Blarney Stone
The Cave
The Lone Star
The Pig & Whistle
The Savoy
The Town Pump
Tonite

OTHER LOCATIONS
Aquatic Barn (Berkeley, CA)
CBGB's (New York)
Golden Gate Aquatic Barn (San Francisco)

BAND INDEX

This is not meant to be an inclusive list of all the bands that were active during the summer of 1981.

It is only a list of the bands mentioned by name in *Desperate Times*.

CONTRIBUTOR INDEX

Made in the USA
San Bernardino, CA
27 July 2015